TOYS
GO TO WAR

ON THE TITLE PAGE. *Tank target from the rare 1940 Louis Marx Co. Exploding Anti-tank set is
one of the best examples of WWII-era toys. The use of metal for its parts, alas, was soon to be banned.*

PICTORIAL HISTORIES PUBLISHING COMPANY, INC.
713 South Third Street West, Missoula, Montana 59801

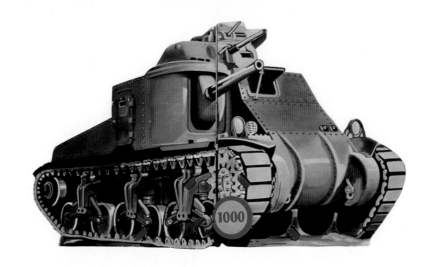

TOYS GO TO WAR

WORLD WAR II MILITARY TOYS, GAMES, PUZZLES & BOOKS

by Jack Matthews

CONTENTS

Louis Marx "target" metal soldiers came in different sets. Immensely popular with today's collectors because of their lithography, they are highly authentic.

ACKNOWLEDGMENTS

THE ENCOURAGEMENT and cooperation I received in researching and writing this book have been most heartwarming. In addition to many long-time friends (some of whom I've never met), the staff at the Library of Congress, the Smithsonian Institution, and Chicago's historical society were most helpful.

A number of people helped me prepare this book by furnishing information and ideas, photographs and encouragement. They are listed below. For those I may have inadvertently omitted, please chalk it up to a failing memory. My heartfelt thanks to you, too.

Special thanks must go to a few whose expertise and friendship were of inestimable help. To my mentors, Richard O'Brien, the Godfather of American toy soldier research, and Harry L. Rinker, the Grand Guru of small collectibles, thanks for lending your vast experience and candid advice to this newcomer in the field of publishing. To my old friends and show-going companions Neal Crowley and Ed Ryan—thanks for everything. To "the Colonel," Stan Stanton, my appreciation for giving above and beyond the call your expertise in photography. Cathy Wadley's patience in typing the manuscript also is much appreciated.

I also am indebted to my "Montana crew." Publisher Stan Cohen of Pictorial Histories whose book on the home front, *"V" for Victory*, brought us together; Bill Vaughn and Kitty Herrin of Arrow Graphics; and editor Candace Chenoweth.

A special thanks to *Playthings* magazine for preserving all those wonderful wartime issues, a research treasure trove.

Finally, for their photos, information and support, I wish to thank: Hank Anton, Will Bierwaltes, Merv Bloch, the Danish National Museum, Guy D'Moulin, Perry Eichor, Ken Fleck, Tony Grecco, Ted Hake, Bill Holt, Gene Johnson, Roger Johnson, Keith and Donna Kaonis, Bill Lango, Jim Morris, Bill Nutting, Nat Polk, Ed Poole, Harry Rinker, Jr., John Schmidt, Al Smith, Michael Smith, Steve and Jo Sommers, J.D. Stratton and Lee Temaris.

Particularly gratifying were the acts of those distant, unmet friends like Jim Harman, Ron Fink, Mary Young and Jean Biermeister who photocopied items from their collections for me and, in one case, loaned irreplaceable paper items to a total stranger.

INTRODUCTION

*"When I am grown to man's estate
I shall be very proud and great,
and tell the other girls and boys
not to meddle with my toys."*

ROBERT LOUIS STEVENSON

T HE INTRODUCTION to a book of nonfiction is usually the author's only chance to reminisce. Some introductions are turgid, some succinct. Some are dull, some witty and genuinely interesting. Most are someplace in between. In my extensive library on toys and related collectibles, there are all kinds of introductions and from each I usually glean some insight or recapture a memory. Reading all those introductions also has made me realize just how similar collectors of memorabilia are!

Unlike some of my long-time collector friends (the popular author on toys, Richard O'Brien, comes immediately to mind), however, I don't have an encyclopedic memory of my own toys or play during WWII. Unlike my Texas friend, Ron Fink, I didn't have a mom who saved all my "stuff." I vaguely recall that my treasures were given away or thrown out in my early teens when I lost interest in such toys. In these wonderful, happy years of retirement, however, the memories, more and more, come flooding back. For the most part they are warm and satisfying, and, in Harry Rinker's word, "neat." And they grow and are sharpened by the never-ending hunt for and acquisition of the ELUSIVE WWII toy! If you are like me, I hope this introduction triggers a few fond memories. If you are much younger, then I hope it increases your understanding of what all the fuss was about in WWII.

Perhaps the most gratifying aspect of serious collecting is the friendships one makes over the years. Often these friendships constitute a major part of a collector's social life, and I feel sorry for "closet collectors," the squirrels who acquire in silence and stuff their collections away. This small

The author with his father (in American Legion uniform) on Memorial Day, 1941.

minority misses so much. Half the fun is going on "the hunt" with fellow aficionados and swapping tales of finding treasure for a fantastically low price, which—the proverbial fish story in reverse—gets lower with each telling. Admittedly, there is spirited competition among collectors but, in my experience, it's almost always healthy. More pronounced is the cooperation and guidance among collectors.

After collecting thousands of antique toy soldiers and military tin-plate toys, not to mention assembling an extensive library of books on military history, biographies, old war movies, newsreels and documentaries, I started collecting military toys and related collectibles from my WWII childhood a dozen years ago. They were very cheap then and continue to be relatively affordable.

The unprecedented manner in which the United States pulled together during WWII has fascinated historians and, now as the world commemorates the fiftieth anniversary of the war, is particularly germane. Volumes have been written on the subject, most with wonderful anecdotes based on oral histories and reviews of newspaper and magazine articles. A number are listed in the bibliography. After accumulating a mass of such materials and a broader insight into the home front, the idea of writing a book on WWII toys crystallized as I eased into early retirement in my fifties. Most books on collectibles focus primarily on the items themselves with perhaps a smattering of company histories. Few, if any, focus on the historical framework and the events that affected their creation and production. And none I have analyzed have included an in-depth study of the toy industry.

My first reading of a war-era *Playthings* magazine, with its numerous columns and reports on toy industry activity, finally gave me an approach. I decided to weave an anecdotal history of the home front and its effects on the toy industry into a picture book on WWII toys. I would relate how toy entrepreneurs reacted to wartime events, government regulations and the American mood.

My research involved a careful review of six years of *Playthings* and *Toys and Novelties* magazines, together with contemporaneous weekly and monthly news magazines, and wholesale and retail toy catalogs. The material is vast and fascinating. These sources may be found at the Library of Congress.

After Pearl Harbor, the American people felt threatened by invasion, bombing, espionage and sabotage for only about a year. Thereafter, government and the media had to keep patriotic fever alive. While the bulk of Europe, Russia and the Pacific were in conflict, the United States, as one noted historian has observed, was fighting, in part, on imagination alone. From an economic standpoint, these were "happy" years for many American citizens. For those who did not suffer in combat, lose a loved one or spend long periods away from home, the war years were far better than the Depression.

As children, we were totally caught up in the war, but it wasn't the war our parents knew. In our minds we created our war the way we wanted it to be—it was a game of toys and play and no one really died. Although we listened to the news on the radio with our parents and older siblings tracked war theatre campaigns on wall maps, for the most part we had no real knowledge of the details. Nor did we care. Geographic locations were fuzzy, political and ethnic causes totally obscure. We were far from the killing and bombing, and so for most American children the war was a huge game and the war years actually a fun time. This may sound terrible but, in perspective, it is true.

Victory over the scheming, devious, barbaric enemy was everything and the lack of durable metal toys soon meant little—we made do with what was available. We dug trenches and foxholes; trees became aircraft observation posts. We made machine guns, rifles, cannons and pistols out of wood and nails, created rank insignia from pieces of cardboard, fastening them on our sleeves and collars with rubber bands and safety pins, and yelled countless times, "Bang—you're dead." "No I'm not! You missed me!" Emergency rations—saltines, raisins and peanuts-were hidden under porches and front steps. Egg and tuna salad sandwiches sustained us "in battle" and were washed down by Orange Nehi and Dr. Pepper.

We did all these things, all day long, almost every day. Our mothers didn't mind; after all, we weren't underfoot. Even when we played indoors, it was war toys that kept us occupied: punch-out battle stations, composition toy soldiers, games of strategy, patriotic puzzles, and military adventure books. Then, on Saturday, we went to the matinee to see the most recent release—all about war.

Combining these memories with information and photographs is what this book is about. I hope you enjoy reading it as much as I have enjoyed researching and writing it, not to mention searching for all these marvelous toys. Three cheers for the Red, White and Blue!

JACK MATTHEWS
March 1994

The author in the summer of 1942 with his latest flying model creation.

This book is dedicated to my Meriam,
who makes everything in my life fun

and to the memory of my mother.

VERONICA BERNICE BRUCKER MATTHEWS (1892–1985), who enter-
tained WWI troops in New England as a member of an all-girl man-
dolin band; who taught me the lyrics of patriotic songs of WWI as
she banged them out in the key of C on our old upright piano; who,
with her sisters, my Aunts Irene and Alice, bought me a wonderful
selection of wooden and cardboard wartime toys; and who never once
thought that playing with "military" toys was bad for a child,

and my father

EVERETT CHARLES MATTHEWS (1897–1945), Corporal, U. S. Cavalry
1917–1918, proud Commander of our local American Legion Post
when, in the thirties, it ran the Klu Klux Klan out of our small New
England town; Assistant Chief Observer, Town Unit of Aircraft Warning Service, WWII; and who died on VJ-Day, 1945,

and to all who have served!

A masterful Fredric C. Madan cover for Merrill coloring book series published between 1942 and 1944. See pages 168–69.

1

A History of World War II Toys

In the early 1940s, Tillicum marketed a boat set that capitalized on the popular theme of home defense and stateside preparedness.

ON SEPTEMBER 1, 1939, Hitler invaded Poland and World War II began. In America, the Great Depression was entering its eleventh year. While things were starting to look up, one in five Americans was still out of work. Over half the country's population, some seventy million people, lived on farms or in towns of fewer than ten thousand inhabitants. Six out of ten homes lacked central heat, one in three families used an outhouse and 40 percent lacked a bathtub or shower.

For Christmas 1939, toy industry polls indicated that the most popular presents for boys were "Erector Sets," "Lincoln Logs" and, perhaps, a cowboy suit complete with shining metal pistols. Girls wanted "Raggedy Ann and Andy" dolls, an "American Girl Sewing Machine," and a black-faced doll named "Topsy."

On the east coast of the United States, the biggest single entertainment interest continued to be the New York World's Fair, which had opened at Flushing Meadows, Long Island, on April 30, 1939. It was twice the size of the earlier west coast fair, the Golden Gate Exposition at San Francisco. Several million people eventually attended the World's Fair. Its huge Trylon and Perisphere dominated the advertising of the year and appeared on many of its toys, much like Disneyland artifacts do today.

The preceding decade, during which the entire industrialized world had experienced a severe economic depression, was a period of significant social, technical and political change for the American people. The airplane, motorcar and radio were relatively new and fascinated the public including the children. Planes, especially those reflecting popular current aviation events and developments such as the setting of new speed records (Steelcrest's Lockheed *Sirius*), technical developments (Wyandotte's excellent pressed steel gyroplane and autogiro), and the highly popular inauguration of Pan-American's overseas Clipper flights, dominated the male child's fantasies. Great transportation and aviation toys by Wyandotte, Tootsietoy, Hubbley, J. Chien, Strauss, Keystone, Kenton, Gray Iron, Arcade and others,

thrilled many a child. A check of toy industry catalogs of the era shows a preponderance of airplane toy ads followed by metal cars, trucks and trains. Very few were military toys with a few exceptions like the Marx "Doughboy Tank" that featured a World War I vehicle with pop-up gunner.

Until the latter part of the decade, except for the cheap "dimestore" slush-cast toy soldiers, civilian transportation toys dominated the toy market for boys as they had in the boom times of the 1920s when Buddy L. and Arcade were the top of the line in the metal toy field.

There were some exceptions. Mc-Gloughlin's cardboard soldier folders were popular and odd military toys such as the "Victory Painting Set" did appear from time to time. McDowell Manufacturing Co.'s "Mystery Gun" game of early 1930's origin had some rather odd target combinations, i.e., Zeppelins and turn of the century ships.

But in the mid 1930s there was generally a strong overall feeling against war toys. In 1935 a *Fortune* magazine arti-

DEFENSE ON THE SEA
BEGINS ON THE SHORE

WWII posters are considered to be among the best examples of 20th century illustrators' art. They are currently being reproduced on everything from T-shirts to coffee mugs.

Left
Louis Marx & Company's late prewar military toys included an array of boxed tin-plate tanks of varying sizes, large airplanes, and trucks.

cle reported that until the Italian-Ethiopian War military toys hadn't "had much popularity since the World War." While reporting on some possible exceptions, such as the Marx "G-Man Machine Gun," the article concluded that the toy makers were somewhat schizophrenic on the subject. The Toy Manufacturers Association in 1935 went out of its way to assure customers by appropriate publicity that its Christmas line had nothing more martial than cowboys and Indians playthings. When Gimbells advertised military toy machine guns, a slew of people wrote in to complain that it ought to be ashamed. Due to protests, General Foods removed cut-out soldiers from its Post Toasties cereal boxes. On the other hand, the major companies observed that the cheaper retail outlets, like W.T. Grants and F. W. Woolworth Company, were selling slush-cast "dimestore" soldiers like crazy and that Marx and other tanks, a flop a year earlier, were selling well. Sears Roebuck and Company added a few war toys at a time. So, gradually, the military toy line increased.

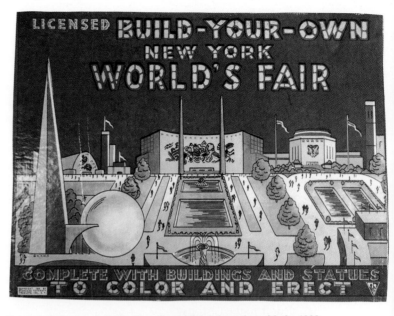

Toy manufacturers capitalized on the public's infatuation with the 1939 New York World's Fair. This color and punch-out set is typical, and reminiscent of the complex paper models that are popular today.

As was the case for all companies depending on the discretionary consumer dollar, things were generally tough for toy manufacturers during the Depression. For most people, after taking care of food, clothing and lodging, there just wasn't much left over to spend on toys. Richard O'Brien's superb history, *The Story of American Toys*, describes in detail the

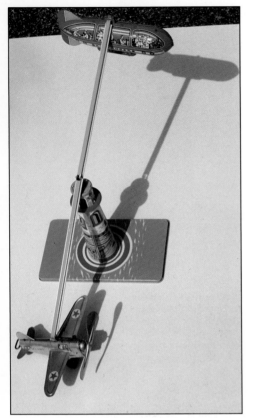

Until the late 1930s civilian toys dominated the market with a few exceptions, such as Unique Art's "Sky Ranger." This novel toy continued Unique Art's tradition of fine tin-plate toys and had some of the best lithography and box-art ever seen.

difficulties of many of America's metal toy manufacturers. Only the strong like Lionel and Marx survived the decade. Outstanding companies such as Metalcraft, Republic, Converse, and Sturditoy all faded. Companies at the lower end of the price range just made it. They did so by cutting marketing costs and using the cheapest available materials such as scrap metal. Marx, for example, did no major institutional advertising, had an extremely small sales force, and did not produce expensive catalogs.

The economic outlook in America started to improve in the late 1930s, and world events strongly influenced the gradual increase in toys of a military nature. The commencement of World War II in 1939

did not come without warning. The Italian-Ethiopian War, which resulted in production of specific toy soldiers relating to it in both the U.S. (Barclay and Grey Iron) and Germany (Lineol and Elastolin), started in 1935. Japan invaded China in 1937, and Italy, Germany and Russia tested many weapons in the Spanish Civil War.

These preliminary mini-wars created a rather bizarre collectible for children in the form of the now rare "Horrors of War" gum cards. Produced in 1938 by Gum Inc., the small picture cards were immensely popular with kids although parents detested them. The cards could never be marketed today. Scenes showing dogs eating dead bodies, body parts flying through the air, hangings, mutilation, and decapitation so outraged parents that a disclaimer, "To Know the Horrors of War is to Want Peace," was printed in large letters on the reverse of each card. The very explicit printed description of the horrible events depicted on each card, however, was retained. It's interesting to note that while the Japanese were always depicted as the barbarians in the Sino-Japanese War cards, the Italian and

Gable and Spencer Tracy in MGM's marvelous *Test Pilot*, and heartthrob Robert Taylor in *Flight Command*.

Book publishers sensed a subtle change in public isolationist attitudes and started reissuing early twentieth century military fiction series for boys with new dust jackets. Saalfield Publishing Co. reissued its popular Fiction for Boys series. Dick Prescott's First (through fourth) Year at West Point (copyright 1911), Dave Darrin's First (through fourth) Year at Annapolis (copyright 1910), and the Battleship Boys at Sea, etc., series (copyright 1910) took on new life with text unchanged but with new marketing. They were sold right through World War II. The archaic title and story line of *Submarine Boys on Duty* or *Life in a Diving Torpedo Boat* (1909) didn't appear to affect its sales in the 1930s and 1940s.

As the thirties ended and the war in

Franco forces were shown as the good guys in the Spanish and Ethiopian conflicts—perhaps a symbolic comment on the yellow peril scare of the times.

Germany's emergent Nazi Government remilitarized by 1936 and annexed Austria and part of Czechoslovakia in 1938. Having just fought a European War less than twenty years earlier, U.S. citizens overwhelmingly refused to be drawn into these foreign conflicts. Hollywood, usually an accurate barometer of the public mood, produced only a few war movies in the early to mid 1930s and those involved stories of World War I heroism. By the mid to late thirties, however, things slowly started to change. Films about Army, Navy and Marine training, often featuring the combination of Jimmy Cagney and Pat O'Brien (Cagney usually got the girl) and others with Wallace Beery, a Naval Reserve pilot himself, were very popular. These "A" films often featured actual newsreels of the annual maneuvers of the Navy's Pacific Fleet. Aviation films in particular were box office successes. Children developed an interest in military events after viewing Warner Bros.' *Devil Dogs of the Air* (1935), Universal's *Wings over Honolulu* (1937), Clark

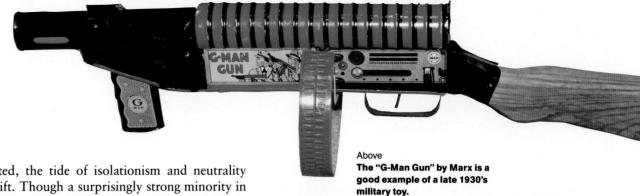

Below
The plot of Whitman's Better Little Book, *Dan O'Dare Finds War*, cloaked growing anti-Fascist sentiment by having the unnamed Allies defend "Librania" against the "Swazis."

Right
Saboteurs were not just figments of the public's imagination. Prior to Pearl Harbor numerous accidents involving U.S. industry and transportation were of a highly suspicious nature. When five mills of the Freestone Rubber Company in Fall River, Massachusetts, burned to the ground in the fall of 1941 and destroyed one-eighth of the nation's strategic rubber supplies, Navy Intelligence strongly suspected sabotage. For just one dollar, Gold Medal's "Federal Agent Finger Print Outfit" gave kids a chance to catch enemy spies.

Above
The "G-Man Gun" by Marx is a good example of a late 1930's military toy.

Europe started, the tide of isolationism and neutrality started to shift. Though a surprisingly strong minority in the U.S. were not put off by Hitler, anti-Fascist sentiment increased, although it was still considered unpopular to mention specific aggressors by name. It didn't take much intelligence, however, to figure out who the publisher or film maker really meant. Whitman's Better Little Book entitled *Dan O'Dare Finds War* was a prime example. "Dedicated to the brave defenders of Finland," the book's plot involves a huge army of "Swazis" invading little Librania. The Allies, who saved defenseless Librania from the evil aggressor, were unnamed but their Admiral in Command had the very English-like name of Basil Heathcoate. The Swazis, coincidentally, spoke German—"Ach Du Lieber"!—and wore German WWI helmets. Their planes, identical to the German Stuka dive bomber, had insignia with four lines that when connected make a swastika. So much for editorial neutrality!

Hollywood, which a few years earlier had been leery of propaganda films since Germany and Italy were important markets for the studios, gradually changed also. Early in 1939 Warner Bros. produced the first explicitly anti-Nazi Hollywood movie. Earlier films in 1938, mostly about spies and espionage, simply had failed to identify the threatening foreign power although when the villains were Oriental, it didn't take any imagination to know to which Far Eastern country the yellow peril referred. Warner's *Confessions of a Nazi Spy*, based on an actual recent FBI arrest of German agents, dealt with American "front" organizations, terrorism of German-born U.S. citizens ("You have relatives in Germany?"), secret codes, and stolen plans for battleships and sabotage. It had everything needed to excite the imaginations of red-blooded American kids. Suddenly toys like Marx's "G-Man Gun" and Gold Medal's "Federal Agent Finger Print Outfit" took on new meaning. Now a child could go after enemy spies instead of American gangsters, most of whom already had long since been put away by J. Edgar Hoover's intrepid G-men. Other Hollywood films adding to the increased public concern in 1939–40 were Hitchcock's *The Lady Vanishes*, a great spy thriller, *Foreign Correspondent, Mortal Storm, Four Sons,* and *Escape.* While dealing with an earlier war, the 1938 remake of the World War I flight epic *Dawn Patrol*, and *The Fighting 69th*, both actively portrayed pro-war sentiments.

How did the toy industry react? While toy items remained overwhelmingly civilian, an examination of the trade press and catalogs in 1939–40 demonstrates how things were changing. Included in Buhl Sons Company's 1940 wholesale catalog were a twelve-piece "Navy Fleet" by Tootsietoy and two "Coast Defense" forts and an air-

craft carrier and submarine by Keystone. "In keeping with a leading topic of the times," read the copy, Tillicum had a "National Defense" set of wooden boats. The aptly named "Trap-A-Tank" race game had a similar military theme. When the handle was turned, the cardboard center obstacle course vibrated and advanced the wooden tanks up and over the traps to the finish line. This game in good shape will cost over a hundred dollars today.

The Buhl catalog also illustrates several boxed military sets by Auburn Rubber that today are found rarely. Six different sets, in colorful boxes with the pieces tied-in standing up, include a tank set, an artillery set, and two different first aid and soldier sets.

Strombecker, the premier manufacturer of pre-cut wooden assembly kits, had a 1939–40 line that featured three cannons, five Navy ships, and four military aircraft, several of which like the Bell *Airacuda* and Boeing's *Flying Fortress* were quite new in America's defense arsenal.

Gray iron Ethiopian war figures. The equivalent German-made composition figures by Lineol are quite rare. That of Emperor Haile Selassie sells for one thousand dollars.

Left

By 1940 defense items were beginning to creep into the pages of the Christmas catalogs. Buhl Son's wholesale catalog featured thirty-five military toys. As the catalog went to press in the spring, these toys probably were designed a year or more in advance.

7

THE EVE OF WAR

THINGS REALLY STARTED popping in 1940. The depression had peaked in 1938 with eight to twelve million people out of work; now employment was up. In early 1940 economists were predicting that the country would be out of the woods by the end of the year. While the average median annual income was only $3,000, you could buy a lot for your money. Steak was twenty cents a pound, a loaf of bread, eight cents. A year-old used Dodge car was $900, gas was fourteen cents a gallon and a matinee movie was fifteen cents.

It was as if the nation was getting over a ten-year case of the flu. Defense jobs were starting to open up and there were almost a million men in the service. Workers were starting to spend. For the first time in many years, they began to buy watches, jewelry, kitchen appliances and toys for the kids. New Year's Eve 1939 was the best one that a recovering America had observed since the crash of 1929. Though Germany had started to occupy central Europe and Japan was conquering China, most Americans still went about their everyday business. The phony war was still in effect in Europe and the London Blitz had not yet started. It is not surprising therefore that 67.4 percent of the populace, according to a Roper Poll, was opposed to taking sides. Things changed rapidly, however. Just a few months later, in May, the exact same percentage of people polled actively favored giving substantial help to besieged England —a complete 100 percent turnabout of public opinion.

Three major events were to occur shortly that would affect the national mood even more dramatically. On August 27, Congress enacted the first peacetime draft in the nation's history. Sixteen million men got draft registration cards. In the summer of 1940 the London Blitz started, and the picture of valiant Londoners surviving the nightly Ger-

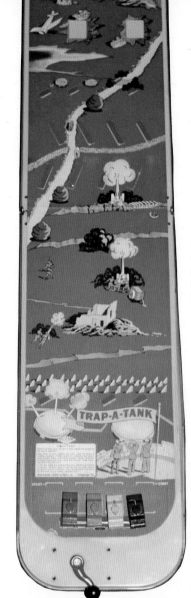

Wolverine's "Trap-a-Tank" was a variation of popular greyhound and horse racing games. In good shape this game will cost over a hundred dollars today.

man bombings as dramatically broadcast by Edward R. Murrow and Quenton Reynolds significantly increased the nation's negative attitude toward the Nazis. Finally, in November, President Roosevelt won an unprecedented third term in the White House against a strong Republican candidate, Wendell Wilkie. This mandate allowed a much more aggressive national defense posture on the part of the Administration.

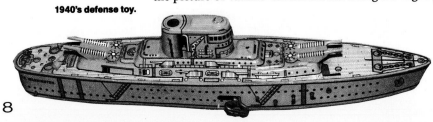

1940's defense toy.

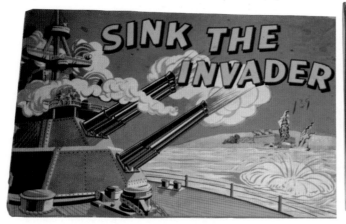

Baldwin's "Sink the Invader" game had fiberboard ship targets that could be sunk by its patented Gatling gun-type cannon. Guns from Baldwin's sets often show up at shows with reproduction dowel bullets.

The nation was slowly, but surely, moving toward a wartime footing, notwithstanding FDR's campaign pledge to keep American boys out of foreign wars. Defense was becoming an important theme, and defense plants were springing up all over the landscape as the armed forces expanded. Shortages started to occur gradually. Silk stockings were tougher to get since silk was used in Air Force parachutes. By the end of the year, 1940 retail sales and Christmas toy sales had set a record. While America was quietly gearing up for war, the public seemed to ignore that cold reality and just to enjoy the beginning of the newfound "end of the depression" prosperity. After those cruel long years, maybe it was natural to want to think that the whole defense boom would go on for years, without war.

How did all this affect the toy industry? Beginning in mid 1940 and continuing up to Pearl Harbor, items of a military nature quietly were introduced into toy lines by a number of manufacturers, book publishers and puzzle makers. Reflecting a continuing sensitivity to mothers' complaints, in many instances the toys were referred to as "defense" items, not "war toys." In the case of metal toys, pedal cars in the form of airplanes, army trucks, tanks and ambulances were among the offerings. New games based on defense themes were offered by several firms. Many more small metal toys of a military nature were made. Even rubber balls and balloons, it was reported, started sporting patriotic red, white and blue themes with pictures of the American flag, airplanes, ships, tanks, soldiers, sailors and aircraft.

Start your own WAR BOOM

with STEELCRAFT PEDAL PROPELLED WARPLANES

For the award of the "hottest" wheel goods items of the year, Steelcraft nominates these sleek, exciting airplanes: "U. S. Pursuit" and "Spitfire." Authentically styled, dramatically executed, these ships are definitely headed for the "best seller" class. With juvenile interest focused so sharply on war-in-the-air, they are "natural" centers of interest for your wheel goods displays—both in your windows and on the floor.

These planes are only two of the twenty new 1941 additions to the famous Murray Ohio line of bicycles, velocipedes, autos,

wagons, and miniatures. The entire line will be displayed at the Toy Fair. Put this in your date-book as a "must." *1941 will be another Steelcraft year.*

A word about our production capacity. Our new bicycle plant, approximately twice as large as the old one, insures adequate capacity. The space formerly devoted to bicycles has been added to toy production, thus substantially increasing those facilities.

If you are unable to attend the exhibit, we will be glad to send you our complete catalog and price list.

An excellent ¼-scale cast model of the "U.S. Pursuit Plane" by Steelcraft is sold today as part of a miniature pedal car series. Or, collectors can order this pedal plane restored for $5,000 from the *Tailwinds* aviation gift catalog. The antique pedal plane measures 45½"L×13½"W and has a 35" wingspan. It comes in silver baked enamel with vermillion and blue trim.

9

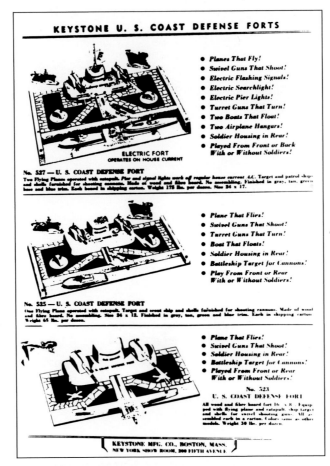

KEYSTONE U. S. COAST DEFENSE FORTS

ELECTRIC FORT
OPERATES ON HOUSE CURRENT

- *Planes That Fly!*
- *Swivel Guns That Shoot!*
- *Electric Flashing Signals!*
- *Electric Searchlight!*
- *Electric Pier Lights!*
- *Turret Guns That Turn!*
- *Two Boats That Float!*
- *Two Airplane Hangars!*
- *Soldier Housing in Rear!*
- *Played From Front or Back With or Without Soldiers!*

No. 527 — U. S. COAST DEFENSE FORT
Two Flying Planes operated with catapult. Pier and signal lights work of regular house current A.C. Target and patrol ships and shells furnished for shooting cannons. Made of wood and fibre board. No assembling. Finished in gray, tan, green and blue trim. Each boxed in shipping carton. Weighs 175 lbs. per dozen. Size 34 x 17.

- *Plane That Flies!*
- *Swivel Guns That Shoot!*
- *Turret Guns That Turn!*
- *Boat That Floats!*
- *Soldier Housing in Rear!*
- *Battleship Target for Cannons!*
- *Play From Front or Rear With or Without Soldiers!*

No. 525 — U. S. COAST DEFENSE FORT
One Flying Plane operated with catapult. Target and scout ship and shells furnished for shooting cannons. Made of wood and fibre board. No assembling. Size 34 x 12. Finished in gray, tan, green and blue trim. Each in shipping carton. Weight 65 lbs. per dozen.

- *Plane That Flies!*
- *Swivel Guns That Shoot!*
- *Soldier Housing in Rear!*
- *Battleship Target for Cannons!*
- *Played From Front or Rear With or Without Soldiers!*

No. 523
U. S. COAST DEFENSE FORT
All wood and fibre board fort 16 x 8. Equipped with flying plane and catapult, ship target and shells for swivel shooting guns. All assembled each in a carton. Colors same as other models. Weight 30 lbs. per dozen.

KEYSTONE MFG. CO., BOSTON, MASS.
NEW YORK SHOW ROOM, 200 FIFTH AVENUE

Keystone's "U.S. Coast Defense Forts" were part of its heavily publicized "Home Defense" line. The forts catapulted planes and had docks for Keystone's famous line of floating boats.

Baldwin Manufacturing Company Inc. of Brooklyn, New York, an industry leader, was typical of those who quickly added to their line. Several of its offerings reflected defense themes. Its boxed target game, "Sink the Invader," had marvelous box art and contained a number of typical fiberboard ship targets that could be sunk by its patented Gatling gun-type cannon in which wooden shells were fired in rapid secession by a crank. The same type of gun in various sizes and shapes was used in its boxed "Coast Artillery Cannon" set, "Coast Defense Gun," smaller "Coast Defense" set, and "Coast Defense" and "Coast Artillery" games. All were variations of the same cannon and target theme.

Keystone of Boston touted its own "Home Defense Program." Toy buyers were urged to seek Keystone's "Preparedness Display" at the 1940 Toy Fair. Advertised as the world's mightiest array of modern toys that "fittingly interpret the spirit of our times," the line included realistic coast defense forts, exploding battle fleets, and shooting submarines. "Planes

Baldwin's stand-up fiberboard and metal "Par-A-Shoot Target Game" came with a standard cork-firing rifle popgun.

that fly, swivel guns that shoot, turret guns that turn, floating boats, airplane hangers, soldiers' barracks . . . sound effects," said the ads. What more could any kid want? To complete its pitch, in the same ad Keystone called its line of doll houses as "the homes that are well worth defending." "Little girls keep house while the little boys defend their families . . . with military equipment illustrated," the ad continued.

The pre-Christmas issue of a national magazine in December 1940, had a several page spread on Christmas toys that is illustrative of the new emphasis. While mostly illustrating the more expensive toys sold by the huge and famous F.A.O. Schwartz store in New York City, it did show two pages of the cheap American "dimestore" soldiers. The article pointed out that "with Germany blockaded almost all toys today are American made." While most of the toys pictured were still the traditional ones, unlike a few years previous, several were military in nature including a nurse doll, diving submarine, and peddle pursuit plane. A separate section of pictures featuring only British toys displayed a marvelous tin-plate British Blenheim bomber, parachute troops and a William Britain's antiaircraft crew, gun, and range finder. In comparing the previous year's English output, the authors noted a change from "Maginot" fortifications and tanks to "air raid" toys. Said the magazine, "Children in air-bombed Britain want air raid toys—planes, parachutes, airfield, antiaircraft guns and air raid shelters."

By 1940 the great cast iron toys of the twenties and thirties had generally been phased out due to cost and other factors. Zinc alloys, pressed steel and tin had emerged as the dominant toy materials with increasing use of the new plastics. There were some wonderful metal military toys and games produced in 1940 and 1941. Louis Marx and Co. did some of its best work in that time span. One of the most highly sought after sets is its large 1940 boxed "Anti-Tank Set" complete with a tin-plate exploding

Above
"Invasion" was a popular theme for board games in 1942. "Par-A-Shoot" and "Sky Chute" are two examples.

Baldwin's military toy line was the best of the prewar era and usually illustrated America repelling invaders by land, sea or air.

tank, targets and metal soldiers. When the wooden shell hit the target spot on the bottom of the spring-loaded tank, the tank broke apart. Scores for toppling the soldiers with similar hits were lithographed on the base of each soldier. The soldiers in the set were from a line of Marx 3½-inch, flat tin lithographed soldiers produced until the late 1930s in various sized box sets entitled "Soldiers of Fortune." These sets came with either a pop-up gun or cannon. In one set, the box itself was the "Fort Dix Barracks." These figures, numbering about fifty, are collected avidly.

Another rare and outstanding boxed Marx target piece is its "Air-Sea-Power" set with spring-loaded ships that explode when hit by ball bearing bombs dropped from the plane. The large revolving drum "National Defense Anti-aircraft Gun" on tripod by Marx was based on parts from earlier G-men Tommy guns. Also nifty was the automatic self-loading machine gun that fired ball bearings at a box-like tin-plate target on which airplanes were suspended.

Another great toy featured was a tin lithographed army train in 027 gauge. While expensive and increasing in price, these toys can be found and are highly popular with today's collectors.

Numerous other metal, pressed steel and tin-plate toys produced in 1940-41 included Tootsietoy's thirteen piece convoy set and twenty piece camouflage Army sets, all of which came in vivid display boxes; Arcade's cast metal "Hudson Bomber," "P-XL Rubber-Tired Howitzer" tank in red and green (of all colors) or green and brown (that's better!) camouflage; Wolverine's "Mechanical Battleship" (with windup motor that powered a spark-firing rear turret; Hoge Manufacturing's "Automatic Rifle" (actually a revolving cylinder Tommy gun) with four-color battle scene lithography; Kingsbury's large, heavy gauge steel Army and

Manufacturing Co., which made a line of assorted five-inch plastic toys cleverly marketed under the Wannatoy name. Wannatoys sold in the five and dimes and were carried by some major chains; Montgomery Ward sold a set of eight for 89 cents. Early plastic toys tended to be monochrome, light and somewhat brittle and cannot be compared with today's intricate and detailed moldings.

Until rubber was severely rationed, companies continued to use it in the manufacture of toys. Molded Latek Products ("Kaysam"), Auburn Rubber and Sun Rubber used it in various trucks, tanks, planes, submarines, soldiers and ambulances.

In 1940 the war in Europe was escalating rapidly. More than one country a month—Denmark and Norway in April, Holland and Belgium in May, and Paris in June—fell to the enemy. Germany's attention turned to Britain: the attack on the RAF airfields commenced, followed by the London Blitz. The only bright spot was the successful evacuation of 330,000 British and French troops from Dunkirk.

Patriotism followed suit in the United States. The National Anthem now was played at every Broadway show, and many large motion picture theatres throughout the country also played it. It was reported that hayfever sufferers substituted "God Bless America" for the German "Gesundheit!" when sneezing. With seventy percent of Americans favoring foreign aid, particularly to Britain, the Roosevelt Administration was

Above
Another example of the late-thirties transition to war toys.

Left
The rapid mobilization was even reflected in comic books.
© 1941 FUNNIES, INC./NOVELTY PUBLISHING
PREMIUM GROUP/CURTIS CIRCULATION
CO./STAR PUBLICATIONS

antiaircraft defense gun trucks; Wyandotte's Army Engineer Corps truck with canvas top and its foot long pull-toy (a tin aircraft carrier with six planes). Arcade's cast tank was particularly neat. When five ball bearings were dropped in a turret hopper and a side crank turned, the tank fired away! It came in large and small versions.

Plastic military toys in the early 1940s included a "Victory Squadron" of four small, red plastic planes that were mounted on a card. A similar five-inch card featured a plastic P-39 *Airacobra* fighter in red, blue, yellow and green. Boats were made by various manufacturers including Dillon-Beck

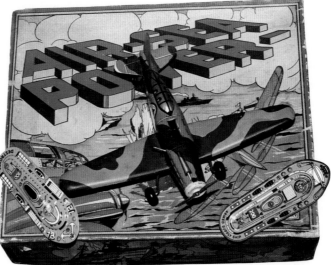

Right
Another exciting game by Marx was "Air-Sea Power." Players dropped ball bearings from a plane onto ships that were spring-loaded so as to explode with lifelike violence.

able to push through the sale of fifty old destroyers to the English Navy and to sell from U.S. arsenals what small stockpiles of World War I weapons were available. Slogans such as "Defend America by Helping Britain" and "British America's Thumbs-up RAF Cavalcade" appeared on domestic matchbook covers; these covers long have been collected by Americans of all ages.

Events in Europe started influencing the children and young adults' publishing field in early 1941. The very popular Crown Publishing series on the war adventures of one Dave Dawson started that year. Nineteen forty-one saw Dave Dawson and his pal, Freddie Farmer, fighting for the British against the Nazi hordes (yes, they were now named) in *At Dunkirk, With the RAF, In Libya,* and *On Convoy Patrol.* In the nonfiction area, Whitman's Guidebook Series of seven-by-three inch hard-bound pocket books commenced with three late 1940/early 1941 issues. Variations of *War Planes of the World,* in which German, Japanese and Italian planes were not shown as enemies but as part of an overall review, were featured. Whitman's earlier editions (1938–39) of slightly larger books on the various services sold well according to trade press and catalog ads. Informative books on our armed forces such as Rand-McNally's *Guardians of America,* which stressed the President's hemispheric defense theme, were published. All of this activity was indicative of rapidly increasing public awareness of and interest in world military and political affairs, a distinct change in just a few years.

As 1941 moved along, America gradually and modestly moved toward something of a war footing both in terms of public attitudes and home front events. President Roosevelt, now safely elected to his third term, frequently talked about

Germany and Japan as aggressor nations and potential enemies. In his famous "Arsenal of Democracy" speech, he cautioned that rationing of consumer and luxury goods might be required. The Four Freedoms were promulgated. The Lend-Lease Act was proposed to get around the provisions of the Neutrality Act that banned military assistance to nations at war, i.e., England. Japan and Germany made the Administration's effort much easier; Japan moved into Indo-China and Hitler invaded Yugoslavia in the spring. Belts started to tighten. Presaging the actual controls that would come a year later, a shortage of steel and tin due in part to events in the Far East started to pinch the American canning industry. All metal started to be diverted to the increasing defense effort. An embryonic system of material priorities began to grow in Washington and even to be formalized to some degree by irritable Harold Ickes, the grumpy, but highly effective, Secretary of the Interior.

Jumping the gun on competitors and getting a big publicity boost in the process, Wrigley's Chewing Gum sold its stockpile of 500,000 pounds of aluminum foil to the War Department. (Wrigley already was planning to convert to the superior cellophane wrapping.) Lucky Strike Cigarettes sacrificed its popular "green" package, which used certain scarce metals in the ink, and instigated the slogan "Lucky Strike Green has Gone to War." This slogan gained the American Tobacco Company years of good will. It was the first of its

The Marx "Army and Navy" revolving shooting gallery came with a revolver and pistol that fired rubber-tipped parts. All boxed military target games and large target tin-plate guns produced by Marx are very difficult to locate today.

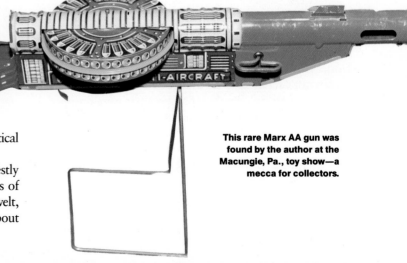

This rare Marx AA gun was found by the author at the Macungie, Pa., toy show—a mecca for collectors.

kind and soon was copied by hundreds of manufacturers, including toy makers, that had to switch to defense and war work.

The increasing shortages of basic materials gave birth to the age of plastics, and plastics started replacing hard rubber, which increasingly was needed for defense items. The plastics originally used in hand telephones, fountain pens and car steering wheels started turning up in a variety of other items including kitchen utensils and toys. Beton Plastics' line of toy soldiers was in major wholesale and retail catalogs all through 1940 and 1941.

A frightening development in 1941 brought the war home to Americans on the east coast. The beginning of

what German U-boat commanders called the "happy time" saw numerous torpedoed and burning British ships in the tanker lanes from Florida to Cape Cod. Tourists saw the fires, bathers felt the oil slicks, and newspapers and radio continuously reported the fact that in the first three months of 1941 Nazi subs sunk more than one million tons of British shipping.

The first use of priority items came in 1941. Essential cargo shipping items were considered strategic, as were materials in short supply such as tin, rubber and leather. Toy industry leaders began to be concerned. *Playthings* magazine, which along with *Toys and Novelties*, was the main trade press of the American toy industry, reported in its Washington Newsletter section that the industry could look

This Page
Marx airplanes and tanks are as popular now as they were during the war. Prices for them have tripled in the last few years.

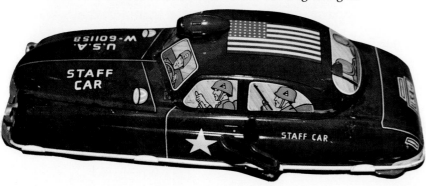

15

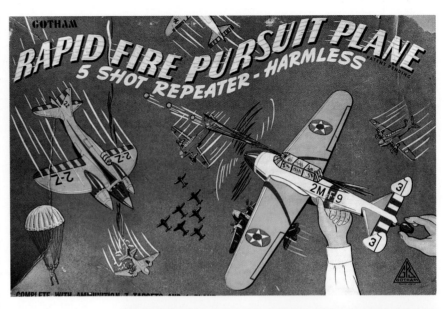

forward to little aid in obtaining scarce defense materials. The initial focus was on how many steel and electrical toys would be available. How about cellophane for packaging? The Office of Production Management (OPM), newly formed but quite active, formed several industry subcommittees to determine the material needs of various industries, toys included. *Playthings* was guardedly optimistic that supplies would be adequate but for the first time urged the use of substitute materials.

Some industry leaders were taking no chances. Bernard Gimbell, one of the successful brothers who owned eleven major department stores, anticipated early wartime shortages by several months. Disregarding the advice of his economic advisors, Gimbell borrowed twenty-one million dollars to build up his inventories of soon to be scarce items. Gimbell's stock of silk stockings lasted well into 1943. For several months after the war started, the only place one was sure to get an expensive, all metal, all electric train was at Gimbells—it had essentially cornered the local markets.

Some other retailers had the same foresight. Sometime later, but well in advance of its competitors, Montgomery Ward purchased the entire Marx inventory of trains and toy railroad accessories when Marx switched to war work. Claiming to have in stock "more than three times as many toy trains, cars and toy train accessories as we have ever had on hand at any one time," Ward's 1942 and 1943 catalogs still were illustrating such items. Proudly reporting its Marx purchase of toys "made before the war [with] no priorities to buy them," Ward quickly pointed out that the metal accessories could be used with any make of train. What a coup! To illustrate how important this single purchase decision was down the road, a 1943 Montgomery Ward catalog with fifty-seven pages of toys showed no metal toys except for the Marx train items.

In late 1941, as the inextricable trend toward American involvement in war continued, *Playthings* conducted a survey of leading toy makers, wholesale houses, mail order

16

concerns, and chain and department store representatives as to what was likely to happen in the upcoming year as a result of the national defense program. Sources in the fields of marketing, transportation and basic materials were consulted as were governmental representatives. A number of predictions were made based on the information collected. As unemployment rapidly decreased, the first and foremost change was to be an increase in demand and mounting sales. Second, substitutions in materials would be required and changes in toy design that required tool and die changes would be few. Third, game production would increase. Fourth, wooden toys would be scarce and, fifth, overall prices would slightly increase. Strangely, no real shortage of metal toys was predicted.

From June to November, ten U.S. merchant ships were stopped and sunk by German U-boats and the destroyer *U.S.S. Kearny* was torpedoed. U.S. troops landed in Iceland. Nonetheless, at home it was all business as usual. As the Christmas season approached, some industry adjustments were being felt and the public was starting to get a little nervous, but the national mood was still upbeat and optimistic. As to the prospects of war, people were not concerned. All that changed early one Sunday morning.

Above
Composition and clay soldiers would replace those made of metal.

Below
Hollowcast "dimestore" figures by Barclay and Manoil.

17

WAR: THE CAT HAS JUMPED

MOST PEOPLE in their forties remember where they were when President Kennedy was shot. Older people also remember what they were doing early on December 7, 1941. In the Philippines, General Jonathan Wainwright jiggled the telephone to call his aide. "Johnny," said the General, "the cat has jumped." The "cat" consisted of 350 Japanese planes in two waves that sank or seriously beached and damaged five U.S. battleships, eleven smaller warships, heavily damaged three more battleships and wiped out two Army airfields, killing in the process over 2,000 military and fifty-eight civilian personnel.

On the mainland, reaction to the Pearl Harbor attack varied. A New York couple sitting down to their Sunday roast chicken dinner thought it was another Orson Wells "Invader from Mars" radio hoax. A Palm Springs, California, girl wondered why you had to "spoil a perfectly good Sunday afternoon worrying about it." In Florence, Alabama, a thirteen-year-old boy warned his neighbors that the

"Japs had bombed Pearl Harbor and are heading for us on Four Mile Creek!" That evening in Hawaii, a sentry at Schofield Barracks near Pearl Harbor, understandably nervous, challenged a noise three times with a, "Who goes there?" When he got no answer, he shot his own mule. "We'll kick their teeth in!" a Pittsburgh steel worker said, which just about summed up the sentiments of most Americans. A West Virginia lad was quoted as saying, "Good, now we can whip their ass."

Within twenty-four hours, war had been declared and approved by the Congress with only one dissenting vote. Almost immediately there was an unprecedented degree of unity of purpose throughout the country. Only 2 percent of those polled opposed the declaration of war. Commenting on the new mood, the New York Times reported, "You could almost hear it click into place." The usual Congressional extremes of hyperbole for once matched the country's mood, particularly after the evil Nazis joined the foe. Said a Representative from Virginia:

> It is a war of purification in which the forces of Christian peace and freedom and justice and decency and morality are arrayed against the evil pagan forces of strife, injustice, treachery, inhumanity and slavery.

Tin Pan Alley songwriters, as usual, moved quickly. "You're a Sap Mr. Jap" was copyrighted late on December 7, 1941. "Good-bye Momma, I'm Off to Yokohama" followed soon after. "Good-bye Dear, I'll Be Back in a Year for I'm in the Army Now" was just a wee bit off the mark in terms of predicting the length of service in a war that was to last over three and a half years.

Optimism and the initial euphoria faded rapidly during the winter and early spring of 1942, however, as Japanese victories in the Pacific came quickly and overwhelmingly. Allied forces were routed everywhere. Wake, Guam, Manila, Singapore, Bataan and Corregidor fell. Eighty-seven more U.S. ships were sunk off the east coast.

Soon after the outbreak of war, government officials called for more vigorous action on the economic front. First to feel the effects was the automobile industry. The head of the War Production Board (WPB) had a simple solution: the complete shutdown of all work on automobile production for the duration.

No More Metal.
L81, The Toy Limitation Order.

IN MARCH the newly passed War Powers Act gave governmental materials allocations the force of law and provided the enforcement weapons. Soon a series of L and M orders rolled off the WPB's presses. The L (limitation) Orders generally applied to finished production and the M (conservation) Orders to raw materials. By June 1942 there were 133 L Orders and 160 M Orders in effect along with nearly six hundred supplements and amendments thereto. They were issued in chronological order. These orders constituted an unprecedented tinkering with the vast and complex U.S. economic machine, but were absolutely necessary in an all out war effort. It has been stated that each order affecting a particular industry or industries was like turning a switch or a valve. The purpose, an officer said in a speech, was to insure that materials coursing through a diverse nationwide production machine emerged as a needed tent or rifle rather than breadboxes or picnic tablecloths.

These L and M Orders affected the most critical materials and industries. The toy industry was about two-thirds of the way down the list. The WPB order that was to govern the raw material used for toys for the remainder of the war was L81 and was issued on March 31, 1942. The order, with the exception of a very short phase-in period stopped production of toys made of metal including the critical components of steel, tin, copper, brass and lead, as well as those made of certain plastics, chemicals and oils, and other peripheral, but essential, components. Only seven percent by weight of any kind of metal was allowed in toys for the duration of the war. Major elements hit by the order, which was not unexpected, were mechanical and electrical toys, soldiers, bicycles and tricycles, skates, pistols, rifles, cars, trains, trucks, airplanes and the like. Educational toys, games, puzzles and dolls, categories that traditionally con-

stituted over forty percent of industry production, were largely unaffected.

One major interpretation of the order, however, did result in a less dramatic effect on the availability of metal toys for the remainder of the year. Completed toys in inventory could be sold and did not need to be converted to other uses. More importantly, until June 30 manufacturers could continue to make toys from materials on the prohibited list from any raw materials that they had in inventory and from any materials that had received any sort of "processing." Many metal toys, therefore, remained on shelves for several months in 1942 and were marketed in the trade press. The Butler Bros.' 1942 wholesale catalog, while featuring many of the newer war toys made from "nonessential materials" such as wood, continued to offer many Marx, Wyandotte, Wolverine, and Baldwin toys and games made of essential materials. Butler informed buyers that planning the 1942 series of catalogs was particularly difficult because of the uncertainties of manufacturing, production and shipping, and that the situation had forced it to eliminate a number of its major lines of metal and rubber toys. It went on to say that it was making a "special effort" to show some of those lines in its pre-Christmas catalog. What was happening was obvious. Major wholesalers were competing for the remaining stock of popular metal toys. While it was a seller's paradise, it clearly was a situation in which none really wanted to be. Thus, in certain toy lines, particularly where some companies anticipating restrictions had stocked up, the short term impact on others was severe.

It is hard to trace from contemporary records and trade press reports which manufacturing companies and retailers initially faired better than others. The press did report that buyers from "large organizations" had anticipated shortages and lines that seemed most likely to be affected and had placed large orders for "real goods, rubber toys, mechanical and steel toys and train sets." As compared with some industries, i.e., autos and major home appliances where production of the product was banned completely and the industry converted 100 percent to war work, the effect on most toy makers overall was not nearly as drastic for some time. At

During 1941 and 1942 the pages of women's magazines were crowded with pictures of society matrons and debutantes dressed in volunteer service uniforms. Paper dolls followed suit.

least continued production of the general product was allowed. That was, of course, putting the best face on things. The Office of Civilian Supply (OCS) did list toys among forty-eight items under "minimum civilian consumer requirements [since toys] are needed for children's recreation and welfare, and will not require critical materials and can be produced by noncritical labor."

The New York City Toy Fair, which always occurred in the spring, commenced in 1942 just three weeks before the metal ban went into effect. The trade press reports, comments and predictions concerning the effects of the upcoming metal ban are interesting. In most cases, the writers hit the nail right on the head. Government priorities, they said, will cause manufacturers and buyers to face the problem of finding new items or lines to replace those that were no longer available. The Toy Fair thus presented an opportunity to take advantage of the emergency circumstances and to discuss cooperative measures with each other. Early evidence of how U.S. toy makers already were coping with shortages appeared here for the first time. That year's Toy Fair, said one, "will be a visual example of the American Toy Manufacturers' ingenuity in a determination to produce toys with a realization of the country's need for war materials and the need for playthings to sustain home morale." And so it was.

Wooden tanks, airplanes and "jeep" cars were prominently displayed. Skineateles Handycrafter's "Midgie-Toy" line of small automotive wooden military toys made its debut as did many other wooden toys. Selchrow and Righters' "Empires" board game and the Dave Dawson line of military games started a popular trend in the spring that continued right through the war. Along with Milton Bradley's "Fighting Marines," "Bataan" and "Ferry Command," "Secret Bombsight," "Sky Chute," and "Air-Raid Target" kicked off the target type games so popular with the under twelve crowd.

Early wartime use of cardboard for punch-out and cut-out military toys and dolls took some months to develop,

but in 1942 the industry did give us the "U.S. Army Infantry and Action Set" and Samuel Lowe Co.'s creative "Sailors and Soldiers" punch-out books. A few military paper dolls made an appearance in 1942 contemporaneous with the organization of the various new women's uniformed services and civilian "home front" organizations. Lowe's "Girls in Uniform" paper doll set is a prime example. The use of paper as a substitute for strategic materials was on its way.

The second major wartime governmental intervention in the free enterprise system occurred on April 28. Intended to halt a rapid increase in the cost of living, General Maximum Price Regulations froze prices, with a few exceptions, as of March 1942. Due to the seasonal selling patterns of the industry, this put retailers in a squeeze since spring wholesale prices were higher than Christmas holiday due to volume buying. Thus, the public now was paying more than it had quite recently. This anomaly was corrected somewhat in the summer when more detailed price regulations, including procedures for obtaining price approval for new products or increases for old ones due to cost increases, were issued. While trying to hold wartime inflation down overall, the Office of Price Administration (OPA) attempted to be reasonable and to give manufacturers prices that reflected their production costs plus reasonable markups, while at the same time to maintain prices within a range that was on a competitive production price level.

While state and regional OPA offices had strong enforcement authority to issue warning notices to price violators and to seek court license suspension orders and fines, a detailed review of available historical materials does not disclose any significant violations by the toy industry. They were good, patriotic citizens. Individual price orders for new toys started flowing in summer 1942. Most applications were approved (nine of the first twelve were for wooden toys) and by the holiday buying season, things were on their way to being sorted out. As in most instances, makers and buyers, wholesalers and retailers learned to cope. In fact, it was reported that with the price situation clarified buyers were again active by early fall and road salesmen were "taking orders as fast as they could write them."

WAR WORK AND THE TOY INDUSTRY

BEGINNING SLOWLY in late 1940 and increasing throughout 1941 to mid 1942, many toy manufacturers gradually shifted to full or part-time production of war materials. By the spring of 1942, just about every company with suitable facilities at least was planning for war production and taking the steps necessary to make appropriate plant and equipment conversions.

Companies who previously made playthings from copper, steel, aluminum, rubber and other critical materials started turning out life rafts, bomb parts, radios and metal shells. Those who had worked principally with wood, leather, cloth, glass, paper and plastic produced uniforms, containers, packs and ammunition cases. By mid 1943, when the toy industry's shift to war work was at its peak, it was estimated that about fifteen percent of the toy companies were producing about five thousand different items for the war effort. The industry had, in truth, gone to war!

Comparatively few toy makers had shifted to war work during World War I, a fact that applied to most American industry. This was due to the fact that America entered WWI so late and hence, during their brief one year involvement, most of the material used by American troops overseas was made abroad.

In the fall of 1942, *Playthings* published a special section in its October issue entitled "Playthings Presents 'The American Toy Industry at War.'" Even though wartime censorship limited, in some cases, exact details as to what a particular plant was producing, this article is fascinating reading for those interested in the history of particular toy companies or for collectors who specialize in certain toys.

In a few instances, the process of conversion from toy making to partial or full war production literally occurred overnight because machines and facilities were in place. Most factories, however, had to acquire new machines and equipment to meet their contractual obligation with the

A feature article in the October 1942 issue of *Playthings* magazine publicized the important war work being done by various toy makers.

government, and that process usually took three to four months.

The list of companies producing war materials included most of the industry leaders. Many produced war items that were a natural extension of their peacetime line. For example, Auburn Rubber, famous for its soldier sets, shifted 100 percent to war work and turned out rubber parts for boats, tanks and planes. Eagle Rubber Co., Ideal Novelty and Toy, Sun Rubber, and Oak Rubber, all makers of rubber dolls, toys, balloons and like products, readily converted to the manufacture of life preservers, inflatable boats, weather balloons and raincoats.

WHEN OUR TOY RUBBER SOLDIERS COME MARCHING HOME . . .

bringing all the Auburn Products with them . . . .

. . . we will extend to our customers the same spirit of helpful service that won loyal friends in the past. Friends who graciously accepted the many curtailments imposed by conditions of war.

When peace returns we are keyed to expand our previously comprehensive line of rubber toys, sales, heels, taps, fly swatters and other popular items to meet all requirements of eager postwar markets . . . a bigger and better Auburn Line definitely in step with the faster tempo of days to be.

Now Auburn equipment, manpower and skill are devoted to shaping the tools of victory. We are proud of that and would not have it otherwise

But soon, we hope, the sun will rise on an Auburn Plant busy once more with toy soldiers that will tramp into the hearts of glad children . . . busy again producing handy domestic, everyday things designed to make life more liveable.

Auburn
RUBBER CORPORATION
AUBURN, INDIANA, U. S. A.

Auburn Rubber converted entirely to war work and produced rubber parts for boats, tanks and planes. Like many companies, Auburn took out ads to let their customers know that they were still around. After the war Auburn did return to the production of rubber toy soldiers but gradually lost its market due to the emergence of new and better plastics.

Manufacturers of displays such as Co-operative Displays Inc. and Visual Instruction Systems had no experience making toys, but once they began to make aircraft identification silhouette models for the armed services, they discovered a civilian market for such items due to the home defense scare. Both made similar sets, with names such as "Sil-O-Models," available to the toy retailer. In many cases, the same machines could be used in the manufacture of defense and civilian items, and when new machines were needed, they were installed with an eye toward easy conversion to peacetime uses.

On the other hand, many famous names shifted to totally different work. Arcade began to produce airplane parts and ship fittings; Milton Bradley, ordnance and aviation parts; Fisher-Price, ship fenders, large glider parts, and pistol and radio specialized chests; and Lionel Trains, precision navigation instruments.

The war work of several well-known companies was classified. Included in this category were Louis Marx Co., Buddy L., Wolverine, Grey Iron, Ohio Art, Hubbley, J. Chein, All-Metal, and Unique Art. Hubbley, for example, made bomb skids, Grey Iron made bomb racks and bomb skids, and Louis Marx made shell casings.

Many companies, proud of their efforts, took out ads in the trade press to reflect their wartime production. Their purpose was two-fold, particularly for those that had shifted one hundred percent; they needed to let their toy customers know that they were still around and that they would be back after the war. Some such as Eagle Rubber and Strombecker could show what they made for Uncle Sam. Others, like Lionel, could not. In either case, the text of these "Remember Us" ads was similar: "Uncle Sam Comes First," "Uncle Sam is our No.1 customer today, but he's not buying Lionel trains," and

"After Victory is won, Eagle will quickly have ready for you all our products which were so popular before the war."

Production awards to toy companies secured major publicity. By fall 1942 the coveted and rarely awarded Army-Navy "E" award for production excellence had been awarded to four toy factories engaged as prime contractors and the related maritime industry "M" award given to a fifth. *Playthings* devoted two full pages of text and photos to a story on A.C. Gilbert Company's receipt of the "E" award. Unique Art, one of very few manufacturers to receive two such awards, also received significant coverage. Impressive local award ceremonies, intended to spur employee morale and production, and featuring bands, high-ranking military officers and, naturally, the ubiquitous politician, were common.

In most cases the companies receiving these awards were those that had converted one hundred percent to war work. A prime example is Steelcraft (Murray Mfg. Co.), which, in addition, had lost thirty-five percent of its work force to the services. Noting that he was prohibited from giving any details as to Steelcraft's wartime activities, the *Playthings* reporter couldn't resist stating that he was sure that Steelcraft's efforts were "effective and will help in bringing down the inevitable downfall of Hitler and Hirohito."

Although the 1942 F.A.O. Schwartz Christmas Catalog still offered shoppers a few metal toys, the majority of items were made of nonstrategic materials such as wood, cardboard and cloth.

SHOPPERS STORM SHELVES

THE FALL 1942 buying and selling season was right on projection with the largest gains made by stores located in areas with significant war work. Early shoppers had the edge, and by late November had just about cleaned the shelves of all toys made of restricted materials that had been produced and stockpiled prior to the spring governmental bans. By Christmas Eve there were very few stores that had any wheel or steel toys, sleds or train sets remaining. High-priced metal toys enjoyed their best sales since the stock market crash of 1929, but it was the last Christmas for two years that metal toys were available.

The F.A.O. Schwartz 1942 Christmas Catalog is illustrative of the retail mix of unsold metal toys and those made of the noncritical materials. Among stockpiled metal toys were three different Lionel train sets, a movie projector, Scout Morse code signalers, a few metal target sets and a full page and a half offering of William Britain's cannons, vehicles and soldiers plus two Dinkey sets of *Hurricanes* and *Spitfires*. This was probably all that was left of the last 1940–1941 shipments of metal toys from England. The majority of Schwartz catalog items used wood, cardboard and cloth and military pieces were numerous. Several pages showed wooden ships by Tillicum and Strombecker, airplanes and tank/vehicle kits, numerous military games, and a wooden "Victory Train Set" pull-toy for the tiny tots. The famous line of Schwartz wartime uniforms and nurses outfits made its first appearance along with "Air Raid Warden" kits and various wood rifles, pistols and machine guns. Gone were the days when Schwartz was criticized for selling a toy machine gun!

Late Christmas shoppers found only the new toys of wood and cardboard that had been rushed to production in the spring. But due to the innovative use of such materials and some fall promotion of the new toys, the encouraging note was that the noncritical materials toys were received enthusiastically by most holiday shoppers. This made toy manufacturers quite optimistic for 1943.

Playthings reported that by January 1943 over one thousand buyers were consulting with suppliers as to 1943 requirements. In order to give manufacturers as much time as possible to produce their goods, their consensus formed the basis of what would be produced during the year. Games, puzzles and military toys were being counted on heavily to produce high volume for department stores; many of which had elected to depart from long standing practice and to maintain year-round toy departments. Particularly with respect to games, puzzles, books and creative toys and toy kits, the thinking was that severe restrictions on pleasure driving and travel in general, coupled with normal weather conditions would provide an excellent market for home entertainment playthings.

THE WAR TURNS

THE MID-YEAR of the four year U.S. involvement in World War II, 1943, proved to be the year in which the war turned in the Allies' favor. Though due to America's massive production capability, there never should have been any real doubt as to the final outcome following its entry into the war, the early setbacks throughout 1942 were not heartening. The year 1943 was to change all that. The year started with the surrender on February 2 of Germany's Sixth Army before Stalingrad, which began a growing Russian counterattack on the Eastern Front. As the year progressed, the unprecedented and massive buildup of American production capacity led to total employment, high wages and, apart from the admittedly serious effects of rationing, significantly improved prosperity on the home front. All of the civilian and military training programs started in 1942 were in place in 1943. Most, but not all, of the bugs in home front defense, in rationing and in the

This advertisement for Buddy L was found in a 1943 issue of *Playthings* magazine. It assures consumers that in spite of the metal restrictions the quality of the Buddy L line remains high.

23

by increased enforcements and Allied air supremacy so that by mid May the Battle of North Africa was over. Rommel was defeated and almost 300,000 Axis prisoners taken.

In the Pacific, although still a secondary theater, results were mixed after the overwhelmingly U.S. Naval victory at the Battle of Midway in June 1942. After horrific fighting, both ashore and afloat, the Battle for the Solomon Islands finally ended after several months with the skillful Japanese evacuation from Guadalcanal in the last week of February. Historians believed that not since the English-Dutch Wars of the fifteenth century had two such powerful navies engaged in such a prolonged, intensive and destructive naval campaign as took place in these restricted waters. Honors were approximately even in the skill and gallantry displayed. The slim margin of overall U.S. land and sea strategic success was basically due to numerical superiority in men and equipment. This relatively small campaign with its numerous land and sea battles had totally preoccupied the U.S. populace for over six months! The key to all of these changing fortunes was the famous Casablanca Conference at which Roosevelt and Churchill and their Combined Chiefs of Staff plotted future Allied operations. While militarily the net result of the ten days of intense meetings was a strategic compromise both in terms of timetables and objectives, the two major decisions reached governed the entire future of the war. The first was the proclamation of an Allied policy of unconditional surrender of their enemies. The second, confirmed at the later Washington Trident Conference in May, was the reaffirmation of the decision to concentrate the basic Allied effort against Germany and the European Front.

All of this was reflected in a predictable increase in home front morale. After the past year of early defeats and later decidedly mixed results, it was somewhat overdue. Hollywood, as usual, did its share. At the high end of the movie scale was the excellent *Hitler's Children, The Moon is Down, Assignment in Brittany, Air Force, Above Suspicion,* and *Bombardier*. The excellent *Five Graves to Cairo*, with the sinister Erich von Stroheim as Field Marshall Rommel, was released in May and reflected the ongoing North African campaign that held the public's attention.

By that spring Grade B double feature war "quickies" were churned out weekly. Some weren't bad, although titles

thousands of wartime regulations governing every day life, work and leisure had been worked out. Thus, 1943 was the first full year of war when everything fell into place. We were 100 percent at war.

U.S. and British setbacks continued during the early months of 1943, particularly in the U-boat war where shipping losses continued to be horrendous. But, evolution of the escort carrier hunter killer groups and increased air patrols in the Azores and Bay of Biscay gradually increased kills so that by June we had won the Battle of the Atlantic. Early U.S. setbacks in North Africa were overcome rapidly like *My Son the Hero, Hangmen Also Die, The Purple V, I Escaped From the Gestapo, That Nazty Nuisance, Hitler's Madman, Mister V,* and *There's Something About A Soldier* left something to be desired. PRC's made on a shoestring release, *Miss V from Moscow,* is considered by many critics to be the worst WWII movie ever made. But good or bad, if one wants to get a flavor of the times and what appealed to the home front audience, it is essential to view some of these mid war films.

On the toy front, it was clearly to be the year of cardboard and wood — with no apologies. Typical was Woodburn Mfg. Co.'s line of cardboard "Rap-A-Jap" punch-out units. Colorgraphic's "Young Patriot" line, which kicked off about the same time, was somewhat better and in the same price range. Colorgraphic's vehicles and ships rolled on wheels and did things: turrets rotated, propellers spun, planes dropped bombs, and guns shot shells. One got a good bit more for his nickels and dimes with the "Young Patriot" all-action line. Colorgraphic even put the inside of some of these box covers to good use. It printed a list of the cost of the actual equipment included in model form. Statements also were included exhorting parents and kids alike to buy war stamps and bonds, help scrap drives and conserve food.

Continuing a trend that started in late 1942, toy merchandisers stressed the military motif, particularly since it was becoming more apparent that interest in military playthings was rapidly increasing among girls as well a boys. Merchandisers urged tie-ins with military events and suggested window displays that included the use of montages of newspaper headlines of battles and victories. Since soon there was a toy reproduction of almost every military weapon, the dealer had toys on hand to deal with every event. World maps surrounded by military toys were useful in making eye-catching windows and counter tops. The trade press and Toy Trade Association gave very detailed suggestions to local retailers as to how to set up such displays and the items to include.

As the war progressed, a few "child-affect" issues relating to war toy production surfaced. Not remotely on the level of the analysis to which we have become accustomed in recent years and of a different type entirely, these studies nevertheless indicate that even then there were those who

Quickie flicks such as *Mister V* often were made in a week on a budget of about $50,000. These films typically made generous use of newsreel footage.

rounded by war news, war work, relatives in the service, mothers in war plants and volunteer work. "They can't help knowing about the war. They're in it too," stated the magazine. It actually felt that many war toys were quite constructive, particularly those of an educational nature such as map sets and construction kits. Offering constructive play with war trucks, tanks, guns, soldiers and boats, allowed children to work off vague and undefined worries. By relieving tension "they are leading healthier lives . . . [and] are feeling more of a part of the family," concluded the report.

Mothers, responding to the poll, overwhelmingly agreed. Examples included the intelligent observations that "[children] play with them [war toys] and discard them just as they do any other toy"; "a child has to learn to live in the world as it is"; "war toys have a place in the child's education." One wonders how such a poll would turn out today, although as Kipling pointed out so well, it seems that opposition to war in times of peace is usually forgotten when war comes.

On the technical side, a number of Government Agency orders governed the toy industry's manner of doing business, many based on experience of the previous year. One, L219, aided small retailers by placing limitations on the amount of inventory that could be stockpiled by companies having large net sales. The small town, independently owned toy store, or the toy "department" of a drug or appliance store (another place where toys often were sold in those days), now had essentially the same opportunity to obtain toy merchandise from wholesalers as the big guys. If the latter's inventory exceeded the new percentage limits, they simply could not buy additional items for the next quarter until their supplies came down to the new formula.

The inventory problem highlighted another wartime effect on industry buying habits. For over fifty years, America's toy buyers for large and small companies alike, made a pilgrimage to New York City, the mecca of the American toy industry, during the first four months of the year. There they saw and judged the new products, made their selections and placed their orders. This time initially was chosen since much of the merchandise, ordered from display samples, was of European origin and had to be made and shipped in time for arrival prior to the heavy fall pre-

were determined to worry about such matters. The *Women's Home Companion* (WHC) magazine felt compelled to employ a child psychologist to do an in-depth investigation and report on the attitude of American mothers toward war toys for kiddies. Articles reflected the "strong partiality" of little boys for uniforms and, heaven forbid, the trend for girls to buy "WAAC and Red Cross costumes just as enthusiastically as their brothers are going for military playsuits." Prominent psychologists were consulted and their response—surprise, surprise!—was that it was natural for children to imitate the wartime adult world environment.

WHC was generally in favor of such toys. It reached the imminently logical conclusion that kids were sur-

This Recent Eye-Catching Window Installed at F. A. O. Schwarz, Featuring Sil-O-Models

SCHWARZ' WINDOWS DEPICT CURRENT EVENTS

Stand on the northeast corner of Fifth Avenue and 58th Street, in New York City, and you will not need a radio or newspaper to keep you informed of either world or local events. Just one glance at the unsurpassable toy windows of the F. A. O. Schwarz toy store and it is easy to tell whether the circus is in town, if there is sailing in Central Park, whether school is about to open, etc., for Schwarz windows are noted for depicting current events.

One of the most recent and interesting windows was given over to a feature display of Sil-O-Models in keeping with the stress that Schwarz is putting on military playthings. Recognizing the demand for military toys and the delight as well as the value of being able to identify airplanes Schwarz arranged a window with Sil-O-Models mounted on a big white wall board in the background. Models hung suspended from the top of the window, were massed on the floor and two doll aviators were shown as though using a Sil-O-Model set. The window attracted a great deal of attention and stimulated sales. The installation appears herewith to show just how F. A. O. Schwarz used the Sil-O-Models to good effect.

So intense has become the demand for military playthings, particularly those dealing with airplanes, that F. A. O. Schwarz has installed an exceptionally good display of Sil-O-Model sets on the spacious second floor. Here the airplane models are shown against a pillar and a counter is filled with an assortment of Sil-O-Model sets.

Sil-O-Models are the product of Co-Operative Displays, Inc., Cincinnati, Ohio, and in the short time they have been on the market have proven to be favorites not only with the children but

The Display Devoted to Sil-O-Models on the Second Floor of the F. A. O. Schwarz Toy Store. Note How the Pillar Is Used to Attract Attention to the Merchandise. Different Box Sets on the Counter Afford Customers a Wide Selection

models, U. S. Army models and foreign models, there being five assortments altogether.

Sil-O-Models are on display in New York City at the showroom of J. Warreny Wiley in the Fifth Avenue Building.

KIDDIE'S FASHION SHOW BY GRAND PRODUCTS

Kiddie's Fashion Show is the latest number to be added to the fast growing popular line of Grand Products, Inc. This new item has been designed so as to enable children to dress a doll in a variety of smart ensembles. Various effects are made possible by the interchanging of dresses and accessories; and, further, children can design their own clothes for the doll. Dresses and costumes are quickly and easily changed simply by slipping a skirt, blouse and accessories over the doll figure and selecting a hat to complete the combination. Kiddie's Fashion Show comes in an attractively designed three-colored display box, 18½ x 10½ x 2½ inches. Included in the set are: 7¾ inch doll body made of heavy fibre board, beautiful doll head with cotton wig and hand-painted face. Silk evening gown, cotton party dress, sports costume with arms attached. Assortment of neckpieces and headwear. Kiddie's Fashion Show is now ready for immediate delivery and may be retailed for approximately $2.00. Grand Products are also the distributors of the Princess Ann Dolls, seven inch composition dolls in a variety of beautifully designed costumes; and of Ti-Nee-People, beautifully dressed cardboard miniature dolls for use with doll houses or as decorative figures. The Grand Products' line is on display at Tom McGinty's showroom, Room 406, Fifth Avenue Building, 200 Fifth Ave., New York, 10, N. Y.

Please Use New Post Office Station Designations on All Letters

TOYS and NOVELTIES—August, 1942

All equipment necessary for a Children's Army is appealingly displayed in this Jordan Marsh toy window in Boston. Uniforms, tanks, planes and trucks dominate the scene. Small flags fly overhead at rear, over several sketched Civilian Defense activities

Stress the Military Motif

THE PLACING of emphasis on the military motif during the month of August is one way of maintaining the present business pace. Interest in military playthings is at a high peak; and the demand for these items continues to grow with each successive action on the part of our armed forces.

Fortunately, there is an abundance of merchandise that can be used in the promotion of military playthings which appeals to both children and grown-ups. To mention a few of the items there are: die-cut cardboard toys, dolls, guns, boats, soldiers, nurse and doctor outfits, puzzles and games. Moving this merchandise from the counters to the hands of the consumers can be accomplished by tying-up the promotion with events of local and national interest.

The store, or some civic organization, can sponsor a War Bond drive

to purchase some specific piece of armament in the name of the community. As a tie-in the retailer can install a window filled with military playthings and posters urging support of the drive. A feature, which will keep interest alive in the display, is to have a chart in the shape of a thermometer for recording the day by day progress of the drive. As a means for stimulating further interest, prizes in the form of military toys could be awarded to the children selling the highest amount of War Bonds. Small daily newspaper advertisements featuring toys and the War Bond thermometer will strike a responsive chord on the part of the public.

Tie-In with Headlines

Each and every day newspapers carry headlines telling of bombings, sea engagements and clashes between armed forces. Inasmuch as there are

toy reproductions of almost every military weapon the toy dealer is in a position to tie-in his promotion with the headlines. In the center of a window place an elevated platform with a jig-saw puzzle map of the world for a backdrop. Flank the platform with all types of military toys, dolls and games. Make use of the newspaper headlines in the following fashion: For example a headline might read: "U. S. Planes Bomb Naples."—Cut out the headline and affix it to a red, white and blue bordered poster on the platform. Surround the poster with airplanes (die-cut cardboard, scale model, wood, etc.) similar to those reported to have taken part in the raid. Have a streamer leading from the headline to the geographical location of Naples on the jig-saw puzzle map. Indicate with small signs the retail prices of the planes and of the various sets from which airplanes can be constructed. Follow the same procedure in regard to headlines telling of sea engagements or troop clashes, substituting for the planes ships, soldiers, tanks or big guns as the case may be.

Any drive or special activity on the part of the local Office of Civilian Defense can be dramatized by showing military toys in a window along with articles used by Air Raid Wardens, and the Auxiliary Police. In this connection special emphasis can be placed upon helmets, uniforms, whistles, ambulances, fire engines, doctor's and nurse's kits.

It is the writer's observation that children under the age of seven play not so much with guns, tanks and planes as they do with doctor's and nurse's kits. These youngsters seem to prefer treating the "ill" and the

Playing with Soldiers Is a Popular and Entertaining Pastime

(Please turn to page 39)

Christmas toy season. Year after year, however, the importance and attractiveness of U.S. toys increased while the demand for foreign products decreased.

Around 1900 this informal spring period, usually in April, came to be known as the "Toy Fair," so-named because of the famous European Toy Fairs held in Leipzig and Nuremberg, Germany. Early attempts to hold regional U.S. fairs in Chicago and San Francisco to save travel time, prior to the advent of regular commercial airline service were successful for a while. Gradually, however, for planning purposes and convenience of all concerned, it became apparent that a single buying period at a known, unchanging location afforded the most economical and satisfactory method of selling and buying.

The trade press gave toy retailers detailed suggestions on setting up displays that tied in with current events.

27

Another reason for the evolution of this major, one-time, one-place a year, three to four week toy buying season was the fact that during these years, long before the modern-day toy chains like "Toys-R-Us," the majority of stores handled toys, dolls and games only on a part-time basis during the holiday season. Thus, toy buying often was done by sales representatives and consumer product buyers whose main specialty was totally unrelated, e.g., the buyer's biggest job was the purchase of sewing machines or dresses.

The war put something of a crimp in this method of operation. Long distance transportation was at a premium. It was very difficult, though not impossible, for buyers at a significant distance from New York to get there by train or bus. Flying was almost out of the question. And, as for private cars, few toy buyers had the gasoline priorities that would allow much long distance travel. While many wholesalers continued to make their selections and place their orders with on-site inspection of the sample, many large retailers and most of the smaller concerns more and more were coming to rely on the wholesalers and middlemen. Thus, for example, the publishers of the Billy and Ruth catalog served as a vital go-between for the very small local retailer and the major wholesalers and manufacturers. These smaller retailers usually received reasonably dependable deliveries, significant transportation savings and, over the long haul, about the same prices.

Particularly in wartime, manufacturers tended to prefer dealing with the wholesaler. Although they perhaps had to sell their products for somewhat less per unit, the additional overhead expense associated in dealing with smaller retailers oftentimes offset this factor. In addition, large carload and truckload lot buying cut distribution costs. These days, when the independent retailer has all but disappeared from the American scene in many communities and we are forced to rely on the chain, all this may appear basic. But in 1938, right before the start of WWII, of 1,770,355 retail stores of all kinds in the United States, over 1,600,000 were independently owned and they sold over seventy-seven percent of all finished merchandise in the country.

There were many large wholesale houses located in major population centers throughout the U.S. in those years, including Butler, Buhl, and Seigal. Copies of their wartime catalogs are difficult to obtain and are expensive. Even the Library of Congress and the Smithsonian have but a very few. While pricey, wartime Christmas toy catalogs of the major retailers, such as Sears, Montgomery Ward, F.A.O. Schwartz are easier to find with diligent effort.

These catalogs make for fascinating analysis. Several dozen pages of toys usually are featured, along with numerous other military or service-connected collectibles of the period. The twenty-seven page wartime catalog of the N. Shure Co. of Chicago, a seventy-five-year-old firm, is illustrative of the offerings of these purveyors of smaller general merchandise from altimeters to wrenches. Very little furniture, appliances or clothing were offered. In the toy section, several hundred items were shown. The manufacturer's name was seldom listed (usually in the case of kits it was Ott, Comet or Strombecker) and prices almost always quoted per dozen. Just reading them makes the collector's mouth water—a dozen Wyandotte punch-out "Naval Patrol" boxed sets sells for $21.00 and there is a whole page devoted to Milton Bradley wartime games.

The "packager" who simplified the complex process of buying holiday toys for the part-time toy retailer had been around for some time, but the most well known and successful was the "Billy and Ruth" toy distribution plan of the Supplee-Biddle Hardware Co. of Philadelphia. It had its origin in 1927 when the firm, seeing an unmet need after a year of intense market research, published its first Billy and Ruth catalog. In effect, the book was a compact toy catalog listing and illustrating reasonably priced toys for all age groups. The characters of Billy and Ruth were presented to the public as two average children who had assisted Santa Claus in making his toy selections.

The plan was simple: Supplee-Biddle selected about two hundred toys and printed an attractive, cheap-paper catalog. Participating dealers ordered as many catalogs as they wanted for free distribution to the store's walk-in customers. A large space was left on the cover for local printing of the retailer's name. The dealer did not have to order all of the merchandise pictured, but most did since it was preferable to be able to back up any advertising piece with merchandise. It was estimated over five million toys were sold by the Billy and Ruth method each year. The average price of a Billy and Ruth toy was one dollar with many selling well below that figure. It was a very clever toy selection, geared specifically to the lower and middle class consumer, the exact opposite of the top of the line, pricey F.A.O. Schwartz, New York City approach. After fourteen years the plan was widely accepted. At the start of the war over eleven wholesalers cooperated with Supplee-Biddle and over a thousand small retailers nationwide participated in the plan each year.

Had it not been for Billy and Ruth, the parents of millions of kids living in the small communities of America during those years would never have had such a wide selection of playthings. Gas rationing would have prevented many parents from driving the long distances required to get to the big city department or toy store. Sears and Mont-

gomery Ward were the mail order alternatives, but that process lacked the advantage of eyeballing the goods. Billy and Ruth handed the local drug or hardware store a ready made mini-toy department on a platter each year.

An examination of the 1943 catalog gives an excellent overview of what was available in lower price toys. Of over 350 toy items featured, only one had any significant percentage of metal. Of over 105 toys for older kids, thirty-five were purely military in nature. Significantly, a comparison of the Billy and Ruth catalog with the Sears, Montgomery Ward and F.A.O. Schwartz catalogs for the same year shows almost no overlap between them. Illustrative items in Billy and Ruth were "Bomber Ball" and "U.S. Air Force Target" games, $1.00 each; "Junior WAAC" kit and "Junior WAACS Sewing Set," $1.00 each; "Commando Periscope" and "General Punch-Out" set, 50 cents each; "Junior Bombsight" and "Torpedo Action" games, 29 cents and $1.00, respectively; "Ski Patrol Boat," 35 cents; and "Sub-machine Tom-E-Gun," $1.00.

As 1943 progressed the continuing increase in the massive U.S. production effort caused numerous problems for the U.S. toy industry. Probably the major problem, not unique to this industry, was the severe manpower shortage as more and more people were drafted or went into critical and higher paying war work. The problem was predicted to get worse and thus, in the spring and summer months, toy manufacturers tried to produce and ship as much as they could with what remained of their ever eroding experienced work force. When combined with delivery delays caused by wartime transportation priorities, the manpower shortage caused a serious problem particularly for smaller manufacturers. It was a tough nut to crack. The supply of younger men and skilled workers such as tool and die makers and machine operators was limited, and the government's War Manpower Commission had detailed regulations that, in conjunction with draft deferment policies of the Selective Service Commission, actually allocated the worker supply. The toy industry obviously was deemed to be one that simply had to get along without this type of manpower. The effect was to force certain younger, but experienced labor units out of the industry and into critical jobs that carried draft deferments.

The only solution for the industry was to turn to per-

An early war ten-cent envelope toy. Not many have survived.

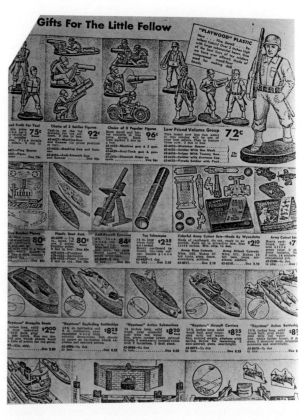

sons not subject to the draft, i.e., women, overaged men, and the physically handicapped. It quickly did so, and with some positive results, far less turn-over with older workers, for example.

The spring 1943 Toy Fair illustrated the continuing success of the industry in adapting itself to the use of substitute materials. The battle of the punch-out kings continued. Colorgraphic, which claimed to be the first to design, manufacture and sell cardboard Army, Navy and Air model sets in 1942—"First on the market, first in sales appeal, first in the hearts of young Americans"—introduced several new

"Young Patriot" boxed sets in a series of multipage color ads. Its major competitor, D.A. Pachter Co.'s Build-A-Set line, also became quite aggressive. Both companies emphasized furnishing large window and counter point-of-sale displays to their retailers.

Some novel toy and craft products were introduced in spring 1943 and increased emphasis on production of old standbys became apparent. On the new side, the clever use of ceramic and plaster of Paris-type materials was seen in some new sets. They seemed to be highly popular. Detroit Toy Company used ceramics in producing a line of fine,

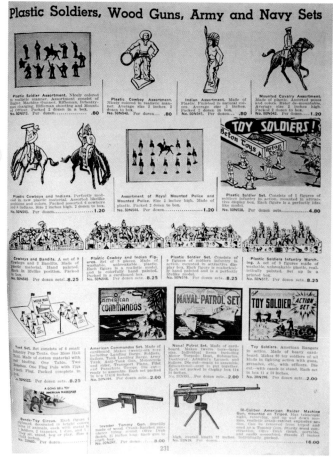

unpainted figures of a standing sailor, soldier, marine, aviator. The figures were five inches high and came with brushes and a palette of "non-poisonous" watercolor paints. They were sold in single, double and triple sets at fifty and seventy cents and a dollar.

Carvatoy, sold by Roni Studios of Whitestone, N.Y., launched its "carv-it, color-it" plastic-of-Paris line in March. Ten to twelve inches high, the line featured action poses of a WAAC, a WAVE, a soldier with machine gun, a sailor loading shell, an aviator and a tank. "Carvatoy" really should have been called "Sandatoy"; no carving, cutting or

sculpting was required. Instead one had to sand down the rough, unpainted figure to prepare it for painting. Brushes and paints were furnished. Children enjoyed displaying the figures on their dressers or mounting them on ashtrays, bookends and the like.

Carvatoy's exclusive distributor, the New York toy wholesaler George Bargfeldt Corp., launched a national contest in which local retailers awarded prizes for the most creative adaptation of a Carvatoy figure. A thirteen year old from the New York suburbs won Macy's contest by using the Tommy-gunner to produce a highly imaginative book

OUR TOYS *are* Sensational
THE TALK OF THE TOWN
WHEN YOU PAY US A VISIT
YOU'LL FIND THE BEST THAT'S AROUND

Above and Below: Two of the Streamers in the Billy & Ruth Ad Kit

THIS IS AN OFFICIAL
Billy & Ruth
HEADQUARTERS *Store*

Get on the BILLY and RUTH Band Wagon — and come to Christmas City!

BILLY and RUTH and TERRY
with GREATEST TOY SHOW on EARTH

M. A. PACOSA & SON
EXCHANGE STREET
CHICOPEE, MASS - PHONE 114

Boys and Girls BE SURE TO SEE OUR HOBBY ITEMS!

HI-YA PALS COME IN AND LOOK AROUND

Girls BE SURE TO SEE OUR LOVELY DOLLS

In addition to the catalogs, participating Billy and Ruth dealers received a kit of advertising materials containing newspaper "ad mats," price cards, and an assortment of banners and streamers for use in windows or to hang over the isles or on counters in the store.

frame for his aunt featuring her serviceman son's photo. He got his picture in *Playthings*, but it isn't reported what his prize was . . . maybe some free Carvatoys?

Also new was the Electric Corporation of America's use of Allied invasion and naval task force themes. These themes reflected the start of the use of American forces in more positive, offensive roles.

The popularity of wartime juvenile fiction, first introduced in 1941–42, continued to grow so much that many toy departments decided to create children's book departments. Publishers quickly reacted to the demand and arranged special wholesale deals and marketing services for toy buyers. Ads by major publishers such as Whitman's and Rand-McNally started appearing regularly in the trade press.

Topical military games continued to be popular. Following up on its best selling "Bataan," Milton Bradley introduced its smaller "Battle of the Tanks." This game quickly capitalized on the first American ground activity of the war in the European-African theater. The game, said Milton Bradley, gave its player the opportunity to re-enact the same kind of battle that had produced headlines. "Kamerad! Just

like North Africa!" said the trade ad. "M-4s vs. the Panzers." "Events of the real war." The fact that our green troops got their clocks cleaned at Kasserine Pass, resulting in a major shakeup of the U.S. command and that the British did 90 percent of the fighting in the theater, does not get mentioned in the game instructions, a far cry from today's involved and historically accurate computer and board war games. "Battlefield," a captive type game by Illinois Game & Toy, had the same North African tank theme, at least according to the box art. Only the pickiest of kids would have noted that the *Dauntless* dive bombers pictured were not used in North Africa.

As the Toy Fair ended, buyers (and sellers) adapted to wartime conditions. Buying early on a large scale, especially with respect to popular items, was the prudent thing to do. Thus, most companies placed the majority of their orders in April. The sharp wartime rise in employment and much higher salaries in defense work, caused many larger toy retailers to stay open year round as newly employed people in defense plant jobs spent money quickly. As soon as goods were received, they were placed on the retail counter.

All of this, coupled with packaging materials shortages and transportation delays—bad in the east, worse in the mid and far west—made the planning of a consistent production schedule chancy. Many manufacturers, through no fault of their own, had to notify accounts that they were

The trade press constantly emphasized the important war work being done by toy makers.

Above

Retailing at one dollar, "Bild-A-Set" was a tremendous buy and led the way in sales of punch-out toys during the 1943 Christmas season.

Right

Typical of advertising in the winter of 1943 was Dave Rapaport's pitch for his new line of cardboard "Rap-A-Jap" punch-out units. These three early sets did attempt to emphasize military realism, but soon were improved upon greatly by other companies. Woodburn prided itself on featuring not only infantry figures but also specialists such as signal corps and radio units, parachutists, motorcyclists, and medical corps.

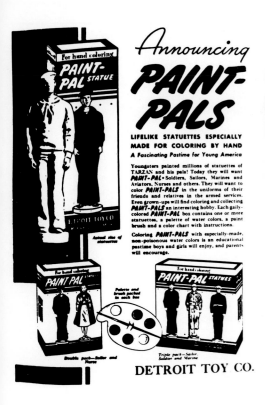

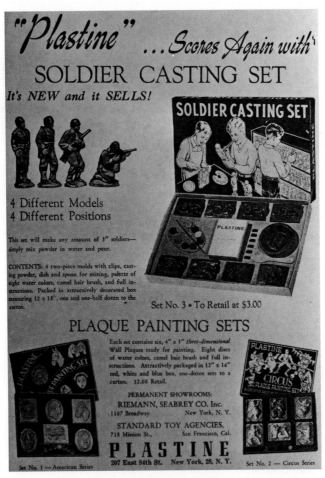

Above Right
By the spring 1943 companies such as Detroit Toy Company, Plastine, and Roni Studios were making use of ceramic and plaster of Paris-type materials to produce military figures for painting. Unfortunately, few such figures have survived.

Far Right
Advertisements for small book sets in *Playthings* magazine show military fiction prominently displayed.

able to make only partial deliveries on large, early orders. On both sides, everyone did the best they could. But as in most cases during World War II, most everyone accommodated to these wartime difficulties with a certain amount of understanding. "There's a war on you know!"

War news kept getting better as the year progressed. Sicily fell to Allied forces on August 17. Italy, having overthrown Mussolini a few weeks early, surrendered on September 8 and was invaded the next day, the first invasion of the European mainland. Italian-American immigrants who had suffered some wartime ostracism from native American's were thrilled by these events. A window display featuring toy punch-out cardboard soldiers aided one New

York barber in publicizing the good news. "Invasion" became a new word in the toy field. We began to see "Secret Invasion" target games and "Invasion Battle" punch-out sets and like items as more and more public discussion was had concerning the upcoming attack on Europe, Hitler's fortress.

War bond drives reached a peak during the year. Many in the bigger cities featured large military parades. The Armed Forces assisted by furnishing vehicles, tanks and artillery for these events. It was the first, and perhaps only time, many kids had an opportunity to see the real thing up close. Once wounded veterans started coming home the toy industry made thousands of toys available for use in rehabilitation programs. Products submitted for pricing purposes to the Office of Price Administration were stored and, thereafter, at company expense, distributed by the truck load to hospitals where they were used in rehabilitation courses, as prizes in quiz shows, or distributed by servicemen visiting children. This highly popular program in which the industry took great pride necessitated additional shipments of supplies and sample items and continued right to the end of the war.

Wartime enlistments and the draft also took its toll on toy executives and sales personnel. The trade press regularly featured photos and write ups on their "boys" in the services, many of whom were in active combat. Decorations for heroes were reported proudly. Many found work in the military quite similar to their peacetime industry jobs. Probably the closest one could get to an easy transition was the senior executive of a model making company who served as a naval officer in charge of the Navy's aircraft identification model program.

By fall, bulk toy purchases by retailers having long since been made, the Christmas selling season began. The serious shopper was finding it extremely difficult to find suitable purchases in this the third Christmas and second full year of the war. Books, movies and other amusements of all kinds stayed in great demand but were sometimes difficult to get. And, with respect to toys, consumers knew to expect substitute materials. Thus was born, in the absence of actual goods, the gift certificate.

There was one other major casualty on the toy front that year. For the first time, the annual Macy's Thanksgiving Day parade kicking off the holiday shopping season was canceled due to wartime circumstances. In a full page newspaper ad, Macy's explained in rhyme its many reasons, i.e., no rubber for the balloons, in a lengthy poem. Some of its more poignant lines reflect the times:

> We also want to help defeat the Axis.
> So we're glad to wait until the war is
> over when we'll stage the Big Parade
> again.

> And welcome back oh joy of joys four thousand Macy's girls and boys [employees] who have gone to war. Oh, what a day when they come marching home to stay.

Macy's probably had the best wartime toy department set up of all. It changed its popular long-time 1930's Flash Gordon holiday attraction to a "Flash Gordon Commando Headquarters." For twenty cents, a child got a ticket that entitled him to a trip through headquarters and a visit with the commandos. The child walked up a ramp where he was met by a soldier who escorted him to a mock-up plane that rolled to Buck Rogers Headquarters, where he met Buck in person. He then went along a walkway maze lined with scenes showing the commandos getting ready for raids. At each full-scale diorama scene, our youngster got a pocket of authentic wartime photos showing actual commandos in action. An occasional visitor received a gold bullet entitling him to a special gift. The entire section featured a vast array of military toys and games of wood and card-

Businesses tried to out do one another with homemade displays for holidays such as the Fourth of July. The best often got desirable coverage in the local newspaper or even, as is the case in this instance, in *Life* magazine.
NATIONAL ARCHIVES

35

board available for purchase. What a trip that display must have been for a kid!

A check of Sears, Montgomery Ward and Billy and Ruth's 1943 Christmas catalogs indicates the best sellers nationwide in various categories. "Blockade," "Ranger Commando," "Sea Raiders," "Conflict," "Battle Checkers" and various "Spot-Em" aircraft I.D. games were the rage in games. In forts, various Built-Rite and Keystone models topped the list; in punch-out, Built-Rite's "Young Patriot" and "Bild-A-Set" led the way. In kits, Joe Ott, Cleveland and Strombecker were the big names. With respect to wooden toys, the catalogs featured numerous ratchet machine guns, rifles, Tommy guns, tanks, trucks and planes from various makers. Military uniforms for children, army nurse and doctor kits, and blackout and air raid warden items were all popular. Books and puzzles, many of a war adventure and scenic nature, were high on most parents' shopping lists. Due to spring buying by the stores, supplies of both were quite adequate.

The December issue of *Children's Activities* magazine made toy recommendations that were relied on heavily by many parents. This year the editors featured "Built-Rite Forts," "Daisy Chattermatic" sub-machine guns and rifles, army periscopes, map framing and blackout kits.

Norma Electric Corporation, whose production of Christmas electric light sets had been stopped by war work, but who continued to produce wooden toys placed this poetic ad in *Children's Activities*:

. . . my sister and I   For one night will come
wait still in the dark   When all men are free
see only the blackness . . .   The whole city will twinkle
And see the guns bark   For sister and me.

AS 1944 OPENED the Axis were on the defense. The German gamble in Russia had been lost. After horrendous battles, the largest in history, the Nazi's Eastern Front was crumbling. Italy was out of the war, North Africa cleared and the Mediterranean completely opened. In the Pacific, as the year opened, the Rising Sun was beginning to set. While major land battles had yet to be fought, the U.S. Navy was substantially stronger than a year earlier and U.S. subs were taking a high toll on Japanese merchant shipping.

Much was left to be done. Despite the ravages of huge Allied bombing raids, the German economy still was producing war materials at ever increasing rates. The Gallop poll in mid January 1944 found that more than half the country thought that the war would last more than a year, although no one had any doubt as to who would win. Patriotism remained sky-high. The eighty-year-old widow of a Civil War Confederate General working in an aircraft plant in Atlanta was quoted as saying: "I am going to assist in building a plane to bomb Hitler and the Son of Heaven [the Japanese Emperor] to the Judgement Seat of God."

The increasing air of optimism regarding an end to the war was reflected in toy industry trade press articles. While no improvement was anticipated in the many problems that had plagued manufacturers in the shortages of raw materials and labor, thoughts were starting to turn to peacetime conversion and transition matters. *Playthings* editorialized that even if the "Nazis surrender in the next six months, the priorities needed to rebuild Europe and to thoroughly trounce the Japs who are a fanatic, dastardly and formidable foe" would result in no marked changes until 1945. The article was right. Still, committees were formed to predict and plan for the immediate postwar period.

New toy products for 1944 were variations on earlier successful themes. Numerous new paper punch-out vehi-

Doctor and nurse's kits included all the appropriate bandages and armbands as well as candy pills and cardboard scissors!

Spring-loaded target games were popular throughout the thirties. Only the lithography needed changing. This version by Wolverine has an odd scene of a warship firing on a passenger liner.

Early plastic HO Scale
airplanes were made in
bright primary colors.

cles, ship and toy sets and wooden guns, ships, and tanks were produced. The hardest job was probably that of the marketing people who were called upon to think up new names and subtle variations on the same theme. Nonetheless, people continued to gobble the stuff up and sales continued to rise over the course of the year and to exceed $300,000,000. There were a number of reasons for this new record, not the least of which was the record number of births. Increased purchasing power was another. Just prior to the war, there were over 13,000,000 unemployed. During the first three years of the war, there was virtually full employment and war workers were taking home wages beyond their fondest dreams. Parents and relatives showered toys on children who had been denied them during the depression. Distance was no object. Jim Morris of Vicksburg, Mississippi (whose toy collection is now so big he had to build a museum to house it), treasures a picture that was featured in the local newspaper. It shows the Morris children holding early wartime toys bought from funds sent home by their dad, an officer with General Patton's famous Third Army.

The big news of the year, and of the war to date, was the long-awaited massive Allied invasion of Europe. On D-Day, June 6, 1944, 176,000 Allied soldiers swarmed ashore at Normandy. A few days later, WWII's most famous war correspondent, Ernie Pyle, walking in the wreckage of Omaha Beach on what he called "a lovely day for a stroll" found an unused American tennis racket brought ashore by an infantryman, reflecting, he wrote, the optimism of American youth.

New toy companies continued to emerge. A comparison of 1943 and 1944 toy advertisers in *Playthings*' Market Place Index is illuminative. Manufacturers of airplane construction kits increased from eight to twenty-two and book publishers showed an identical increase. Fourteen companies making die-cut cardboard toys were listed in 1944; there had been no listings at all in early 1943. Reflecting the continuing need on the home front to stay at home, the game category went up over fifty percent to sixty makers, and puzzles went up thirty percent. Listings doubled for makers of wooden guns, holsters and pistols. Sadly, several categories ceased to exist; iron, metal and rubber toys left the Index until war's end.

Notwithstanding the temporary scare brought on by the German's Christmastime offensive in the Ardennes forest, the Battle of the Bulge, optimism concerning an early end to the European conflict remained high. Christmas toy sales were terrific as customers became fully adapted to the substitute materials. They had no choice. The Billy and Ruth catalog for 1944's holiday season had no metal toys. It also reflected the beginning of a phase-out of military toys (down considerably to only twelve items) and a phase-in of more peaceful items similar to those available before the war. The toys selected by *Children's Activities* magazine indicated the same trend.

As 1945 opened, the end was in sight in Europe. By March, Allied Air Forces had virtually crushed the once proud Luftwaffe and had run out of strategic bombing targets. General Patton and others had crossed the Rhine and by April, for all practical purposes, the once mighty German army had collapsed on all fronts. Russian and American forces had joined up on the Elbe River. Notwithstanding the great war news, an unexpected event in early spring devastated the nation. On April 12, FDR, whose rapidly decreasing health had been kept from the country—he couldn't shave himself and had been sick and coughing heavily for months-died suddenly of a stroke at Warm Springs, Georgia. Ironically, only three days earlier, the first shipload of returning American POW's from liberated German camps had reached the U.S. One month later, on April 30, Adolph Hitler committed suicide in his Berlin bunker. As it turned out, none of the three tyrants in the "Hang the Tyrants" game got hung. Emperor Hirohito (not really a tyrant as it turned out) died in his bed at a very ripe old age. War in the West officially ended at midnight, May 8, 1945. The war with Japan was to go on for only four more months.

Though the beloved Spring Toy Fair, scheduled for March 5–17, 1945, was canceled for the first time in forty years due to a governmental travel restriction order in January, its cancellation didn't affect buying all that much. As the war in Europe ended, notwithstanding the unfinished business in the Pacific theater, more and more the toy industry's focus shifted toward implementation of peacetime production and toward responding to changing consumer demands. A long-awaited announcement by the War Production Board, issued on May 10, lifted the general restrictions on the use of metals for toys, effective July 1, 1945. After that date, mills could fill any orders for metal goods to the extent that they did not interfere with government priority orders already in hand. Anticipating some summer production of bicycles, trucks, cars and other metal toys, some retailers tried to get an edge on the competition by adopting priority plans for good customers who signed up early with a hefty down payment. But most suppliers urged a first-come, first-served policy, stating that their experience had been that priority lists caused customer resentment. They were right. As metal goods started slowly to trickle back on the shelves, little advertising was needed. One store got three dozen pair of roller skates in and put them on a back shelf for a promotion later that spring. They were spotted by a sharp-eyed kid, the word got out, and within a few hours the whole lot was sold.

As a few foreign made toys began trickling in from England and liberated areas of Europe, the OPA found it necessary to regulate price markups on such imports. *Toys and Novelties* issued a strong warning to toy buyers to stay away from "enemy" imports. It predicted that following the total end of hostilities, the situation would be as after World War I when practically every exclusive importer of German toys went out of business due to the fact that the American people would not buy German toys. Many department stores in the early twenties, stuck with large supplies of such toys, publicly burned them to reestablish themselves in the eyes of the boycotting public. The article reviewed the practice of Japan in the 1930s of producing cheap reproductions of U.S. toys, even down to the "Made in U.S.A." on the box, an alleged reference to a fictitious town in Japan called Usa. The great American toy industry, opined the magazine, should not be obliged to compete with goods made by "cheap, rice-eating labor." It concluded:

> We may be sure that those whose sons . . . have fought in France . . . will have no use for any item that bears the German or Japanese label after this war. Those dealers who made the mistake of buying such goods will be obliged to follow the examples of those who made a similar error after the first World War.

How wrong the editorial writers were. European and Japanese industry rapidly was revived by American aid. Within a few years, the F.A.O. Schwartz catalogs were full of the famous German Hausser-Elastolin soldiers, forts and vehicles so popular with upscale American consumers prior to the war. Postwar Japanese tin toys, particularly robots, soon were very well made and today command very high prices.

As the European troops trickled home, island after island in the Pacific fell to MacArthur's forces and Japan was relentlessly bombed by the new B-29 Superfortress. Naturally, the media's focus shifted. Unique Art, whose series of wartime ads in the trade press were creative and eye-catching, immediately shifted its attention. From an ad showing its trademark, the "Merry Juggler" clown, "in the forefront of every Invasion" from Africa through and right up to V-E Day, it jumped to a headline reading, "Your old friend is now Tokyo Bound." Unique had manufactured over 100,000,000 hand grenades, AA shell percussion fuses and, late in the war, the B-29 firebombs that devastated Japan. Its wartime production ad theme was, "Ordnance for the duration, mechanical toys for Peace."

Toy industry executives called to the colors started returning to civilian life. The *Playthings* and *Toys and Novelties'* sections of serving industry personalities were filled with photos and short bios of returning veterans. Many were decorated for heroism. The son of the president of the Los Angeles Craftsmen Guild Company had to bail out of a B-17 over occupied Europe and make his way to safety through enemy lines. Later, he served as head of toys and crafts research and design for his family's firm.

Industry planning for the immediate postwar future became important. What will happen, asked game and puzzle makers and book publishers, when gas is plentiful and people do not have to stay home so much? How will the shift of millions of high-paid workers in wartime industries with plenty of overtime pay to low-paid workers in peacetime jobs affect discretionary consumer buying?

Fortunately for the toy industry, the late war baby boom, which was to continue well past the war years, guaranteed a demand for toys for several years. Said *Playthings*, with a photo showing a couple looking longingly at a Built-Rite cardboard Tudor home, "Where there are homes, there are children, and children must have toys."

This punchout, pop-up, cut-out item was perhaps the best all-around toy made during the war years.

But what kind of toys did parents wish to purchase? During the war years, there was clearly an overwhelming tendency to buy toys, games and children's books with a combat motif. After the war, it was predicted there quickly would be a desire to forget war, and the old toy standbys again would become very popular, particularly with the return of metal as a raw material. Even as the war progressed that spring and summer, the catalogs and ads increasingly changed from forts to doll houses, from soldiers to dolls, from tanks and bombers to trucks and airliners.

Some military toy staples were destined to remain popular. Toy soldiers were high on the list. Five years after the end of the war, F.A.O. Schwartz still prominently featured four military uniforms for children, only two less than in 1942. The only difference in the 1950s was that the kids got promoted; the naval officer of 1942 became an admiral and the pilot, an Air Force colonel.

Some manufacturers just made simple changes in existing stock. John W. Hill's "Ranger Bow Gun," a heavy, wartime fiberboard pistol gun that shot cardboard bullets, quickly became, in fall 1945, the "Robin Hood Bow Gun." The gun was exactly the same; only the printing and embossing and the box cover were new.

VICTORY

BY AUGUST, it was all over. The long-awaited and much-feared invasion of Japan with over a million U.S. casualties estimated never happened. The most closely guarded secret of the war, the U.S. "Manhattan Project," was the development of the first atomic bomb. Even MacArthur didn't learn of it until late July.

Embroiled in one of the most hotly debated ethical questions of all time, newly installed President Harry S. Truman, over the objections of his top two generals, Eisenhower and MacArthur, decided to bomb Japan. On August 6, a twenty-nine-year-old Army Air Force Colonel from Illinois, piloting a B-29 bomber named after his mother, dropped "Little Boy," the uranium version of the bomb on Hiroshima, Japan. Nine days and one atomic bomb later, dropped on Nagasaki, it was essentially all over.

The United States, many historians believe, came out of the war in better shape than when it went in. In one perspective, the war years were happy years for the tens of millions who took part in the unpredicted prosperity following the great Depression. The intense patriotic fever that gripped the country has never occurred again, and a lifelong devotion to country was formed by those who were children during the war. Everyone believed that they had shared in victory. It has been observed that for nearly every person, particularly the impressionable young who watched, then recreated wartime activity in their play, World War II has a special appeal. There was real national purpose without dissent. The nation had confronted identifiable, non-controversial enemies, yet had escaped many of the horrors of war that had befallen the rest of the world. In a way, it could be said that the United States population for the most part enjoyed itself against the common foe: war bond rallies, rationing, substitute materials, school stamp programs, scrap lines, victory gardens, air raid drills, airplane spotting, model plane making, countless war films and tunes showed that all were caught up in the war effort. We beat Hitler and Mussolini and Tojo. Our fathers, uncles and cousins came marching home. So did Auburn Rubber's toy soldiers and Unique Art's mechanical toys. Said an ad in *Playthings* in the fall of 1945, the Merry Juggler was "Home Again."

POSTSCRIPT

MOST WARTIME CONTROLS came off quickly. The Truman administration's commitment to the hated price controls and some rationing continued for over a year until the 1946 elections caused President Truman to abandon the entire program, even though black marketeering and inflation plagued the country. The transition to peaceful toys occurred almost overnight. Within a few months, the great majority of the toys, games, books, puzzles—all the terrific military things that had kept children so enthralled during the war—now dealt with non-martial subjects. The Sears and Montgomery Ward catalogs for Christmas 1945 showed only a few military items, mainly some surplus helmets, plane and tank model kit stock, and wooden rifles and machine guns. Billy and Ruth turned completely peaceful that Christmas. They had only seven military toys in their whole catalog. What a change! The war was over and along with American troops and equipment, toys, too, finally had come home.

These items reflect a lucky home whose soldier boy fulfilled the poster's wish by coming home safely.

2

The HOME FRONT

Advertising agencies put their heads together to come up with plenty of heartwrenching and evocative ads for war bonds. The caption for this one was "Don't Let That Shadow Touch Them; Buy War Bonds."

THERE WERE NO GERMAN land-based aircraft in WWII that could come close to hitting a target on the eastern seaboard of the United States, and the Kriegsmarine never operated an aircraft carrier. The public, however, didn't know this. *Air News,* a "definitive" aircraft magazine of general circulation, in a late 1942 issue, advised that Germany had several long-range bombers that easily could span the Atlantic, drop tons of explosives on U.S. cities, and return to their bases. Air warning spotters soon became the most popular (and unnecessary) part of the U.S. Civil Air Defense effort.

Over 600,000 spotters, with their own special insignia and armbands, were enlisted in the Ground Observer Corps. Together with the Aircraft Warning Service under Army jurisdiction, they served in posts located across the U.S. and every six to eight miles along the Eastern, Gulf and Pacific coasts. Their mission was to report every plane in the sky. Not one spotter ever saw an enemy plane!

Flying officer Naburo Fujita of the Imperial Japanese Navy was the only enemy pilot to bomb American soil. Flying unseen at night and piloting a Zero float plane carried by the sub I-25, he dropped small incendiary bombs on an Oregon forest in November 1942. Coincidentally, during the heyday of blackouts, he honed in on the beam of the Cape Blanco lighthouse. The same year Japan also launched nine thousand large balloons carrying thirty-pound bombs intended to start forest fires. They miscalculated and the balloons were launched during the winter and early spring snow and rainy seasons. Some three hundred did reach the U.S., but only one exploded; as a result six people on a church outing were killed in Oregon. The only other reported bombing of continental U.S. soil occurred in 1943 when an *American* plane from a Texas training squadron dropped six bombs right in the middle of Boise, Oklahoma. Luckily, no one was injured.

In February 1943, a national magazine ran a special cover story on the efforts of spotters in the small town of Kent, Connecticut to vigilantly protect the American skies. The article explained how adult spotters, working in pairs, two to four hours per week, telephoned flash messages to regional tracking centers where, as in the case of German attacks on England, the plane's track was plotted and its identity determined.

Since there were no limitations on a spotter's age and often girls and boys were deemed superior as spotters (they had better hearing and eyesight than many adults), hundreds of thousands of children aided their fathers and big brothers in this aspect of the war effort. Everyone took the job very seriously. The spotters did serve one very useful purpose: by keeping track of planes and systematizing identification, they put a stop to false reports of enemy planes that triggered air raid alerts and caused widespread panic.

The toy industry was quick to catch on and to produce numerous plane identification books, charts, games and other items to involve youngsters in this defense effort. After a while, very few kids failed to distinguish a Heinkel 111 from a B-25.

One of the most popular of the spotter toys was "Plane-O-Graph," a large, rotating-dial fourteen inches in diameter. This spotter's aid was produced in 1942 by a New York company aptly named Plane Facts Inc. Another big seller (due in part to the fact that it cost only a dime), was Leo Hart Company's "Junior Aircraft Warning Service of America." The kit contained all the paper items needed to start one's own "official" observation post. Included in the envelope were thirty-two photos of planes, a large identification chart, a "Height Finder" (if the observed plane fit in a certain size circle it was considered to be at a listed altitude), a "Flight Direction Indicator," an Observer Handbook and Report Book, an ID card, and a cardboard arm-

This painting, used as a full page ad for General Electric during the war, showed the "Spotters' Guide" wall chart from the Leo Hart kit posted on the wall of a basement rec-room.

Above
Colorful and easy to use, the "Plane-O-Graph" probably would have been of more help to the war effort if it had shown enemy, as well as U.S. aircraft!

Right
The cover of Leo Hart Company's "Junior Aircraft Warning Service" kit showed youngsters manning their own "official" observation post.

Far Right
Bombing raids facilitated by spies and enemy agents were a constant theme of comic books and posters.

band that could be held on with a rubber band. The toy was sold throughout the war and was described by Hart in a *Playthings'* ad as "that wartime juvenile success."

Other books and toys contained ID charts as part of a more general theme. For example, the "American in Action" jingoistic playbook contained a full page "Be a Spotter" chart. "Keep a sharp lookout for the enemy in your own neighborhood," warned the manufacturer. Apparently they found it conceivable that the Nazis could have secret air bases located right in our own backyards!

Spotter games were quite popular. Parker Brothers jumped on the bandwagon in the spring of 1943 with "Spotting," a warplane identification game. Although at two dollars "Spotting" was pricey for the times, it was advertised as popular in "every city and town." In 1942 Toy Creations, Inc., a major manufacturer of games, paint sets and dart boards, introduced its large "Spot-a-plane" game. The box cover pictured a large four-engine bomber caught in a spotlight over the New York City skyline.

Two "Squadron Scramble" card games sold by Whitman Publishing Company were also big favorites. These decks had forty-eight cards on which three silhouettes each of sixteen American, British, German and Japanese military aircraft were printed in color. Identifying the various aircraft

made for hours of fun. Incidentally, the player who received the Victory card in the Scramble pack doubled his score.

The U.S. Playing Card Company also produced a standard playing card deck with fifty-two three-way silhouettes of Allied and enemy planes. The literature in the deck indicated that in addition to being useful for normal card games, the pack gave you information of "extreme value" that could assist in spotting enemy aircraft. By covering over the name of the planes, children used the deck to play identification games. Whether it was coincidental, the aces were divided evenly between Allied and enemy planes. This deck was among the more accurate of the card games and "approved" by the National Aeronautic Administration.

Other plane ID toys included "Spotem." Produced by the Electric Corporation of America (ECA), this toy cleverly simulated a cockpit with dials that rotated to show pictures of planes of all nations and data concerning each. The large, six-colored box measured eighteen by fourteen inches and retailed for a dollar. The Genuine Kits Toy Company produced its version of the popular dial format with a large

OFFICIAL KIT

JUNIOR AIRCRAFT WARNING SERVICE
of America

Start an Observation Post!
Here's your equipment!

32
PHOTOS OF MILITARY PLANES
IDENTIFICATION CHART
ALTITUDE HEIGHT FINDER
FLIGHT DIRECTION INDICATOR
OBSERVER'S HANDBOOK & REPORT BOOK
OBSERVER'S ARMBAND
OBSERVER'S MEMBERSHIP CARD
OBSERVATION POST SIGN

A SPY doesn't LOOK LIKE THIS

A SPY may LOOK LIKE THIS

DON'T TALK about
TROOP MOVEMENTS-SHIP SAILINGS
WAR WORK-MUNITIONS SHIPMENTS

Reed Associates' popular punch-out set of famous Allied fighting planes, "3 Flying Models," also contained "American Ace Spotter," a rotating dial made of paper with forty-eight plane silhouettes. The 1944 issue date indicates the continuing popularity of spotter ID toys long after public fear of enemy air raids had dissipated.

wall-hung board called, simply enough, "Plane Spotter." By turning the knob, players could dial, one at a time, three silhouette views of thirty-two different planes painted on the sides of the large dial. Most of these dial toys employed the same mechanical approach and were made of heavy stock paper and cardboard and had wooden knobs.

Even manufacturers of school supplies got involved in the craze. A popular school pencil box was titled "Junior Aircraft Spotter" and pictured various airplane silhouettes. D.N. Robbins' took a simplistic approach; the company merely packaged twenty-five color drawings of planes in

a set entitled "How To Spot It Warplanes." As there was no game involved, it probably was not very popular. Merrill's 1944 "Spot the Planes" coloring book took an educational approach. In addition to coloring the planes, the child could study the three silhouettes and performance data supplied for each plane, and then take a quiz. Answers were provided in the back of the book.

Demonstrating the toy industry's commitment to produce items of proven timeliness and buy-appeal for its retailers, ECA's summer 1943 offerings included an "Airplane Identifier" kit. The kit touted a "magic" airplane identifier, but upon opening the box the child found just an additional dial. Notwithstanding such advertising gimmicks,

Joe Ott Manufacturing Co., the popular model plane kit producer, took advantage of public interest with its "Identoplanes" kit.

45

manufacturers clearly were attempting to gear their offerings to home front trends. They were aided in no small part by the popular print; during 1942 and 1943 numerous articles on plane spotting kept the public's interest high. For example, one magazine ran a cover feature and several major articles on the possibility of air raid attacks. Its March 2, 1942 article went so far as to state that "four-engine Heinkel 177s [could] cross the Atlantic with a heavy bomb load [and] let fly at an East Coast plant." This statement was about 50% off base. The plane and its bomb load would have plunged into the Atlantic about two-thirds of the way across! Further illustrating the temper of the times, another magazine editorialized that in the likely event German crews bombed U.S. cities and, after bailing out, crash-dived their planes, civilians should *not* obey the impulse to "lynch them, shoot them or kick them to death"!

Toy companies were not the only manufacturers to capitalize on the public's interest in aircraft spotting. Coca-Cola, for example, produced a popular, very colorful, seven by four inch, forty-four page booklet entitled, *Know Your*

Advertising informed store buyers that Toy Creations was giving its "Spot-a-plane" game the benefit of one of the most extensive advertising campaigns in game history. The company claimed it had never produced a faster selling game.

Top Right
Although Coca-Cola is including a few WWII items in its offerings of reproduction Coke memorabilia, this colorful booklet, with its outstanding art work by William Heaslip, has not yet been reissued.

Right
Indicative of their popularity during WWII, most "Squadron Scramble" card decks found for sale today are dog-eared from use.

War Planes. Back then, ten cents in stamps or coin bought a copy; today it's highly sought after by collectors of Coca-Cola memorabilia. But even during the war, children avidly collected commercial and advertising pamphlets, booklets, and handouts too numerous to mention.

The prize for the most creative, most guilt-inducing marketing approach must go to the Better Vision Institute Inc. In urging the reader to go to one of its members for an eye checkup and to purchase new glasses, the ad declared in no uncertain terms that defective vision in the spotter's tower was a "betrayal of trust" with the "fate of lives, key production plants, and perhaps the nation . . . at stake."

It is no wonder that the public bought up all these identification games, card decks and cardboard cockpits. "Vision for Victory" required no less!

46

Above
The Lone Ranger radio show offered a "National Defenders Warning Siren" in mid 1941. The plastic siren was actually a cheap bird caller and slide musical instrument.

Red Goose Shoes emphasized their patriotism by urging readers to know the difference between Boeing and Heinkel aircraft.

Left
A full-page magazine ad by Interstate Engineering Corporation kept would-be-spotters informed of the latest American aviation technology.

Of the dozens of coloring books produced during WWII, this one by Merrill had one of the most animated covers. Just look at the steely-eyed determination of the young aviator; what patriotism shows in his face!

47

THE BIG BLACKOUT

Wearing armbands marked with insignia of the Citizens Defense Corps, such as the striped triangle of an Air Raid Warden (left center), instilled pride in those who "fought" on the home front during the great struggle against tyranny.

During and after the London Blitz of 1940, Americans began to worry about U.S. cities being bombed, even though the country was not yet at war. The popular March of Time newsreel shown weekly in all theaters featured one based on the British Air Raid Precautions Service. Entitled *When Air Raids Strike*, it had a profound effect on audiences. Some states and cities, mostly on the coasts, attempted to facilitate civilian preparedness regulations and conduct emergency disaster tests, but the efforts of these local defense committees were, for the most part, a disaster.

The Federal Government was little help. President Roosevelt gradually moved to recognize the rising concerns over civilian defense and finally created the Office of Civilian Defense (OCD) in May 1941. He appointed the famous mayor of New York, the "little flower," Fiorello LaGuardia, who had once read the comics to the kids over the radio on Sunday mornings, as OCD Director. The First Lady, Eleanor Roosevelt, was appointed "Assistant Director in Charge of Volunteer Participation." She enlisted major entertainment and sports figures in the drive to educate the populace in defense measures, but things went slowly. Local councils had poorly trained volunteers. Air Raid Wardens were not supplied with armbands or whistles. Ironically, according to contemporary accounts, the only reliable whistles were made in Japan. Unlike in Britain, gas masks were not available for the public. Air raid warning tests and blackout drills were, by and large, ineffectual. In Washington, D.C., the major

blackout offender during an early drill was the brightly lit building housing the Office of Civil Defense.

One practical problem involved a lack of adequate air raid sirens. The existing sirens lacked range and power. Consequently, often when cities attempted drills, people simply did not know they were underway. Houses stayed lit at night because people had not heard the sirens. Finally, the "Victory" model produced in mid 1942 by Bell Labs solved the problem; allegedly it could rupture an eardrum at one hundred paces.

While the situation gradually got better after Pearl Harbor, people were panicky for a while. On the evening of December 8, 1941, for example, a forgetful merchant at the corner of 4th and Pike in Seattle, Washington, left on his neon sign. His timing was lousy since a blackout drill was underway. Within a few hours, a crowd had gathered, his store and sign were trashed, and pilfering and rioting had occurred. When police arrived to arrest ringleaders, one, a nineteen year old, was defiant. "This is war!" she exclaimed. Even General DeWitt, the commanding officer of the entire Western Defense Command, who should have known better, claimed that thirty Japanese planes had flown over San Francisco on the night of December 8, and that "death and destruction are likely to come to this city at any moment." Afterwards he never explained why the unseen planes (there were none) had failed to drop any bombs. On the east coast, New Yorkers, on the other hand, were their usual blasé selves during an alert the next day.

By all historical accounts, the attack on Pearl Harbor galvanized America's Civil Defense (CD) forces. A strong impetus for action seized the nation. Every hamlet organized committees, and within two months there were over 8,400 local CD organizations. Milwaukee and Chicago warned against air attack. A North Dade, Florida, handbook urged residents to lock their cars so that in the event of an airborne invasion they wouldn't "give easy transport to the Nazis." Blind people, it was suggested, made excellent airborne detectors since they had an acute sense of hearing. Those caught smoking a cigarette during a blackout were subject to a stiff fine. In retrospect this all may seem somewhat silly, but the Civil Defense program united Americans with their government and gave all a sense of purpose.

The tour de force of this popular blackout kit was phosphorus-treated paper that glowed in the dark. The kit remained popular for some time, due in large part to the Good Housekeeping Seal of Approval it was awarded.

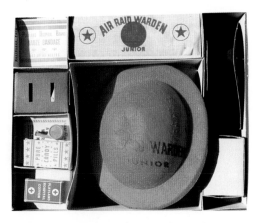

Above
James McGowan Associates' air raid warden kit was advertised extensively in contemporary comic books.

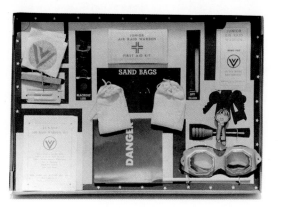

Left
New York Toy and Game Mfg. Co.'s terrific "Junior Air Raid Warden Set" contained almost everything needed to equip an air raid shelter.

Again the toy industry was not left behind. In discussing window displays and toy promotions, the marketing experts urged tie-ins with bond drives and special activities of the local Office of Civilian Defense. Toys were displayed "along with articles used by air raid wardens and the Auxiliary Police," and helmets, uniforms, whistles and doctors' and nurses' kits were emphasized. New York Toy and Game Mfg. Co.'s "Junior Air Raid Warden Set" tied right in. A marvelous

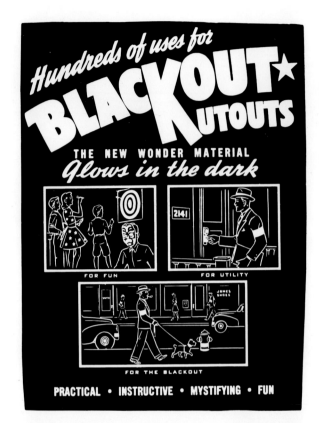

Left
Left
A pamphlet included in the "Blackout Kit" described over hundred uses for the glow in the dark material, uses not limited to civilian defense. Its clever marketing appealed to both children and adults: parents could light up door locks during a blackout, children could play darts.

Left
As was the case with Milton Bradley's "Blackout—Today's Game of Thrills," a striking box cover aided the sale of "Air Raid Warden." This great Milton Bradley game, however, doesn't show up in the 1943 trade press ads, testifying to the decrease in civilian concern.

Above
The object of this dice game was to blackout your section of a "brilliantly lighted metropolitan city" with black squares.

toy, it contained a first aid kit, memo pad (with spares for "sector notes" and "raid reports"), storeroom keys, screwdriver, goggles, a red danger flag, insignia armband, clip, miniature sandbags, whistle, blackout light and instruction sheets. All these items except the whistle and screwdriver shaft were made of paper, cardboard or wood, an excellent example of a mix of the small allowable amount of metal with nonstrategic materials.

A companion piece released by James McGowan Associates consisted of a similar variety of pieces in a large valise.

Included were a cardboard gas mask, a plastic whistle, a red felt "Junior Air Raid Warden" helmet (the better to be seen in the dark), and Playland Hospital brand gauze bandages, boxes of "pure" candy and sanitized hospital cotton. (It is assumed that the latter items were also included in doctor and nurse Kits by the same maker.) The Pledge of Allegiance to the flag was inscribed in large letters on the inside box cover.

FAO Schwartz created its "Air Raid Warden Set" in 1942. From the wide, web belt inscribed "Air Raid Warden" in large letters, hung a variety of working items, including a Hubley metal .45 cal. pistol in a white western-style holster. One wonders who the play warden was supposed to shoot. Never catering to the blue collar crowd, Schwartz sold top of the line toys of every variety. This set sold for a pricy $5.57.

"You owe it to your Uncle Sam to know just what to do in the event of an air attack," reads this comic book advertisement. Owning this kit assured a young man that he would "become the most popular boy on the block."

AMERICAN WOMEN IN UNIFORM

The figures presented on this page show American women in the uniforms authorized for their various types of war work. Never before in the history of the country have women played such important parts on the war front and the home front and enlisted in such numbers as today. This wholesale volunteering for war work releases large numbers of men for the actual business of fighting.

Member of the WAC—Woman's Army Corps.

Member of Women's Auxiliary Ferrying Squadron (WAFS)

Member of American Women's Voluntary Services.

Member of the WAVES—(Women's Reserve of the Naval Reserve)

Red Cross Worker

Army Nurse

Navy Nurse

Civilian defense worker.

Member of Red Cross Motor Corps.

SPAR Coast Guard Auxiliary

Red Cross Nurse

Member of Red Cross Nurse's Aid Corps.

Marine Women's Uniform

Right

value to the manufacturer. The Billy and Ruth catalog also featured this blackout kit. An updated 1943 version, the "Junior Blackout Kit," capitalized on wartime concerns by including an air raid booklet and airplane ID silhouettes.

Game makers, too, did not ignore Americans' interest in civil defense. Milton Bradley, the country's largest manufacturer of games, marketed a blackout and an air raid warden game. "Blackout—Today's Game of Thrills" was first produced in late 1939, well before U.S. entry into the war. "Air Raid Warden" came on the market in 1943. This game of "intense interest, dramatic suspense, and exciting action" had a dedication that easily could win an award for marketing hyperbole:

"Air Raid Warden" is dedicated to the thousands of patriotic men and women whose unheralded, unselfish service is the very core of the democratic way of life. For them, no bugle blows, no medals decorate them, but in the dark watches of the night, under starry skies or storming clouds, their steady reassuring footfalls beat out the credo of America: "We're watching! We're ready! All's well!"

Although aircraft identification and air raids objects occupied the top toy spots throughout the war, other aspects of civil defense did not go unrecognized. Just a few months after Pearl Harbor, the Office of Civilian Defense adopted

One of the more popular sets was "The Blackout Kit" produced in 1942 by the Vernon Company of Newton, Iowa. Its popularity hinged on the clever use of phosphorus-treated paper tape. The kit was advertised widely and sold in major retail chains, and was recommended by the Child Training Association, the publisher of *Children's Activities* magazine. Editors assured parents in the regular "Selected Activity Toys" section, that the phosphorescent material was harmless since the "light emission was visible to the eye at not more than a few yards." Since many parents relied heavily on these semi-official recommendations, they were of immense marketing

PAPER DOLLS in UNIFORMS of the U.S.A.

6 DOLLS

ARMORED DIVISION, TANK

AIR RAID WARDEN

AIR RAID WARDEN

Left
These dolls from Saalfield's "Uniforms of the U.S.A." set demonstrated the versatility required of woman volunteers. She might don an Air Raid Warden's uniform by day, an evening gown by night.

Far Left
Even bubble gum cards sought to demonstrate the importance of educating children on the realities of wartime and of including them in readiness preparations. © GUM, INC.

regulations that allowed toy and hobby manufacturers to obtain licenses to reproduce, fabricate and sell its fifteen different patented insignia. These eye-catching insignia soon became familiar to all Americans. They consisted of various red symbols located within a white triangle on a blue circle: a red ladder represented the Rescue Squad; an airplane the Bomb Squad; a lightning bolt the boys and girls Messenger Squad; and a coffee cup the Emergency Food and Housing Corps. The license application had to contain appropriate sketches of and data concerning the product, and the "ethical character" of the item was taken into account before the license was

issued. A 5% royalty fee was charged, payable, naturally, to the U.S. Treasury.

Paper doll producers were among the many to take advantage of this opportunity. A fascinating piece was Saalfield Co.'s handsome boxed set, "Paper Dolls in Uniforms of the U.S.A. (#S-592)." The colorful box top showed fourteen civil defense insignia and the contents included various civil defense uniforms for women. Similar dolls were contained in two large, colorful booklets produced by Saalfield: "Air, Land and Sea Paper Dolls (#S-313)" and "Victory Paper Dolls (#S-2445)." Both sets contained numerous representations of civil defense insignia.

A DEATH TRAP SET BY THE **7**th COLUMN

Samuel Lowe Publishing Company's "Girls in Uniform (#L-145)" paper doll set gave its dolls names. "Eleanor" worked for the OCD, and "Edith" was a member of the American Women's Volunteer Service (AWVS). (If photo magazines of the time are indicative, the AWVS was very popular with socialites, debutantes and aspiring Hollywood starlets!) Another Lowe set (#L-1048) featured "Babs," an ambulance driver.

Jack and Jill magazine also underscored the importance of civil defense by featuring a couple on their paper doll pages. Mrs. Burns could be dressed in an air raid warden uniform; both Mr. and Mrs. Burns, in Victory Garden outfits.

Significantly adding to children's knowledge of civilian defense and enhancing their imaginative play, were the Handbook of Civilian Defense and the Handbook of First Aid from Whitman Publishing's popular, small, bound handbook series. Intended for all ages and first released in mid 1942, they had chapters entitled "The Duty and Destiny of Every American," "Civilian Morale in Wartime," and "What **YOU** Can Do." Other subjects included defense work, home defense, and air raid protection. Similar civil defense booklets were advertised in comic books and shown on Gum, Inc. bubble gum cards. Even home safety was pro-

moted; one ad showed a war worker about to slip on dime store soldiers a negligent child had left laying on the stairs.

Both adults and the government took seriously the child's role in civil defense and the general emotional impact of the war declaration and early war news on children. In the spring of 1942 the Department of Labor issued a five-cent pamphlet entitled "To Parents in Wartime." Prepared by a psychologist, the booklet recommended that the realities of war and defense be included in family life as rapidly and routinely as possible. It proceeded on two theories: that children could be taught not to fear and that education was important. Parents of younger children were advised to make wartime conditions and civil defense a game.

Life magazine did a fascinating three-page pictorial spread on this approach entitled "Children in War" in its March 30, 1942, issue. A Queens, Long Island, family with two small children is shown playing "air raid shelter" under the dining room table. The kids are wearing Churchill suits, tin hats, and armbands. "Like a picnic to the kids is a family dash to the cellar for a practice drill," reads the copy. "They carry food [in this case a box of Graham Crackers], a flashlight, their favorite toys." The parents, properly praised for "fostering a sense of family solidarity," are shown including the children in measuring food supplies and in hanging up blackout curtains, and accustoming the children to being in the cellar for long periods.

One photograph shows father and son engaging in a naval battle on the living room floor. A Keystone catapult aircraft carrier is shown prominently. Contrary to postwar child psychologists who have railed against "warlike" toys, the experts of the time believed that playing with war toys often helped little boys release hidden anxieties by acting them out. (Little sister, on the other hand, usually was photographed playing army nurse with a favorite doll, perhaps so that she would be a more practical patient in case she was hurt in an air raid.)

Notwithstanding all the publicity, private and public air raid shelters were never built on any scale in the United States. In some cities, buildings were designated as shelters simply by the use of the large "S" on the front. None of the public's interest or concern, however, was lost on the clever entrepreneurs in the toy industry.

Mom Gave Away My Toys

Today Lionel trains sell for hundreds and thousands of dollars, as do countless other prewar metal toys. Scarcity has much to do with the high price for such collectibles.

In the summer of 1942 the War Production Board instituted a mammoth, well-advertised national metal scrap drive to cope with increasing shortages of steel, aluminum, rubber, priority metals, and particularly tin due to the Japanese occupation of Southeast Asia. The drive was something in which every American could become involved and has been called the biggest scavenger hunt in the nation's history. Attics and basements, farms and apartment buildings were combed for pots, pans, old overshoes and anything else that could aid the war effort. Britain and some of its commonwealth nations, such as Australia, had been doing the same thing for some time. Acting as a role model, Princess Elizabeth had donated many of her playthings. Needless to say, countless metal toys were included in America's bounty.

This so-called "conversion" of raw materials into strategic weapons had started a few months earlier. For example, since April 1, 1942, if you wanted to buy a tube of toothpaste, you had to turn in an empty tube. Since this measure, one of the first of its type, was not well publicized, druggists had some pretty angry customers on their hands for awhile. It was reported that dry cleaners were exacting the same tribute for wire coat hangers.

The government swiftly learned its lesson and, again with the help of the media, massive publicity was given to the salvage drive. "Get in the scrap" became a rallying cry, and soon youngsters were very active in the drives. Popular news magazines of the day focused on celebrity participation and had marvelous photos of odd items being turned in. Westbrook Pegler, the famous columnist, was pictured following up on his unusual suggestion that car owners remove and turn in the bumpers from their automobiles. Boston society, we are told, had a scrap party that took in, among other things, an 1880's Gatling machine gun!

Under a plan originating in Nebraska, newspapers, states, localities and organizations awarded war bonds and other prizes for the most scrap collected. Then national competition with plenty of publicity got underway. Boy and Girl Scout and Campfire Girl organizations were particularly active; drives were organized down to the street and block level. It was downright unpatriotic not to participate, and in those days, patriotic was truly the thing to be.

In just a few months, over thirteen million tons of scrap were turned in, and not just metal and paper. Housewives

The little boy in this 1943 Spartan Radio ad looks as if he really wants to give away that toy train. And why not? Spartan's ad offered this encouragement: "Remember— you boys who toss your precious toys on the salvage heap—they'll be coming back, all gay and new. Meantime— Thumbs up for Victory."

A media blitz helped to ensure the success of the scrap drives by focusing on the critical importance of contributions to the war effort. Many posters were directed toward children's participation.

stored fats and grease in cans to turn in for use in making ammunition. "Scrap your fat, just scrap your fat," urged Tin Pan Alley. By year's end, another 17,000,000 tons of metal scrap were in hand. So active were the home front scavengers that at first officials could not handle the load and scrap piles around the country grew larger and larger. The Boy Scouts collected so much paper—150,000 tons—that their drive had to be suspended for a time. By the end of the war, half the tin and paper, and much of the steel needed for the war effort was obtained in this way.

Scrap drive slogans began appearing everywhere: on posters, pins, blotters and matchbook

Slogans promoting war bond and scrap drives appeared everywhere and were collected enthusiastically even during the war.

covers. The latter were the most propagandistic and colorful. "Get in the scrap—save wastepaper and old rags," "Help win the war—Save Fats—America's bullets are fired from explosives made from your waste fats and grease," and "Sell your iron and steel—it makes Guns, Tanks and Ships," screamed the matchbooks. Such momentos are prized highly today.

As the war progressed, paper became scarcer for a variety of reasons. Massive troop buildups in England for the Normandy Invasion precipitated what was probably the most prodigious packaging and shipping job in history. Although packaging for civilian purposes was restricted, a shortage nonetheless occurred that necessitated a major paper drive in Spring 1944. The nation's needs had jumped from five to over eight million tons, an average of seven pounds per person per month. The quota was more than met. Kids were the mainline troops, serving as Junior Salvage Wardens. Again, the Scouts were deeply involved. Receiving the "Boy Scout General Eisenhower Waste Paper Campaign War Service 1945" medal for collecting a thousand pounds of paper was a grave honor.

Scrap collection soon made the game scene. Perhaps the best of the genre in light of completeness and educational value is Milton Bradley's "Get in the Scrap (#4487)" game produced in 1944. The game traces scrap from the home to the collection center to the furnace. Backing up the game board's admonishment to "Play it! Do It!", a booklet entitled "How To Do It and Why You Should" was included in the box.

Jack and Jill magazine commenced a Scrappers Club story in November 1943. During the six-month run, a grandfather helps the neighborhood children organize a scrap gathering club. The paper dolls that accompanied the story were shown collecting tin cans.

In hindsight, if today's collectors could roll back the clock, they probably would have been less willing, as kids, to discard their toys. Perhaps they even would have culled them from the scrap heaps and replaced them with additional pots and pans. But, the sacrifice was for a great cause, and the one thousand pounds of waste paper needed to garner the General Eisenhower Service Medal allegedly made containers for five hundred 75mm shells.

Rationing was instituted early in the war. Tires were the first to go since Japan had very cleverly, quickly conquered Malaya and the other major rubber producing areas. Tire sales were frozen three days after Pearl Harbor. By January 5, 1942, less than a month later, 5,500 volunteer local rationing boards were in place across the country. First, gas and tires were rationed, then gradually foodstuffs. Food rationing depended on what was locally or nationally available. Australia, for example, situated near the front lines of Pacific area fighting, did not need to institute meat rationing until January 1944, due to its large sheep industry. An increasingly complicated system of stamps and points was used and somehow worked. It was managed by the Office of Price Administration (OPA), the organization that also administered and enforced thousands of price ceilings including those on toys.

OPA was described as a lawyer's heaven. Every regulation had to be discussed by numerous lawyers. "While haggling over legal conundrums in lengthy sessions," reported one magazine, "OPA lawyers munch sandwiches and drink coffee from paper cups." OPA even maintained an infirmary for those "who crack under the strain."

The food rationing system was based on a complicated system that had worked quite well in England and Australia. Australian and U.S. Ration Books were similar in appearance; the small ration stamps showed pictures of tanks, planes, ships and guns. To prevent cheating, ration books listed the holder's age, sex, height, weight and occupation. While necessary, rationing also contributed to the upcoming paper shortage; in 1942 rationing books consumed 44,000 tons of paper. By war's end, some 3.5 billion food stamps had been issued.

In the toy industry, the lesser-known Jayline Manufacturing Company, Inc. of Philadelphia beat Milton Bradley to the punch with its 1943 game "Ration Board." All of the game's implements were made of nonstrategic materials; wooden tokens were carved in the form of automobiles and colored paper ration cards were labeled "sugar," "coffee,"

This gem is one of the more readily available of Bradley's WWII games.

Below
Regular Fellers, a popular comic strip, encouraged children to collect scrap and purchase bonds.

58

"gas," and "meat." Each player's trip around the ration board in the little wooden cars followed a circuitous route and was filled with peril. "Ration Board" also featured another of the industry's marvelous wartime art deco box covers.

In spite of food rationing, the U.S. population was fed better in wartime than ever before. In 1945 the Department of Agriculture reported that the public spent more on food and ate more per capita than at any time in our history. Victory Gardens had much to do with this phenomenon.

Shortly after Pearl Harbor, Secretary of Agriculture Wickard, recalling the Liberty Gardens of WWI, suggested that consumers who wanted to continue to have fresh vegetables take the heat off farmers, who had to feed the Armed Forces, by growing their own. These plots, called Victory Gardens, soon became the rage. The department issued reams of how-to-do-it material, and within three months, six million amateur gardeners worked the soil. The results were amazing. In 1943, 20,500,000 Victory Gardens were planted and produced almost one-third of the fresh vegetables in the country. Gardeners proudly wore patriotic paper armbands while they hoed and raked.

Gardens were found in the strangest places. In the Bronx, the nuns of St. Patrick's Home for the Aged raised vegetables in a vacant lot; at the Cook County, Illinois, jail, prisoners planted behind the walls of the prison courtyard. (They weren't allowed to grow corn, however, since when tall it might provide ready hiding places for escapees.)

Everyone was busy, the media reported, including the Hollywood contingent whose press agents, as usual, never missed a beat in getting them involved in the war effort. In Portland, Oregon, high school girls were required to tend a 200'×40' Victory Garden as part of their "instruction in the house-wifely virtues."

Paper dolls joined the vegetable growing army. Merrill's 1942 "Victory Volunteers (#3424)" and 1943 "Liberty Belles (#3477)" sets contained victory garden dolls, as did Saalfield's "Victory Paper Dolls (#2445)" issued in 1943 and "Paper Dolls in Uniform of the U.S.A. (#S-592 and S-2445)." Saalfield's 1943 product, "Uncle Sam's Little Helpers (#2450)," is a particularly charming set. It had a large page of costumes for little gardeners complete with seed packets, baskets, wagons and tools. Even the family's puppy and kitten are helping.

Wolverine, Pittsburgh's top of the line prewar metal toy company, produced a marvelous, large boxed "Victory Garden (#179)." The 21-by-14-inch box contained all the ingredients for a real garden: six terra cotta pots, a small wooden pick, spade and rake, packets of seeds for lettuce, radishes, beans, carrots, peas and beets, and an illustrated booklet. The inside box cover contained detailed instructions for indoor planting.

An ad for another hands-on Victory Garden set, "Plant for Victory," appeared in *Toys and Novelties* about the same time. This set contained a packet of Vaughn's tested broc-

SAVE YOUR CANS
Help pass the Ammunition

McLELLAND BARCLAY USNR.

PREPARE YOUR TIN CANS
FOR WAR
1 REMOVE TOPS AND BOTTOMS
2 TAKE OFF PAPER LABELS
3 WASH THOROUGHLY
4 FLATTEN FIRMLY

The War Production Board distributed "Paper Trooper" decals, armbands and other materials to encourage children to aid in the drive. Other children's groups were called "Junior Salvage Wardens." One of their chores was to deliver string to wrap waste paper properly to neighborhood homes.

coli and spinach seeds. It seems quite possible that the manufacturer's choices of vegetable seeds may have hindered sales!

Wartime realities inspired Hollywood to produce several grade B movies. Wallace Beery starred in *Rationing* with Marjorie Main (Ma Kettle) as a tough Ration Board supervisor. One of Laurel and Hardy's least successful features, according to the critics, was entitled *Air Raid Wardens*, and the popular Blondie series included *Blondie For Victory*, which centered on the activities of a local housewives' auxiliary. *Rosie The Riveter* and *Gangway For Tomorrow* also featured the sacrifices of civilian war workers.

Tin Pan Alley geared up its song factory quickly. Scrap

drives inspired many back room Mozarts to write such forgettable tunes as "While Melting Away All Our Memories," "Cash For Your Trash," and "Junk Ain't Junk No More Cuz Junk Will Win The War." In the Victory Garden category, everyone sang along to "Get Out and Dig, Dig, Dig" and "Harvey, The Victory Garden Man." The ever popular ditty, "When The Air Raid Siren Sounds," told the public to obey the orders of their reliable block warden.

The songs, the movies, the household products, the slogans, the insignia, the magazine articles and, of course, the toys—all this hoopla fed the imagination and determination of the American public.

Above
Clever packaging tempted housewives to buy patriotic "Victory Pack" waxed paper for preserving their home-grown produce.

Left
Although experience would indicate that many kids used the miniature toy grocery sets of the era to devise their own rationing games, "Ration Board" by the Jayline Mfg. Company is the only WWII toy known to revolve directly around rationing.

Women's participating in civil defense efforts stole the scene in many paper doll booklets, including this set published by Saalfield.

"We'll have lots to eat this winter, won't we Mother?"

Grow your own
Can your own

The media sought to involve all ages in Victory Garden projects, and the outstanding results were another example of the public's willingness to pitch in for the war effort.

These youngsters are carefully selecting seeds for the vegetables they'll plant in their victory garden. FRANKLIN D. ROOSEVELT LIBRARY

In Portland, Oregon, girls get physical education credit by working in the Jane Addams High School's Victory Garden. OREGON HISTORICAL SOCIETY

Today Every Body must be a Fortress . . . fortified to

FIGHT!

Here's the COMMANDO FRUIT to Fortify Every Body with vitamin C

Every Day
DRINK IT!
EAT IT!

FIGHT Colds!
FIGHT Fatigue!
FIGHT Weakness!
FIGHT Infections!
FIGHT Absenteeism!

Fresh FLORIDA GRAPEFRUIT
Rich in "Victory Vitamin C"

THE PHILADELPHIA INQUIRER

With the patriotic fervor regarding food, it is not surprising that there was little evidence of black marketeering during the war. Violations that did occur primarily involved retailers making under the counter deals—mostly for meat for special customers.

62

Toys And The War Bond

"Any bonds today, bonds for freedom, that's what I'm selling, any bonds today." So sang Bing Crosby and Bugs Bunny in a cartoon short set to Irving Berlin's unforgettable music. On the other end of the pendulum, forgettable war bond drive songs included "Get Aboard the Bond Wagon" and "Swing the Quota."

The brainchild of Secretary of the Treasury, Henry Morganthau, Jr., a 1930s foe of Hitler, the several War Bond drives (the name was changed from Defense to War Bonds after Pearl Harbor) galvanized the American people. The program enlisted everyone and contributed mightily to U.S. morale. It gave all the people an opportunity to do something and answered the question, "What can I do to help?"

Hollywood jumped in with both feet and this time really did make an enormous contribution. Major stars like Jimmy Cagney, Dorothy Lamour and Heddy Lamarr blitzed the country in September of 1942 on their cross-country train tour, "Stars over America." In three weeks they personally sold 838 million dollars worth of bonds and stamps. Tragically, Carole Lombard, Clark Gable's movie star wife, was killed in a plane crash on a bond-selling tour; soon after, Gable enlisted and flew bombing missions over Germany.

Most children couldn't afford to buy a bond outright, but millions bought war stamps in ten and twenty-five cent denominations every week, pasted them in "Defense Stamp Albums," and eventually turned the filled booklet in for a War Bond. Earnings from a lot of paper routes and lawn mowings went into the drives. Boy and Girl Scout troops again participated wholeheartedly.

Schools actively pushed stamp purchases and everyone participated in competitions. One class even thought of something that hadn't occurred to the bureaucrats; it collected junk jewelry and baubles so "our boys fighting in the jungles [could] trade them to the natives for food, friendship and help." Another youngster, counting things in the way children like to do, proudly reported that her class had collected exactly

Above
Saalfield's "Our Victory Garden" page is a delightful example of the mood of the times.

Top Left
Kids even gave up their toys for this scrap drive. Larrie Lou Osterman sits on her front steps in McMinnville, Ore., with her toys. OREGON HISTORICAL SOCIETY

Bottom Left
Children who received this Victory Garden set could have the fun of growing their own lettuce, radishes, beans, carrots, peas and beets.

63

9,751 bottle tops. During the war years, school children accounted for more than a billion dollars worth of bonds sold.

Children's Playmate Magazine, a popular monthly magazine for children four to fourteen published since 1910, regularly featured letters from its younger readers in a section called "The Playmate Patrol." Most letters described the writer's war effort activities. In the October 1943 issue, for example, all fifteen letter writers mentioned buying stamps and bonds, air spotting, raising Victory Gardens, canning produce, writing letters to servicemen, and collecting waste fats, paper, scrap, and tin cans and foil. *Playmate Magazine* soon instituted ranks in "The Playmate Patrol." If you bought a bond and your letter was published, you became a First Lieutenant!

Faced with a large advertising bill to promote its various War Bond drives, the government came up with an ingenious plan to convince industry and the media to pay. President Roosevelt himself is given credit by some historians for the idea. He sent a special message to the 1942 convention of the Advertising Federation of America urging it to donate advertising space. An Advertising War Council

Music students of the National Institute of Music and Arts in Bremerton, Wash., show their bonds and savings stamps. FRANKLIN D. ROOSEVELT LIBRARY

was formed consisting of volunteer copywriters. Companies bought and donated millions of dollars worth of free advertising per year. A new Treasury Department ruling allowing tax deductions for such contributions didn't hurt the effort one bit.

In addition to media advertising, countless manufacturers placed various "Buy War Bonds" emblems right on their products, the containers, or the instructional materials accompanying them. Again, comics, matchbooks and milk bottle tops led the parade. The slogan on Swan paper napkins read simply, "Buy bonds and stamps for defense."

Above
Actual toy soldiers were used in bond drive ads.

A matchbook cover carried more graphic encouragement: "Every bond you buy is a nail in the axis coffin."

The toy industry again was at the top of the list of government supporters. The Toy Knights, an association of toy makers and retailers, ran several industry bond drives and, according to the proud trade press, set records for bond purchases. One of the biggest personal sacrifices this active committee made was to cancel its sumptuous annual banquet timed to coincide with the spring Toy Fair. As *Playthings* reported in 1943, this was no time to waste food on lavish dinners.

One of the toy industry's earliest and longest lasting tie-ins with the war stamps and bond effort was also the most obvious—kids' banks. Prime examples were the Well-Made Doll and Toy Co.'s banks in the form of tanks and ships. These novel banks were large; the tank was nine-by-six inches and the ship was nine inches in length. Both items left no doubt as for what any patriotic American boy or girl should use its contents. No Red Ryder BB guns (if you could somehow get them) were to be purchased with these funds. No sir! When the "Victory Ship Bank" was filled with $18.75 in pennies, nickels, dimes and quarters, the box advised its diligent owner: "Go to the nearest bank or post office and purchase a $25.00 war bond." And once was not enough; the child could not buy that favorite toy with his next savings. "Then refill bank with more savings and buy bonds again," read the directions. Similar directions were given on the "Tank Bank" box.

Another terrific bank was the large, ungainly papier-mâché "Bomb Bank." Produced by the W.H. Long Co. and widely advertised in the trade press, ads told kids they could use the "Bomb Bank" to "Bomb the Japs from your own home!" Although it had to be smashed to get the coins out, *Playthings* magazine advised toy buyers that this was a great idea since it "guaranteed repeat sales." Retailing for twenty-five cents in 1943, it was sold wholesale by Butler Brothers for two dollars a dozen.

Well-Made Doll and Toy Company produced two superb war bond banks, the "Tank Bank" and the "Victory Ship Bank." These banks are a dual collectible, sought eagerly by both toy and bank collectors.

Although large and ungainly, W.H. Long Company's "Bomb Bank" appealed to children, perhaps partly because they got to smash it once it was full.

The "Sock the Japs War Bond Bank," made by Lite Products, Inc., was also an eye-pleaser. Red, white and blue and shaped in the form of Uncle Sam's fist, the bank was molded of nonstrategic materials and had to be broken to empty.

Another "composition" bank was the 1943 "Uncle Sam Bank" made by Durable Toy and Novelty Corp. Nine inches high, it came in two models. Number 205 retailed for a dollar (a lot in those days) and was painted red, white and blue. Number 200 was bronze in color and cost half as much since only one color application was required.

The wartime toy bank that because it is made of tin shows up most often at toy fairs these days, is the early war "Tank Bank" of The Ohio Art Company. Made in late 1941

before any metal bans went into effect, it was promoted during the 1941 Christmas season. The trade press didn't link it to early Defense Bond efforts, but Butler Brothers' 1942 wholesale catalog (published in the summer of 1941) did suggest to retailers that it be promoted as a bond tie-in. This tank bank had terrific lithography comparable to a Marx toy, rolled on rubber wheels, and could be used over and over again. Most important, it retailed for only ten cents (a much better bargain than later cheap composition banks) and at six-by-three inches was roughly in-scale for the metal toy soldiers manufactured directly prior to America's entry into the war. Needless to say, children used it as a toy as well as a bank. This popular WWII collectible currently sells for $30–$50.

Richard Appell came out with a line of banks in the shape of an antitank gun, a plane and a cannon. These banks looked more like party favors. The bank section was a red, white and blue striped cardboard tube with a slot that served as the plane's fuselage, the tank's breach, and the cannon's barrel. The antitank gun also shot peas. "Save to buy; bonds for victory," was Appell's slogan.

Finally, in the toy bank line, so-called "Dime Registers" were popular until the metal ban caught up with them. These small, tin, hexagon or similarly shaped, 2½-inch containers fit easily in a pocket or purse and accepted only a dime. Those produced in late 1941 and early 1942 had colorful defense scenes and slogans such as "Keep 'Em Flying" and "Keep 'Em Sailing."

Pencil boxes, pencil sharpeners and other school supplies also stressed the stamps and bond theme. Cheap plastic pencil sharpeners shaped like tanks and planes were produced.

One of the most unusual and fascinating toys made during the war was the "Broadcast Truck." Made of compressed wood, it was eighteen inches long (about 1/10 actual small truck size). It contained an internal plastic tape record that was attached to a rotary disk driven by the rear wheels. This produced a broadcasting effect. Made in 1944 by the Metal-Ware Corporation of Two Rivers, Wisconsin, this toy came in two versions. One had a circular war bond sign on top and was named the "Victory Broadcast Truck." When pulled along it blared out, "Buy more stamps and bonds." The other, the "Safety Patrol Truck," had a similar circular sign on top. It said, "Stop, Look, and Listen." Both come in red, white (truck body) and blue. Only one small trade press ad for this expensive ($2.35) toy is known, in addition to a mention in a W.W. Grainger, Inc. wholesale catalog. While unusual, the trucks couldn't have sold well.

It's hard to assess how many manufacturers actually utilized the buy bonds theme on the box top, toy container, accompanying literature or the actual toy. The latter was pretty difficult to do. While far less than a majority complied, enough did that it is fair to say that the industry's effort was respectable. Its trade press advertising certainly featured the theme and repeatedly urging shopkeepers to tie-in bond purchases with window front and in-store displays went a long way in assisting the overall effort.

Game boxes and punch-out set covers were probably the easiest places to display a war bond slogan. Such ads were usually in the shape of a 1½-by-2-inch red, white and blue shield. The aptly named Victory Toy Company's line of punch-out sets utilized the mottos "Keep 'Em Flying — Buy more U.S. War Bonds and Stamps," "Keep 'Em rolling and . . .", and "Keep 'Em Going . . ." Dave Rapaport made clever use of his name-takeoff theme by displaying this motto on his shield: "Buy . . . Bonds . . . and Rap-a-Jap." Pachter Co. went halfway by utilizing a box cover shield on its "Bild-A-Set Navy Fighting Fleet" punch-out set that stated simply, "Build for Victory." Plane Facts Co.'s ad for its short-lived "Smilin' Jack's Victory Bombers" punch-out

set in *Playthings*, had Zack Mosely's popular comic strip character urging buyers to "Give the axe to the Axis. Buy more War Bonds."

The overall prize for the most slogans goes to the paper overseas cap for children made by Avon Products Company. It had fifteen different mottos and sixteen different emblems on it including "Get those Japs," "We buy 'em. . . . They'll fight 'em," and "Chin-up." First prize for the most selfless motto goes to the W. L. Fuchs Co. of St. Louis, Missouri, whose "Mystery Bombing Puzzle" cover told its prospective buyer: "To avoid over spending, buy War Bonds first."

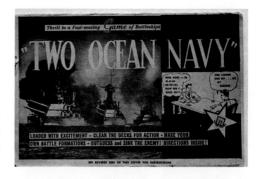

I Left My Heart At The Stage Door Canteen

The title song of this popular movie exemplified the home front's desire to make the off-duty and leave time of the young boys in uniform as much fun as possible under wartime circumstances. Based in New York and Hollywood and staffed by Hollywood movie starlets and New York stage, radio, and big band stars, the famous United Service Organization's (USO) Stage Door Canteens and its attendant publicity helped the whole country to entertain its servicemen in a variety of all-volunteer local clubs, canteens, and "bring a soldier home to dinner" drives.

The USO, staffed primarily by civilian volunteers, performed heroically both at home and overseas. Among other things, it provided game rooms for lonely GIs and furnished games to them. The photo shows a version of the popular pencil games of the day. All you needed to play these simple "square" games on paper sheets were two pencils. Then pencil fights could be played anywhere: in camp, on troop trains, even in a foxhole. Published by Krall Publishing, they prominently carried the USO logo. The USO passed them out free, but they also could be purchased for

The United Service Organization served as an umbrella and helped coordinate support services provided to military men and women and their families around the world.

Saalfield's paper doll page, "Our Canteen Service," provides clothing for volunteers manning a donut and coffee shop. These canteens not only provided nourishment but also company and a friendly face for lonely servicemen and woman.

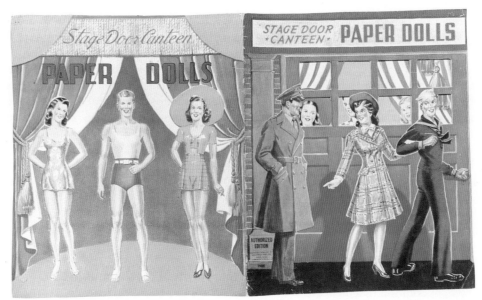

This typical paper doll booklet focused on the friendly nature of services provided by the USO. COURTESY OF MARY YOUNG

a nickel. Kids loved them and with a ruler and a piece of Mom or Dad's stationery, you could design your own once you got the hang of it. Paper dolls appear to be the only other toy capitalizing on this aspect of home front activities.

In 1943 Saalfield published several versions of "Stage Door Canteen Paper Dolls (#S-2468 and 347)." Lowe's set was called "Ruth of the Stage Door Canteen (#L 1048)." Various other sets by Saalfield, Lowe and Merrill contained canteen paper dolls. "Uncle Sam's Little Helpers" had a full page depicting a local coffee and doughnut operation called "Our Canteen Service." Margo Voight's charming "United We Stand" paper dolls booklet had a page entitled "We entertain at the USO." This booklet pictured various Uncle Sam and Revolutionary War costumes. Merrill featured a doll book entitled "Soldiers and Sailors House Party." It contained several formal dress uniforms that were terrific looking but rarely, if ever, worn in the khaki land of WWII.

In its January 1945 issue, Jack and Jill magazine's paper doll series included two pages of soldiers coming home on furlough called "The Homecoming." Several paper doll sets featured military weddings, a popular fantasy for the female preteens of the war years.

A multipage card from the popular series of comic cards for mailing to GIs was entitled "News from the Home Front." In reporting to the servicemen on what was happening at home, the cards' verses sum up the home front effort in an entertaining, red, white and blue way:

There now are air raid wardens
on every block and street
There is a Woman's Army Corps with
uniforms complete
The ladies all are helping out with
Red Cross and first aid
There are lots of Victory Gardens and it's
style to use a spade
The young gals and the old ones are
knitting for the boys
And all the kids are turning in
their tin and rubber toys
The Scouts are selling War Bonds
and stamps in great big chunks
and even Fido's itchin' to start
a-chasin' [Axis] skunks!

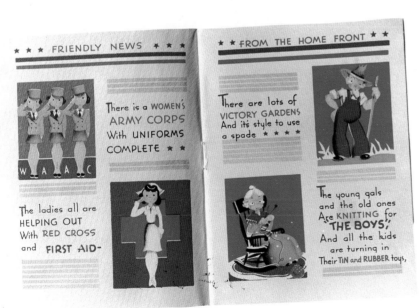

"News from the Home Front" was a popular comics series published specifically for away-from-home GIs. Its lighthearted approach to civilian support services was guaranteed to make U.S. military personnel smile.

3
LESS GAS, MORE GAMES

The effects of gas rationing were severe. Car pooling got its start, and bicycle riding was a necessity, not a sport. In New York City horse-drawn delivery wagons were widely used to replace trucks.

I'll carry mine too!

SARRA

TRUCKS AND TIRES MUST LAST TILL VICTORY

FTER THE START of WWII in Europe, American game makers gradually introduced games dealing with defense and geopolitical aspects of the conflict. Milton Bradley's popular "Blackout" game, which came out in two editions, was first introduced in late 1939. New York's GHQ, Inc. sold "Military Strategy—The Modern Game of War" with cardboard silhouettes of machine guns and other hardware as board pieces. That same year several non-board target games with defense themes also were marketed. Baldwin's all metal "Air Defense (#158)" target game had a swivel gun that shot ball bearings at hinged airplanes and colorful lithography. Other prewar games were "Sunk" and "Admiral"; prewar metal target games included "Attack" by Wiz Novelty Co. and "Aerial Bomber."

The most fascinating late prewar game was the "H.V. Kaltenborn Diplomacy: The Game of Intrigue" by Trend Games Co. Named after a popular radio commentator of the day, it combined international political and trade aspects. Players were given cards signifying characteristic products of various countries. The board showed "neutral" states such as Cuba, and "strategic" locations such as Hawaii. The major nations shown were the U.S.A., Russia, Italy, Great Britain, France, China, Japan and Germany. Since America and Japan were not yet belligerents, the game's authors quite accurately predicted all of the major combatants of WWII. The game sold throughout the war in three editions, club, gift and popular, and ranged in price from $1.20 to $2.50.

Probably the most unpopular set of home front regulations adopted during WWII was that relating to gas rationing. The local Ration Board System was instigated right after Pearl Harbor. The most critical raw material was rubber, and official suggestions for conserving it were made as early as December 1941. Within three weeks, local boards were allocating car tires based on a complicated system of need priorities: trucks used for delivering bee

hives qualified, those delivering pinball machines did not. Each county board's monthly allotment was based on county vehicle registrations. Thus, it was reported, one county in Utah had a monthly allotment of precisely one tire. As more items including typewriters and bicycles were deemed scare, the board's task became much more complex. Common sense usually prevailed as to who got what. Reasons given for qualifying for scarce items were complex, creative and humorous. The system worked, however, because, as one senior official stated, "We learned that the American people are basically honest and talk too much."

Gas rationing was closely related to the scarcity of rubber. It went into effect in nineteen eastern states after May 15, 1942, but was so unpopular that President Roosevelt postponed nationwide gasoline rationing purely for political reasons until after the November 1942 elections. But soon after, every motor vehicle in the country had the notorious "A," "B," or "C" sticker prominently displayed on the windshield. The lowly "A" sticker entitled the owner to a lousy three gallons a week, and also publicly confirmed the official judgment that the car was not essential to the war effort, unlike a doctor's car, for example. Pity the poor owner of a twelve cylinder Cadillac with an "A" sticker.

In addition to severe limitations on gas for the family car, there were restrictions on what a car could be used for and a thirty-five mph speed limit. Contemporary reports indicate that federal inspectors ticketed cars with "B" and "C" stickers (supposed to be used only for essential travel) that were parked at night clubs and racetracks. On the east coast, early in the war, the use of private cars for nonessential purposes was severely restricted. Even driving to

Although recognized as a necessary evil, gas rationing was not popular with the American public. In the east it went into effect in May 1942, the rest of the country was saved until after the Presidential elections in November 1942. A thirty-five mph speed limit also was instituted.

BOARD GAMES

IN THE BOARD GAME category, 1942 saw a number of excellent items including several produced by Milton Bradley. Bradley's games followed the headlines. For example, "Bataan," a board game for two players or teams, was built around MacArthur's defense of the Philippines, the first large scale American battle of the war. Unfortunately, the marvelous box art showing WWI-helmeted doughboys and U.S. planes defeating Japanese troops did not reflect the actual outcome. Three other Bradley games, "Fighting Marines," "Ferry Command," and "Battle of the Tanks," also tied in with current events. Advertising claimed they were as "timely as tomorrow's headline."

Bradley's plant was devoted about fifty percent to war production. Making small wood and metal parts for naval ordnance and aviation uses, Bradley's war contracts required only minor modifications to its tooling and jig machines, but did result in a twenty percent increase in employees.

"Combat Air Trainer" by Lewis Instructor Games was a fascinating piece with far fewer game features than in-

visit a loved one at an army camp was not allowed and, without special permission, similar travel by rail and air was just about out of the question. Although many depression thin wallets were soon stuffed with defense work cash, there was little opportunity to spend it on leisure travel or vacations.

Thus, Americans stayed home during the war, and games and puzzles found increasing favor, particularly in the winter months when outdoor activity was limited in much of the country. The same phenomenon held true for the nearby hometown and neighborhood theater . . . so long as it was within walking distance. Movie attendance tripled during World War II.

Wartime military games fall into two main categories, board and target. The former held favor with both adults and early teenagers while action/target games appealed more to the six to thirteen year old. Bombing games of all kinds were immensely popular.

Many of Milton Bradley's games took current events of the war as their theme. "Bataan," based on events in the Philippines, was a popular target game with the under-twelve crowd.

structional ones. Containing over fifty die-cut planes, bomb-bursts, hangars and targets, its twenty-four page booklet contained complicated instructions for air combat techniques and flying formations.

Two smaller board games were based on the exploits of a highly popular fictional aviation hero, Dave Dawson and his British pal, Freddy Farmer. American Toy Works (ATWO) brought these games out for the spring 1942 Toy Fair and tied them in to the "Young America's #1 Boy Hero"

This page from a wholesale catalog gives an excellent sampling of the games available early in 1942.

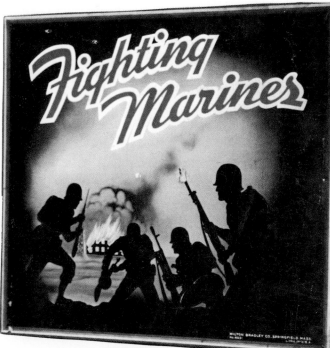

Milton Bradley was the first to produce wartime board games and thus got a leg up on the competition. With but a few exceptions, Bradley's products reflected the high quality for which the company had long been noted.

73

AIR COMBAT TRAINER

This marvelous game came with great bomb spinner dials and bomb angle aimers approved by the National Aeronautic Association. It was recommended by the New York State Education Department for use by all teachers of pre-flight education.

theme. The "Pacific Battle Game" chronicled Dave and Freddy's exploits in that war theatre; the "Dave Dawson Victory Game" covered Allied victories in Europe and the Atlantic. The games were purely fictional since, at that point, the fortunes of war were strictly on the side of the Axis.

"Empires," a Selchow and Righter Co. game, clearly was created prior to U.S. entry into the war. First advertised in January 1942, it allowed up to six players to compete as great powers "trying to conquer everybody in sight." Involving armaments, resources, colonies and campaigns with numerous cards to signify each, it made for interesting evenings of armchair strategy. This game definitely was not for the younger child.

Prior to OPA regulations, game prices did go up a bit due to increased costs of raw materials and labor. Board games, which had averaged about $1.00, went to the $1.19–$1.59 range. Nonetheless, in anticipation of the upcoming metal restrictions, there was very heavy advance ordering of games and wooden toys during the 1942 Toy Fair. In 1943 the supply of paper became somewhat of a concern, particularly with respect to the large shipping containers needed for a gross of relatively large, boxed games. The problem was solved in large measure by simply reusing the shipping container as often as possible.

Some highly technical revised specifications on the composition of so-called paper board did result in some changes in the density and finish of box board. OPA price ceiling regulations adopted in late 1942 included games, and paper restrictions adopted in August 1943 limited that year's usage to a percent of what a particular company had needed in 1942. The only other wartime restrictions affecting game make-up were those imposed over all by Order L-81. Its ban on metal required thereafter that board game implements be of wood or plastic. Metal target games, of course, could no longer be made.

While probably not needed all that much due to the increased popularity of games, a good deal of creative point-of-trade marketing was used between 1942–44. *Playthings* urged that game, puzzle and book displays feature signs and other visual devices featuring current war news stories. This, said the magazine, was "ideal for the amateur Monday morning quarterback who has now assumed the

Produced in 1943 by Penman Co., "Battle Checkers" stayed popular for the duration of the war. This Toys and Novelties magazine ad for the game features a Chicago Tribune column and is indicative of aggressive local marketing.

role of armchair general." By Order L-291, adopted in Summer 1943, the War Production Board limited the use of cardboard in ad displays. This forced retailers to become even more creative. Use of the actual toy in the store window and in displays increased. In the case of games, books and puzzles, the eye-catching, colorful nature of the game box art, book dust jackets and puzzles made the job much easier. In some cases, the shipping carton could be converted into a counter-top display. Continental's "Bombardier" bombsight target game featured this approach.

During 1943–1944, board games continued to reflect all of the rapidly changing developments in the adult world. Those of coastal defense, bombing, plane detection, air defense and world geography predominated. Van Wagen Company's 1943 trio, "Attack," "Defense," and "Pursuit," were typical. "Attack" gave each side tanks, planes, guns and squads of men. Adapted for a wide age range, the game involved fighting across deserts, dodging enemy traps, shooting down planes and capturing men, tanks and guns. "Defense," the naval version, utilized a form of checkers to capture an enemy base and was marketed for teenagers. It came in Pacific, Atlantic and Servicemen's editions. The final entry, "Pursuit," was an extremely simple checkers type game intended for the younger crowd.

Other 1943 battle games included "Pursuit" (Game Makers, Inc.), "Battlefield" (Illinois Game and Toy Co.), "Battle Checkers" (Penman Co.), and "Air Attack" (Corey Games Co.). Along with a terrific cover, "Battle Checkers" had plastic implements of action soldiers, AA guns, tanks, ships, subs and planes. Industry buyers were told that "Battlefield" was designed to encourage youngsters to let off steam by actively taking part in the war situation. They got to capture and release prisoners, form rescues and organize commando raids. For these same reasons, the game also was attractive to adult players.

Since many of the non-spinner, dice-throw type board games were based on variations of checkers, simplified forms of chess, or a combination of the two, the theme of capture and exchange often was involved. For example, Bradley's "Fighting Marines," despite its title, simply involved taking an opponent's pieces off the board and giving them back when one's own men got captured.

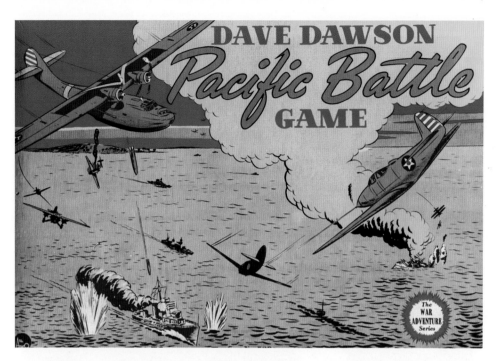

Above
Nationwide marketing linked the "Dave Dawson Pacific Battle Game" to the very popular fiction series for boys. The Dave Dawson games were produced by American Toy Works, the books by Crown Publishing.

Left
"Combat Air Trainer" by Lewis Instructor Games was designed by a former army flyer and came with complicated instructions for air combat techniques. It was said to be endorsed and used by U.S. aviation groups.

75

"Air Attack" by Corey Games Co., a Boston firm, was one of the largest games ever produced and featured one of the most dynamic box covers.

Corey Games' 1943 line equaled Milton Bradley's 1942–43 offerings, both in box art and creativeness. The Boston firm's "Strategy" and "Blockade" were particular favorites. "Blockade," a naval strategy game that combined geopolitical aspects, had a nationwide publicity kick-off featuring celebrities. Press releases and trade press ads featured photos of popular comedians Abbott and Costello engrossed in a game of "Blockade"; popular action film actor Pat O'Brien extolled the virtues of "Blockade" in another ad. The Ice Capades, Radio City Music Hall Rockettes, and famous stage stars allegedly spent much of their leisure time between acts destroying the enemy's fleet and blockading enemy countries. All of this found its way into regional newspaper stories and obviously helped sales.

"Strategy, The Game of Armies" had the most striking and oddest game box art of the period. A gigantic Man-God of War, holding a globe is shown directing mechanized divisions, troops and aircraft. While its monster-like appearance probably scared little children, the game itself was much more mundane.

Milton Bradley's last wartime game, "Bizerte Gertie," was a humorous takeoff on the service nickname of the North African ladies of ill repute. Due to the first major British victory of the war at Tobruk, the U.S. landings and Tunisian campaign, and other developments such as the Casablanca Conference, that area of the world was very much in the news during 1942–43. Feature films such as *Sahara* and the all-time classic *Casablanca* broke all records.

"Bizerte Gertie," slightly risqué but totally harmless by today's standards, was a clear departure from the ordinary war game and from Bradley's usual offerings. It was described by the company as an original idea in merry and brilliant home entertainment. The plot featured buck privates on the loose with a one-night pass and plenty of play money. Our intrepid soldiers (players) are accompanied by Alice the Hound Dog and three fair maids of Algiers: New Guinea Minnie, Sally from Bali and Gertie herself. They try to beat each other to the moonlit beach, there to pitch a little woo.

Interesting wartime variations of popular games were introduced. "Victory Rummy" had cards with cartoons of Hitler, Tojo and Mussolini. "Victo, the Victory Bingo-Game" featured large red, white and blue playing boards. Its twenty-four "Victo" (not "Bingo") spaces contained patriotic slogans from American history such as, "There are no atheists in fox holes" (wrongly attributed to Douglas MacArthur), U.S. Grant's "When in doubt—fight" and, for some strange reason, "Lost time is never found," from Ben Franklin's *Poor Richard's Almanac*.

Several dozen other miscellaneous board games were put out in the 1941–44 period, most dealing with battle themes. Among the most colorful were those produced by Advance Games and All-Fair (E.E. Fairchild Corporation, Rochester, NY). While not made of the best quality stock and selling well below the quality price range of the larger Parker Bros. and Milton Bradley items, their box art was highly indicative of the times. "Let 'Em Have It—Our Righting Rangers" is a fine example. While no copyright date is found, from the scenes pictured it appears to have been produced after the D-Day Invasion. A player reaching a ninety-point score received a medal for bravery and three War Bonds from his community!

Advance's "Bomber Attack" was rather unusual in that the players were civilians who, by spinning the right number, extinguished incidendiary bombs, promptly turned on air raid sirens, and performed other heroic civilian defense deeds for which they were awarded paper War Bonds. On the contrary, landing on the wrong circles meant, for example, that having failed to turn out lights in a blackout, you were jailed for two turns (similar to "Monopoly"). The overall winner received a pair of red and gold American aviators wings.

All-Fair games, though made of cheap cardboard, were quite creative. All-Fair, founded in 1900 by paper box and

Corey Games made extensive use of celebrities in kicking off an extensive nationwide publicity drive for its 1943 best seller, "Blockade." Like "Battle Checkers," this naval strategy game was billed as timely and sensational.

Right

Games by Advance Games and All-Fair often were carried by small drug and candy stories that kept a few shelves of toys and used middlemen such as the Billy and Ruth catalog to obtain their products. These games were of cheaper quality and sold for less that half the price of the Parker Bros. and Milton Bradley products.

Below

Although one might not expect it from the striking, comic-book-style box art, the game of "Strategy" actually demanded a great deal of smarts and concentration. It captivated the imagination of adults as well as youngsters.

novelty makers Harry O. Alderman and Elmer E. Fairchild, was in existence over sixty-five years. In the 1920s it sold numerous novelty "black character" games, now highly sought after. One of its early executives, Herman G. Fisher, later founded popular children's toy maker Fisher-Price. At least five All-Fair war games were produced in 1943 alone, all with identical box and folding board dimensions, a very clever, cost effective manufacturing ploy. "Army Checkers," whose squared board featured large borders with dozens of colorful army insignia, was a simple capture type of game. "Battle" was somewhat more sophisticated. The circular cardboard playing tokens had drawings of men and equipment on them. A form of simplified chess (certain items could only perform certain tasks and move in a certain direction), the object of the game was "to take the sector of enemy territory by capturing your opponent's men, guns and tanks with the least possible loss of your own playing pieces." As did other companies producing lower priced games, All-Fair printed its game instructions inside the box top.

Two All-Fair war-related but not strictly military games were "Game of International Spy" and "Cargo for Victory." In "Spy" four players chose countries, represented by different color board sections, and attempted to capture more spies than their opponents. The ultimate goal, however, was to get your spy on an opponent's picture square represent-

Based on ad repetition it doesn't appear that Milton Bradley's "Bizerte Gertie" sold well. The game's lighthearted theme of dating and romance perhaps was too frivolous for the serious-minded public.

ing that country's capital. Countries representing "Secret Police" complicated the works.

"Cargo for Victory" (subtitled "Freighters Against Submarines") was played out on a world map board. Victory was achieved by scoring the most points, based on cargo ships safely home and, strangely enough, by sinking enemy subs with your convoys protecting submarines. "Bomber-Raid—The Game of Bombers vs. Anti-Aircraft" was a dice game utilizing cardboard airplanes and two cardboard searchlight beams. The play was to pit the planes against the beam, to draw the beam toward one plane while another got through.

Another half-dozen or so lower priced games of this period were a mixed bag. "War Bingo," distributed by Gotham Sales Co. of Chicago, had attractive box art and cleverly substituted squares with war equipment for "Bingo" counters. Lido Toys had two entries: "Jeep Patrol," a spinner game for three players using small plastic jeeps, and "Sea Battle," a naval version.

Samuel Lowe Co. marketed two colorful "double" wartime game sets, "Hornet Airplane Games" and "Land and Sea War Games" for twenty-nine cents. Each had a "catapult" game—really a version of tiddly winks—and a regular spinner game that utilized the same flat circular pieces. Extremely simple in execution, the almost paper-thin playing boards had dynamic air and sea scenes. These sets are quite common today and sell for about twenty dollars. The number that have survived is no doubt due to Lowe's size and paper doll marketing operation.

Whitman, somewhat surprisingly, made several games in the cheap category. Its similar double spinner game set was called "The Game of Battle Stations." Its somewhat earlier 1940 "Battleship Game" was a pegboard game in which two players matched wits on home and enemy boards by calling out attempted "hits," e.g., "B-17," to each other. The player to sink his opponent's entire fleet first was the winner. Other 1940 Whitman cheapies were "Wings of America" and "Dive Bomber."

At the higher end of the price scale ($1.00-$2.00), Parker Bros. issued numerous games between 1940 and 1945. "Ranger Commandos," which came in two different versions, was one of the better wartime games. Included

among its game pieces were small wooden landing craft. "Conflict," its 1940 predecessor, had several dozen hard-rubber game pieces depicting planes, ships, cannon and tanks. Two early 1941 games, "Dog Fight" and "Sea Raider" had soon to be restricted metal airplane pieces. Other Parker games included "The Great Victory Game—Thumbs Up" and 1943's "The Great American Flag Game."

Selchow & Righter Co. had been around since 1867. For the first sixty years of its existence, it produced no games itself but served as a major jobber for other game companies, primarily Milton Bradley and McLaughlin. In 1927 it started producing its own games, and its single wartime entry, "Salute," was one of the best. The dice-move board game was designed to teach children the rank insignia of the various services. In the center of its colorful board was the Commander-in-Chief position. The player reaching that position then led the other players in the Pledge of Allegiance.

Finally, in this board game category, Toy Creations put out a most unusual puzzle game in which speed was measured by a small hourglass device. A small sticker on the box indicated that it was produced for the "Buy to Aid Britain Companies" campaign sponsored by the British-American Ambulance Corps. The game dates to around 1940 and is the only example found of a commercial game specifically manufactured to aid a particular wartime cause.

Enclosed, hand-held BB and marble games, in which the object is to get ball bearings, marbles or other items into holes or slots on a small colorful board, go back many generations. Usually the games were enclosed in five-by-three-inch metal boxes. Both World Wars had numerous versions. Two cardboard, glass and marble types sold by Modern Novelties, Inc. of Cleveland, Ohio, "Put the Yanks in Berlin" and "Trap the Jap in Tokyo," are still easy to find. Later war items included "Trap the Jap" and "Atomic Bomb." Surprisingly, the latter was made by the famous manufacturer of children's chemistry sets, the A.C. Gilbert Company of New Haven, Connecticut.

Easily transportable, small card games of WWII interest were popular with members of the armed forces. "Sigs—The Game of Insignia" and "Squadron Insignia" (by All-Fair Co.) are typical. Also popular were a number of prewar

"Spot the Plane and Win the Game Teaches as You Play," said this item's game board. The "art deco" box makes it a striking game collectible.

Falling in both the propaganda and toy categories, "Victory Rummy," with its cartoon cards of Hitler, Tojo and Mussolini, is a favorite cross-collectible.

paper puzzles and brain twisters packaged by Geo Metrics Co. in a "Serviceman's Fun Kit."

Bagatelle games were small, thirty-by-fourteen-inch versions of regular pinball machines and were sold in toy stores throughout the 1920s, '30s and '40s. With only a few metal parts, Gotham Pressed Steel's "You're In The Army Now" is a great example of a WWII version. Holes signifying higher ranks are interspersed among scenes typical of an army recruit's life: wake-up bugles, aching feet, potato peeling and inspection. Points are earned as higher rank holes are hit; hitting Chief-Of-Staff earns a player 100,000 points! Northwestern Products Co. of St. Louis specialized in these items; cheaper examples were made by the misnamed Durable Toy and Novelty Corp.

This Page
Retailing for less than a dollar, All-Fair games were a good value for the money. Today they can be obtained for considerably less than larger items, but often have tears and torn corners due to the poor quality of the cardboard stock.

This Page
Although the games in this grouping were among the smallest and poorest quality of the era, due to their handsome box art they nonetheless are considered an important part of any WWII game collection.

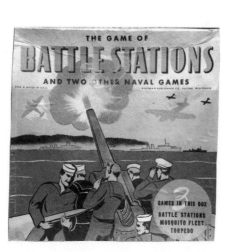

"Ranger Commandos" was a great wartime offering and today is the most widely available of the better war games. It is also the most overpriced. Although asking prices vary widely, is worth about $40.

"Sea Battle" by Kaywood Corp. was a large board game contained in a colorful folder. It was a variation of "Battleship," an old navy game that was played with ruled sheets of paper and a pencil and found in USO game packets throughout the war.

Walco Read Co. and C.H. Taylor, two rather obscure game companies, produced "Magnetic Minesweeper" and "Flagship" in 1941 and 1944.

A number of toy makers including Corey Games Co., producer of "Barrage Game," and the Samuel Lowe Co. marketed games that were versions of tiddly winks. The games sold for about twenty-nine cents.

CONFLICT
Planes—Ships—Guns

This game heavily oversold during the Christmas Season is now again being manufactured in quantity and prompt shipments can be made.

...lict $2. and Commandos $1.50 are among the "Best Sellers"

OTHER FAMOUS PARKER GAMES

...CORPS ROOK SORRY FLINCH MONOPOLY GREMLIN DOGFIGHT PING PONG CAMELOT
...DIG COMMANDOS SPOTTING U.S. SERVICE KIT WITH ACEY DUCEY PIT BUNNY RABBIT GAME, ETC.

...RKER GAMES

This Page

These Parker Brothers' games are solidly made and like those by Milton Bradley, usually are found in excellent condition. Though they often appear on the lists of dealers specializing in games, one will pay a much higher price than if the game can be spotted at a flea market.

This Page and Next
Game cards often displayed airplanes, squadron insignia, and so on, and hence are themselves a popular collectible. Often they are sold separately at ephemera shows without any indication as to their source.

Right
An unusual game with a sticker touting the British-American Ambulance Corps.

Above
The "Army Air Corps Game" by Parker Brothers is one of the best of the spinner board games.

Referred to as "Slidem Solitaire Puzzles," these odd, cheap cardboard puzzles were packaged in sets of three for a dime.

Right
Selchow & Righter Co. capitalized on the American child's fascination with military rank and insignia in "Salute," their only wartime offering. Like their now famous games of "Scrabble" and "Trivial Pursuit," "Salute" was quite instructional.

Right
Somewhat larger than most hand-held games, "Sink the Enemy Navy" is a nine-by-six-inch marble game featuring a B-29 bomber.

Below
The hand-held games illustrated date from the late prewar period and show themes popular before and during the war. None indicate the maker.

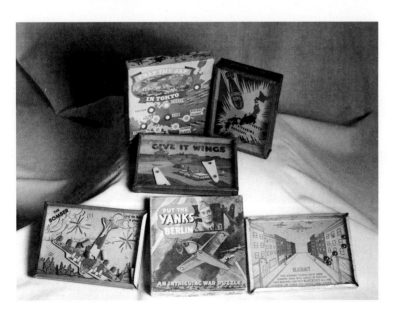

Above
The Service Man's Fun Kit contains a number of envelopes with numerous different "Chineese" type brain-twister puzzles. The cards in Sigs, "The Game of Armed Forces Insignia" illustrate, in color, over 100 different insignia.

Target Games

TARGET GAMES constituted the second major category of wartime games and although Dad probably occasionally took a turn dropping the dart-bomb on Berlin, were marketed essentially for children. Bombing the enemy was immensely popular and constituted the theme of the vast majority of such toys. Since marketing staff had just a few catchy words with which to work, the names of these games were remarkably similar. Shoppers could choose from "Bombs Away," "Bomb the Navy," "Secret Bomb-Site," "Bomb-Sight," "Bombardier's Bomb-Site," "Bomb-A-Jap," "Bomber Ball," "Dive-Bomber," "Bomber," "Victory Bomber," "Push-Em-Up Victory Bomber," "Aerial Bomber," and "Bombardier Bomb." Some of these small in size simply used marbles to knock over cardboard targets.

Many of the target games operated on a simple dart board principle except, in most cases, the board/target was horizontal and the darts ("bombs") were dropped from some device. Toy Creation Inc.'s "Bombs Away" was typical. One dropped four plastic darts from a cardboard box, the "Eagle Bombsight," onto a target on the floor, in this case

Below
The bombing device for "Direct Hit" by Northwestern Products Company was a sixteen-inch wooden airplane that dropped plastic darts out of a bomb bay. The author has only seen this interesting toy offered for sale once.

Scenes of wake-up bugles, aching feet, potato peeling and inspection typify an army recruit's life in "You're In The Army Now." This is a charming example of a bagatelle game marketed during WWII.

Left
The cardboard targets in Transogram's 1942 offering, "Sink the Ship," included American PBY Catalina flying boats and aircraft carriers. Transogram's wartime "Gold Medal" line also included military doctor and nurse kits, and map puzzles.

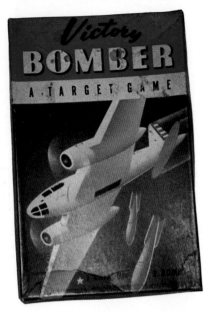

a port city. Scores from one to one hundred were awarded, depending on whether a bridge, pier or factory was hit. Based on the major ad campaigns in the trade press and the frequency with which it shows up at toy shows today, "Bombs Away" was probably the biggest seller of this type. Ad copy reached new heights of hyperbole: "Imagine yourself high up on the clouds . . . with the Eagle Bombsight, blockbusters appear to fall thousands of feet before hitting the ground." (In reality, depending on the size of the player, it was more like four to five feet!) Children quickly learned to weight the dart to make sure it stuck when it hit.

"Direct Hit" by Northwestern Products Company came along quite late, in April 1945. This game took the bombing principle much closer to reality. It had the same floor target, but the bombing device was an actual sixteen-inch

wooden airplane. The same plastic darts were loaded into an open bomb bay held on by a wire connected to a red handle. When one pulled the handle back, the bombs dropped. Pulling slowly made the bombs drop one by one; jerking quickly, it was "bombs away" for all four. Since one couldn't sight as well with the Direct Hit handle, one couldn't be as accurate of a shot as with the angled mirror of the Eagle Bombsight.

Two other horizontal dart target games that were sold in 1944 may have given mother some pause. "Bombardier," the "precision bombing game" by Continental Toys, featured a spring-loaded, forty-inch-high gun that shot a dart

This Page
Due to the nature of the materials used in their manufacture, cardboard and wood target games turn up far less frequently than do metal ones. Knowing children, there's no doubt that these games probably received a great deal of wear and tear due to constant use.

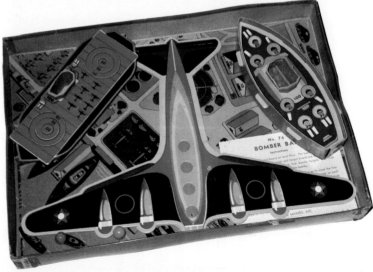

in a "secretly calculated" trajectory ten feet or more onto a large, folding, cardboard target featuring a military coastline. Lithographed in four glossy colors and marketed in an eye-catching action scene combination box and display carton, it was a neat looking toy, the kind that every kid instantly wants, and had all the ingredients for a big sales success. It probably did not make it for two reasons: it was expensive—at $4.95 it was one-tenth the average man's weekly salary—and the risk of putting a baby's eye out with the five-inch, spring-loaded steel dart probably resulted in a veto from many a mother.

"Secret Bomb Site" sold from 1942 to 1945 for one dollar. It had a handle-toggle release mechanism and a unique board with rotating military targets. Note also the large target of "Torpedo Action Game" with shark-like subs, a late war creation of N.Y. Toy and Game Co. Stand-up popgun target games such as Parker's early, magnificent "Wings" were popular, too.

Dart boards also took on a patriotic, action-oriented flavor. New York Toy and Game Mfg. Company, which specialized in dart boards, marketed an interesting variation. A large easeltype box housed a roller that when turned displayed five different bombing targets. New York's line of dart boards exclusively featured "safety" darts with rubber tips. "No steel parts to injure youngsters," read the advertising copy. Included in this line was the attractive

Above and at Left
The "Junior Bombsight Game" is another example of fantastic box art! This target game utilized marbles which, in many ways, worked better than darts.

"Our Defenders—the Game of the Day" was produced during the early to mid 1930s. Though referred to as a game by the manufacturer, Master Toy Company, the box actually contained toy soldiers.

Parker's magnificent "Wings" was a popular, stand-up popgun target game. The scene dates it as late prewar, probably 1940–41. Conforming with prewar sensitivities, the enemy planes are not identified but, painted yellow and red, they certainly would have been easy for our brave AA gunners to spot!

Across the Top
Components of Toy Creation Inc.'s Eagle Bombsight usually are offered separately by dealers. The bombsight box, the bombsight, the "Bombs Away" board and board box all were obtained at different times and places by the author.

The target for the "Set the Sun" dart game has action scenes worth ten, twenty-five, and fifty points and, in the center, a grotesque drawing of a Japanese face worth one hundred points. Sharp, steel-pointed darts came with the set.

"U.S. Air Force" dart board with an eighteen-by-eighteen-inch board that displayed silhouettes of Air Force planes in several colors, and "Dive Bomber Board" with cardboard bombs that released when hit by the safety dart.

Toyad Corporation sold a popular dart board set intended for servicemen. Entitled "Blaze Away," this popular set came in a cylindrical mailing tube and contained two paper targets, one traditional and one of the popular bombing-site type, and two bomb-shaped darts. The set even included eight thumbtacks.

Perhaps the most aggressive, propagandistic dart target game was "Set the Sun [Of A Bitch]." The trade press ad for this game truly reflects the flavor of the times:

> Set the Sun. READY! AIM! FIRE! All of us would really like to fire a round at these yellow "Sons of Heaven." Here's a game that gives young and old the same satisfying pleasure our boys in the Pacific feel each time they score.

No sissy safety darts came with this set—only sharp, steel-pointed ones would do.

90

Left
Another "Bombs Away" game of late-war vintage.

Above
Battery-powered and poorly constructed as it was, "Electric Patrol" by Electric Toy Company is nevertheless somewhat rare and sought after by collectors. On today's market it sells for as much as $500.

The large, clunky, cardboard target for the "Torpedo Action Game" featured shark-like subs and a Rising Sun battleship. The game was a late war creation of N.Y. Toy and Game Co.

Left
Another art deco gem, "Quoits—Ahoy!" was sold during the early and mid 1930s. The stand-up target was almost three feet tall and had swivel sticks that collapsed when a hoop was tossed on them.

4

PUZZLES & BOOKS

Many puzzles featured home front scenes, such as this one of a soldier home on leave. War worker scenes were a popular subject with titles like "We can, we will, we must."

O NE OF THE WORST offenses a youngster could commit during the war was to jostle the card table or other surface on which the omnipresent, incomplete puzzle was laid out. Usually this resulted in messing up the completed portion, knocking pieces on the floor and having to spend time looking for them. There was nothing worse than losing pieces of a puzzle on which the family had spent days.

By 1940, puzzles had been around for about two centuries. John Salisbury, a London map maker, invented a map jigsaw puzzle in the mid eighteenth century to "facilitate the teaching of geography." Due in large part to gas rationing, puzzles became extremely popular with Americans during the war. And, chances were, the puzzle had a military or civilian defense theme.

Manufacturers in the U.S. began active production of puzzles after the Civil War. McLoughlin Brothers pioneered the use of color lithography on heavy cardboard instead of wood; this innovation made puzzles much cheaper and more readily available to the masses. Parker Brothers, Milton Bradley, and Selchow and Righter also had a good share of the market. Imported, unpainted puzzles for very small children, usually of ten pieces or less, were very popular, particularly those made in Germany. Throughout this period, puzzles were relatively expensive. From 1920 on, however, almost all puzzles sold in the U.S. were made in America and were quite inexpensive. Book publishers got into the act in the twenties and thirties, and Saalfield, Whitman and Dell became significant producers of children's puzzles.

New production techniques, particularly intricate steel rule dies that looked like complicated cookie cutters, allowed the production of intricate designs of several hundred interlocking pieces, and giant and jumbo puzzles were born. Though expensive to manufacture, these dies could produce 100,000 puzzles before wearing out. The use of thinner cardboard, i.e., 1/16 to 1/8 inch, resulted in substantially reduced prices. For the price—usually a

quarter—puzzles became a bargain, a factor of real importance during the Depression years.

The years of the Great Depression ushered in what has been called the biggest jigsaw puzzle craze in the nation's history. *Business Week* magazine referred to it as the "Jigsaw Jag." The weekly sales of jigsaw puzzles throughout the United States in 1932–1933 reached six million, a figure not since matched. One company reported selling over a half million puzzles a week. Learned psychologists opin-

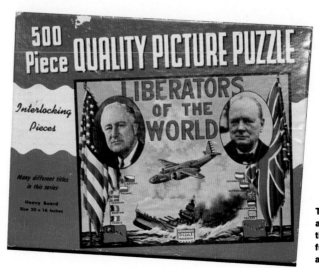

Although after the Japanese attack on Pearl Harbor their significance diminished greatly, battleships remained immensely popular as cover art with puzzle makers.

This depiction of Roosevelt and Churchill as "Liberators of the World" also shows up as a full-page magazine illustration and on posters.

Some puzzle pictures were based on especially commissioned drawings or paintings and some, for example the "Six War Picture Puzzles" set, on color photographs. This photograph is of the Bell *Airacuda*.

ioned as to deep reasons for the craze, but the underlying reason was puzzles were cheap—the cheaper, the better. Newspapers put out weekly jigsaw puzzles; newsstands sold them. Puzzle swap clubs were formed. For little money, puzzles provided a lot of fun over many hours. Also, with high unemployment, people had more time for leisure activities and the whole family could work on a puzzle together.

Radio, too, played a role. The sponsors of popular radio programs gave away puzzles as premiums. Cocomalt, a drink similar to Orphan Annie's Ovaltine, distributed its Flying Family puzzle series. Children who drank the product for a whole month became "Cocomalt Flight Commanders" and earned additional premiums. Their parents had to sign and mail in a weight chart that came with the puzzle.

After WWII started, the public eagerly sought puzzles with wartime themes, and there were a multitude of experienced manufacturers to supply this demand. The early rationing of gas and severe travel restrictions produced the major home front impetus for puzzles, games and books. Several game companies, including Parker Brothers and Milton Bradley, made wartime puzzles as did the major book publishers.

Up to the war years, puzzles typically had depicted scenes from paintings. Landscapes and seascapes were particularly popular, as were portraits, still lifes, maps and other educational subjects. During the defense buildup immediately prior to Pearl Harbor, however, the public's inclination for puzzles with patriotic themes began to grow rapidly. Flags, planes, armor and ships became the subjects that sold. The Statue of Liberty was featured constantly.

One theme that recurred particularly often during 1941–42 was that of battleships steaming around New York Harbor and aircraft armadas flying overhead. Regardless of the manufacturer, the artwork was remarkably similar. Perfect Picture Puzzles produced two such examples. Its "Safeguards of Liberty" puzzle showed the Statue, one battleship and several planes; "Defense of Liberty" had six huge battlewagons abreast steaming up the harbor. TUCO's deluxe "Guardians of Liberty" was much more conservative—there was only one BB in sight. Its "America" puzzle, however, had seven battleships plus about fifty airplanes steaming past the Statue of Liberty. (The statue is about a mile tall!)

Unlike the contents of many games and punch-out sets, wartime puzzles didn't disappoint. Notwithstanding how dull and small the box cover photo or illustration might be, the puzzle itself almost always was very colorful and striking. Many people glued the finished puzzle on a backing and mounted or framed them. Clearly indicated on each puzzle was the title, an identification number, the dimensions and the number of pieces.

Copycat puzzles didn't seem to bother either the manufacturers or the public. Perfect Picture Puzzles' "Keep Em Flying" puzzle had a B-19 flying right to left over the Capitol and a huge American flag. TUCO's "Keep Em Flying" just had the plane flying in the other direction!

WWII puzzles can be divided into two categories. The first, designed for use by children five to eight years of age, contains some of the best and most colorful artwork. These puzzles, which usually came several to the box, were smaller, about ten-by-sixteen inches, and contained about two dozen large-size pieces, a number well within the younger child's attention span. The various puzzles in the Land-Sea-Air Combat series made by U.S. Finishing & Mfg. Company of Chicago are typical. The three sets in the series came in colorful boxes, each containing eight puzzles. The paintings or color photographs of tanks, ships and planes had one-inch borders on the top and bottom showing several different military insignia or aircraft markings. These puzzle sets got a good bit of institutional advertising and retailed for fifty cents.

A bald eagle with wings spread to form the familiar "V" for victory graced the box of U.S. Finishing's "Victory Combat Picture Puzzles" set. Such work is an excellent example of the fantastic box art on which collectors place a premium.

Puzzle manufacturers furnished retailers with large window and counter display cards. "Feature [these displays] and watch your sales sky rocket," proclaims this ad for U.S. Finishing & Mfg. Company's boxed puzzle sets.

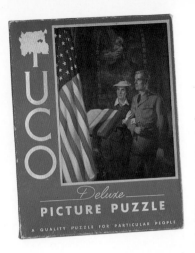   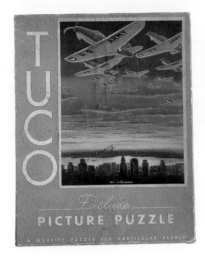 

Across the top
Perhaps due to the millions sold, puzzles are the most easily obtainable WWII children's collectible, and puzzles by TUCO show up most frequently. Those with 250 to 1,000 pieces range in price from fifteen to thirty dollars.

American Boy and Girl Picture Puzzles with box art of A. C. Weems' famous painting, "Tomorrow's Pilot," (see cover) is a personal favorite. Weems' painting captures the child's wonder of those years.

Larger puzzles that were designed for mom and dad and the older children form the second broad category. Among the major manufacturers were TUCO; Jaymar; J.S. Hart; Guild; J. Pressman & Co., Inc.; Whitman; Dell and Perfect Picture Puzzles (Consolidated Box). TUCO puzzles are probably the most sought after by today's specialists. TUCO Work Shops, Inc., located in Sackport, N.Y., was a division of The Upson Company, a wallboard manufacturer. Upson's puzzle business started during the Depression when the budding construction industry became virtually nonexistent. TUCO (a derivative of the parent company's initials) used wallboard as its puzzle material, and its puzzles were unique in several aspects. Since wallboard was thicker than cardboard, the pieces initially had to be noninterlocking. Advertising its product as "a quality puzzle for particular people," TUCO made light of this fact and emphasized that its thicker pieces were easier to handle. TUCO also used a better picture of the completed puzzle for its box art than other makers. They certainly had some of the best original patriotic artwork, and TUCO artists such as Schieder, Mielatz, Lee, Steinke, Slaughter and

Cornwall are well known to today's puzzle aficionados. Common TUCO wartime puzzles today sell at a modest premium above those of other makers.

Perfect Picture Puzzles, a division of Consolidated Box Company, pioneered the use of the "picture guide" on the box cover. Consolidated, formed by a merger of four Boston area box makers in the early thirties, sold both adult and children's puzzles. The former, with a few exceptions, featured battle scenes and were advertised as "card table size." Perfect's line had marvelous titles such as "Down with the Axis" and "America Fights Back."

J. S. Hart Co., maker of paper and cardboard toys, featured photo puzzles. Its "America in Action" puzzles, said the trade press ads, showed the "latest photos of our troops in action." They were, however, among the less creative of WWII puzzles. Moreover, its boxes were of the cheapest cardboard and very fragile.

The Modern Fighters for Victory and Hobby Jigsaw series by Jaymar Specialty Co., Inc. were quite colorful. Jaymar's aircraft scenes had small inserts containing ID data for aircraft spotters and silhouettes. Their advertisements said that these were "puzzles you'll really enjoy puzzling over."

The Jaymar Company had an interesting history. Controlled by relatives of famous toy king Louis Marx, the small

96

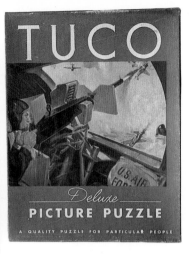
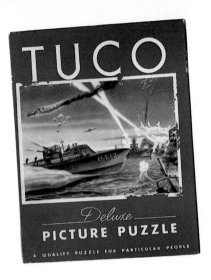

company produced wood and paper toys and entered the puzzle business in 1942. It shared display showrooms with Marx and Marx handled all of its selling. When the metal toy ban idled a portion of Marx' production line, those workers not employed in the company's defense and war contract work were used in Jaymar production. The puzzles, copyrighted by Marx rather than Jaymar, became excellent sellers, a trend that continued long after the war. Jaymar also was one of the earliest Disney licensees, a privilege reflected in its wartime Disney "Gremlins" puzzle that featured Disney-created Navy squadron markings. Ironically, Jaymar survived long after the Marx company's demise was brought on by a series of buy outs and mergers. Today, children's puzzle production constitutes fifty percent of the firm's business.

The production of puzzles by book publishers Whitman, Dell and Saalfield was a natural tie-in. Whitman, a subsidiary of Western Publishing Company started making puzzles in 1925. Whitman's puzzles also were sold under the Gold Seal and Guild names. Many of the illustrations used in the puzzles were taken from Whitman's popular wartime series of illustrated aircraft books for children. Whitman also made an boxed series of eight puzzles featuring "Pictures of our Army, Navy And Air Force in action." Produced in the millions, Whitman's wartime puzzles are

now among the cheapest and most readily available.

Saalfield Publishing Co, founded in 1900 in Akron, Ohio, had been a leader in children's book publishing for seventy-five years. It began making simple children's puzzles and the Interlox brand of adult puzzles during the thirties. During WWII it produced the Victory series, a name also used by J. S. Publishing Corp. of New York City. Saalfield's "Liberators of the World" puzzle showing Roosevelt and Churchill is one of the most difficult of wartime puzzles to obtain in good condition. The scene, also featured in a small, poster-like sheet suitable for framing, appeared in Saalfield's "Quality" line of large, five-hundred-piece puzzles right near the end of the war. The illustrative battle scene showing a single Martin A-26 Havoc attack bomber sinking an enemy battleship followed the toy book tradition of "creative" propaganda. Such action never occurred and several squadrons of A-26's probably couldn't have done the job.

Dell, another large publisher, produced the "All-American Picture Puzzle." Some puzzle makers merely copied wartime scenes from the many series of kids books devoted to the various services, their planes, tanks and equipment. Many of the manufacturers placed the familiar call to buy war bonds and stamps on the puzzle box.

Sometimes puzzle pieces were made in the form of mil-

Everybody wanted to sign up after Pearl Harbor, even this heavily armed, left-handed pre-schooler!

Right
Guild Puzzle's "A Lesson in Patriotism" is a pre-Pearl Harbor puzzle. "Defense" stamps became "war" stamps soon after the attack.

McNally World Map bordered with flags of all the United Nations. With only a hundred large pieces, it was easy to assemble. The "Patchwork" map puzzle kit was the most unusual of all. The box contained four envelopes with ten-by-eighteen-inch airplane puzzles made of very thin cardboard. When these four puzzles were reversed and put together, they formed a giant 20"×36" map of the world containing over 1,300 pieces. The distributor claimed over 90,000 were sold for a dollar during the first month. Our example illustrates an interesting piece of WWII ephemera but certainly a very poor quality product.

Advertising puzzles date from the 1870s. In their hey-

Far right
"Young Commandos" puzzle by E.E. Fairchild Co. is a perfect example of what this book is all about.

itary objects. This ploy delighted kids. J. Pressman's Victory Picture Puzzles (yet another Victory series!) used this technique extensively and illustrated it on the box cover. Note the outlines of cannon, tank, ship, sub, AA gun and planes.

Geography has never been as popular with kids as it was during WWII, and as in earlier times, map puzzles were big sellers. Franklin Mfg. Co. of Philadelphia specialized in them. Its Patriotic Picture Puzzles featured "military and naval maps and pictures." Its ads urged the public to follow the war, to read, and to enjoy geography and become familiar with all battle zones. "Get on speaking terms with Guadalcanal . . . Papua and Stalingrad," they read. At one dollar, its product was expensive but a great help to school children.

U.S. Finishing Co. published, as a puzzle, a Rand

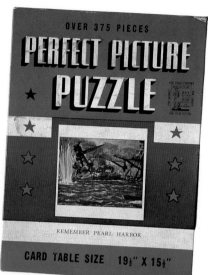

Defense themes dominated the picture puzzle industry. Perfect Picture Puzzle's "Bombs Away" and "Remember Pearl Harbor" flaunt two of the industry's most frequently used subjects.

The Whitman publishing company began making puzzles in 1925. Its WWII Fighters for Freedom puzzle series was unique in that some of the puzzles featured two distinct scenes side by side.

These puzzles are examples of the common practice of using illustrations or photographs from book covers.

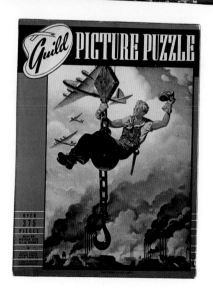

day in the early thirties, hundreds of companies gave away advertising puzzles printed on cheap paper and usually contained in flimsy envelopes. Prime examples are the 1943–44 series that Ward Bakery Co. distributed with Tip-Top Bread. Depicted are scenes of the West Point Military Academy, Annapolis Naval Academy, and the Statue of Liberty. Few WWII examples have survived.

Finally, various kinds of small game "puzzles" that were not of a jigsaw nature were sold in five and dimes, drug stores and gas stations. A typical example is the 1943 "Gambling Mystery Puzzle" made by the W.L. Fuchs Co.

It involved making U. S. planes in an eight-inch square. It was not easy, but if a customer was totally stumped they could mail Fuchs a dime to get a diagram of the correct solution.

Most WWII puzzles for adults that are complete and in very good condition still are modestly priced; missing pieces reduce the price accordingly. Boxed sets of multiple children's wartime military puzzles sell for somewhat more. Since the latter fall more in the toy category, box art and the condition of the box are more important.

100

This is a selection of wartime puzzles from Consolidated's Perfect Picture Puzzles series. Courtesy of Harry L. Rinker, Sr. and Harry L. Rinker, Jr.

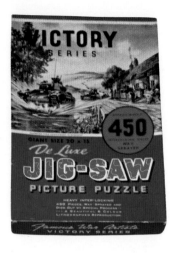

STIRRING ADVENTURES: WWII FICTION BOOKS FOR BOYS AND GIRLS

Red Randall was a human flash. Almost nose to nose, his guns poured lead into the Nip and that killer took it, practically straight in his face. His zero streaked off for a short distance, and then seemed to hit an invisible brick wall. . . . It folded up . . . and fell down into the sea in flames. "Two down, but good," Randall muttered. *Red Randall on New Guinea* (Grosset & Dunlap, 1944)

THINK THAT WAS TOUGH and rough fighting? How about this rhetoric from an earlier war: "The 95th zoomed in the air to meet the foe's gun threat . . . Richtoven's circus soared up there aflame with the killer lust." (*Battle Stories* magazine, c.1930)

During WWII several series of hard-cover fiction books chronicling war heroics proved increasingly popular with young people. Today these books are great, modestly priced collectibles. These stories for boys and a few for girls were a natural offshoot of the adult "pulp" magazines of World War I that primarily featured aviation adventures and were published throughout the late twenties to the late thirties. Selling for ten to twenty-five cents, these nine-by-six-inch magazines gave outstanding value for the money, even in the depths of the Depression. They contained an average of 150 pages and over 30,000 words; they were about one-third the size of an ordinary novel for far less the price. And what titles and covers they had, all derived from full-size paintings: *Flying Aces, G-8 and his Battle Aces, Dusty Ayres and his Battle Birds, Battle Stories, Wings, War Aces, RAF Aces,* and *Sky Fighters.* The heroes tended to have American surnames with a nickname attached; there was Slim Denton, Dixie Darrell, Tex Malone, Gunner Randall, and Wild Bill Hollowell. It seems anything was doable in the pulps!

Grosset & Dunlap of New York, a long-established publisher of children's and educational books, produced the most wartime fiction serials. Its Air Combat Series for Boys featured nine Yankee Flyer books and a marvelous story line by author Al Avery. Typical of these twelve chapter, 200-plus-page books was a *Yankee Flyer in North Africa*. Irishman Bill O'Malley, American Stan Wilson, and Britisher March Allison fly P-40 Warhawks and P-38 Lightnings against the famed "Red Stingers" of Luftwaffe Ace Colonel Fritz Stamer. Our three heroes had been transferred from the South Pacific (*A Yankee Flyer in the South Pacific*) just in time to stop a major German ground offensive. From 1941 (*A Yankee Flyer with the RAF*) to 1946 (*A Yankee Flyer under Secret Orders*), the daring trio fought in Italy, the Far East, over Berlin, in Normandy, North Africa and On a Rescue Mission.

The Red Randall Series was created by R. Sidney Bowen, one of the aviation pulp authors of the thirties. Bowen himself was described as the youngest member of the Royal Flying Corps in WWI and was said to have shot down a number of planes and balloons. Bowen's Red Randall character also got an early start. The seventeen-year-old son of an Air Force Colonel, Red and his pal, Jimmy Joyce, belonged to a flying club near Pearl Harbor and outwitted Jap spy, Kato Harada, thus foiling an invasion of the Hawaiian Islands. "Clever slant-eyed yellow Jap rat," yelled Randall at one crucial point. Harada hissed back, "We Japanese have much to teach you American Dogs." Like all the Randall stories, this first adventure was full of action. Red, described by Bowen as "just a red-blooded American boy, full of pep and ginger and ready and eager to tackle any job," went on to serve in the Aleutians, at Midway, over Tokyo and on New Guinea. Bowen was the master of cliché and propaganda—including the recurring and unproven wartime charge, which kids totally accepted, that Japanese pilots constantly attempted to machine gun helpless parachuting pilots.

Grosset and Dunlap's third series, the Lucky Terrell Flying Stories by Canfield Cook, had the best cover art of the genre. Cook's hero, Texan Lucky Terrell, flew from *Spitfire Pilot* (1942) to *Wings over Japan* (1944). Cook took more than a little editorial license in his plot lines. In *Lost Squadron*, Lucky, now a Squadron Leader, led a group of

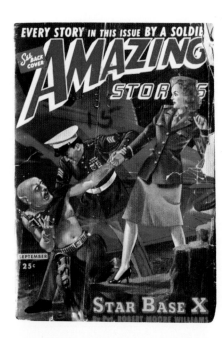

This cover from a pre-Pearl Harbor pulp magazine hints at the typically sensational nature of the contents. © 1944 ZIFF-DAVIS PUBLISHING COMPANY

The cover art work on this ten cent quarterly by Goodman was particularly well done. The artist makes use of an odd combination of WWI machine guns, a Dutch-type helmet worn by the avenging U.S. infantryman, and an enemy dressed in green. © 1942 USA AT WAR

single-engine *Stratohawks*, a fictional plane that doesn't show up in any real life battle, over the Himalayas!

Grosset & Dunlap resurrected seven WWI adventures from the 1930s with new dust jackets in the Air Combat Group written by Eustace L. Adams and Thomson Buitis, earlier pulp authors who, like several of that breed, were former WWI flyers. *Four Aces* (1932) and *Doomed Demons* (1935) are illustrative.

Bowen also authored the most popular fictional series for boys, the War Adventures of Dave Dawson. Alternating between the Saalfield and Crown labels, the sixteen-book series saw Dawson flying and fighting in every theater with many famous units including the RAF, Flying Tigers, Eighth Air Force Command and Pacific Fleet. At Truk, Dave and his British buddy, Freddy Farmer, "chased Jap rats all over the Pacific" making it possible for the U. S. Navy to smash

   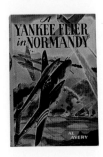

Grosset & Dunlap's Air Combat Series for Boys featured nine Yankee Flyer books, each with a marvelous story line by Al Avery. The rhetoric on the jacket of *Yankee Flyer in Normandy* was typical: "It was only natural that this renowed three man flying team . . . were detailed to fly special equipment to the French underground just a few hours before the Normandy Invasion."

"Nipponese" sea power with the "famous naval victory at Truk." This never happened. Truk was bypassed completely in MacArthur's South Pacific island-hopping strategy.

Whitman complemented its successful puzzle line with a series of boys and girls fiction tales entitled Fighters for Freedom. Unlike the other series, the Fighters series did not involve a continuing hero but rather individual freedom fighters. Four out of the eight were female, a normal ratio today but a most unusual step in the forties. These early pioneers of fictional equality deserve a complete listing: *Norma Kent of the WACS; Nancy Dale, Army Nurse; Sally Scott of the WAVES;* and *Kitty Carter, Canteen Girl* (she followed the troops!).

Roy J. Snell who wrote for several publishers and had a vivid imagination, wrote several of the the Freedom Fighter series. His Sally Scott, for example, was imbued with fighting spirit, handled secret radio messages, sailed on convoys to England and back, fought U-boats and parachuted into the sea. But was it only a coincidence that her

This dust cover recreates the popular image of RAF pilots scrambling for their planes during the Battle of Britain. Hard-cover fiction following the adventures of various heroes, particularly aviators, became immensely popular with young people during the war. These books averaged 150 pages and sold for ten to twenty-five cents.
© 1942 BETTER PUBLISHING, INC.

book's dust jacket alone carried an admonition to "Save Cooking Fats and Grease For Victory"?

Later in the war, Whitman published its In Action! series. This is the neatest set of large, illustrated, heavy paper booklets. If the cover numbers were consecutive, there were twenty in the series including *U.S. Navy in Action!,*

Right. **Unlike fictional hero Dave Dawson, who fought all over the world, Red Randall, the star of a popular series by the well-known pulp author R. Sidney Bowen, never made it out of the Pacific Theatre.**

Below. **A familiar WWI scene—a rear gunner manning a scarf mounting for twin Lewis guns and Fokker D-7 planes—provides the cover art for this WWII monthly publication. It was not uncommon during WWII for publishers simply to recycle WWI stories. Sometimes new dust jackets were produced; sometimes even the dust jacket was unchanged.**

Right. **Grosset and Dunlap's third series was the Lucky Terrell Flying Stories by Canfield Cook. Like Red Randall and Dave Dawson, Lucky fought, according to dust jackets, with "indomitable courage, spectacular flying skill, heroic and dare devil flying, and unforgettable heroism." Wow!**

105

Left and below. **The popular Dawson series was authored by the estimable R. Sidney Bowen and alternated between the Saalfield and Crown labels. The ad from the wholesale catalog indicates that each hard-bound novel ran approximately 250 pages and featured large type. The rarest Dave Dawson books are the last two published,** *Dave Dawson at Truk* **and** *Over Berlin.*

Dave Dawson Books—The War Adventure Series. Assortment consists of 9 titles. With the Pacific Fleet, At Dunkirk, Singapore, With the Commandos, Libya, R.A.F., Air Corps, Flight Lieutenant, and Convoy Patrol. Cloth books, size 5⅝x7⅝ inches. Over one inch thick, thread sewn. Ornamental and reinforcing headbands. Four color jackets, varnished. Titles in ink on front of cloth cover and the backbone. Each book 250 pages or more. Large clear type.

No. 33N22. Per dozen... 4.20

Below. **Whitman's series of boys and girls' fiction tales was entitled** Fighters for Freedom. *Canteen Girl* **by Ruby Lorraine Radford is the rarest book in the series—possibly mothers hesitated to purchase a book with such a title for their daughters.**

Barry Bart and August (Alex) Schamberry did the color covers for Whitman's In Action! series of large, illustrated booklets. These exciting, more realistic illustrations also were used for Whitman's puzzles.

107

Above

These popular WWII titles indicate that not all wartime fiction for young people was written as part of a series, as were the Dave Dawson books, below.

U.S. Marines, U.S. Army, U.S. Fliers, U.S. Submarines, U.S. Solders, U.S. Sailors, U.S. Warplanes, and *U.S. Bombers.* The full size watercolor illustrations, crammed full of action, are the best of their kind. It was as though artists Barry Bart and August (sometimes listed as Alex) Schamberry didn't want to leave a single inch of space unused. The forty-page plots by Roy J. Snell (naturally) and Art Elder, among others, were fictional narratives of various wartime events such as the Allies' bombing raids over Europe without any fully developed or named characters.

Other wartime fiction publishers included Goldsmith Publishing of Chicago with about eight titles, several by the ubiquitous Roy Snell. His *Wings For Victory* had one of the most propagandistic cover art of the war, notwithstanding the total inaccuracy of the aircraft depiction.

Hampton Publishing's 1943 title, *Flying Wildcats,* contained a number of fine short war stories by R. Sidney Bowen and others. Its companion book, *Wings Over the World,* had a host of military and commercial aviation action stories for boys.

Almost all of these children's fiction works still can be found with good dust jackets for modest prices at book fairs and sometimes a flea market. Since the dust jacket cover art is so important to a collection, one should wait for a good copy complete with cover.

The paper stock for books during WWII was quite inferior, and thus has resulted in brittle paper that fades and yellows easily over the years. Many copies found today are torn and damaged. With a little patience, however, a good copy will turn up, and with diligent searching, it is relatively easy to complete substantially most of the series described here for a modest investment. Book dealers, particularly those that specialize in children's series, can be very helpful. Preparation of an advance want list will expedite matters and secure a more prompt response.

Big/Better Little Books

Pioneered by Whitman, Big Little Books and Better Little Books had been around for some time by 1941. Approximately four-by-three inches, these one-inch thick, hard-bound, illustrated novelettes were designed to fit in a big pant's pocket. Kids loved them. Many had "moving picture" illustrations in the upper right-hand page that, when flipped with the thumb, made an action sequence such as a torpedo plane launching a torpedo to sink an enemy ship. In the 1930s, Big Little Books featured fictional movie star exploits and popular comic book and serial heroes like Buck Rogers and Flash Gordon, Don Winslow of the Navy, and various Western stars. In addition to Whitman's two famous lines, there were excellent imitations by other publishers: Little Big Books by Saalfield; Dime Action Books by Fawcett; and Fast Action Books by Dell.

The list of wartime titles is lengthy. Averaging 350–400 pages with color covers and selling for a dime, they were a great bargain, particularly since much like a comic book they could be swapped or loaned. Whitman's usual stable of writers and illustrators of children's war fiction also did these books. R. R. "Russ" Winterbottom is well known for his many stories.

In their reticence to offend Germany and Japan, pre-Pearl Harbor plots were similar to those of the full-size books of the era. In *Alan Pike of the Parachute Squad-USA* (1941), Olaf Anssen, a Norwegian-American parachutist, helps Pike lead raids in an unnamed African country; throughout the entire book the enemy goes unnamed. A few months later, in early 1942, *Windy Wayne and His Flying Wing* prevented a second attack on Pearl Harbor. Wayne was assisted by the United States' new ally, Canada. Author Winterbottom claimed that U.S. losses at Pearl numbered

only one battleship and that "within a week" U.S. forces had inflicted casualties on the Japanese Navy far exceeding America's Hawaiian losses.

Although it had a somewhat superficial plot involving a transatlantic clipper pilot who gets called to active duty and retrained as a dive bomber pilot, *Keep 'Em Flying for America's Defense* (1943) was a particular favorite. Overall, it was a highly instructional, illustrated essay for kids on dive bomber tactics and carrier life.

Currently, Big Little Book and Better Little Book prices are all over the lot—priced at what the traffic will bear. Beware! Many toy show and flea market dealers greatly overprice them.

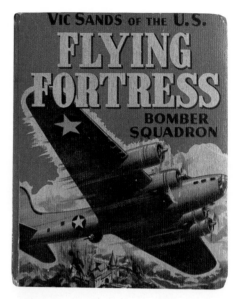

Above

Whitman's line of Better Little Books were copied by Saalfield, Fawcett, and Dell. *Flying Fortress* was a popular title by Whitman.

Below

One attractive feature of Whitman's Better Little Books was the "moving picture" illustrations in the upper right-hand corner.

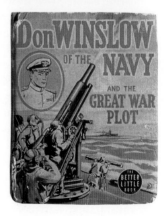

Over four hundred Better Little Book titles were published over the years. The most sought after today are those published during WWII and based on comic book characters such as Buz Sawyer and Skeezix.

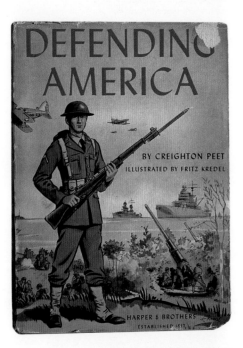

WWII NONFICTION FOR BOYS

IMMEDIATELY PRIOR TO and during the war, Americans of all ages had an insatiable and continuing interest in everything military. Well over a dozen major U.S. publishers fed this need with a varied menu of low and medium priced books on insignia, weapons, ordnance, planes, tanks, ships and all aspects of military life. This discussion will focus on those books that can be described broadly as catering to the younger, under eighteen age group. This is not to say that many adults did not favor these publications, nor that kids restricted themselves just to these books.

With some exceptions, those books favored by the young tended to be smaller in size, lower in cost and somewhat simplified in terms of narrative and illustration. Although not technical manuals, they were highly accurate. Most were written by retired military officials and had forwards written by senior military officers. Like other military collectibles of the period, these instructional books started appearing about a year or so before Pearl Harbor, although three by Whitman that featured the Coast Guard and Army ground and air forces and used actual photographs, were published earlier. The emphasis on WWI weapons and tactics in these books shows how unprepared our forces were just prior to the start of WWII.

The best of the late prewar books, and perhaps the finest children's book on military subjects ever published, was Harper & Brothers' *Defending America*. Published in early 1941, this book had charming text by Creighton Peet—its simple narrative with short paragraphs and crisp, declarative sentences and captions are a prime example of what such books should be like. But its real treasures were the outstanding watercolor and black and white illustrations by noted children's illustrator Fritz Krendell. Needless to say, this book is very difficult to locate today.

Based on the number available at toy and collectible

shows and book fairs, the books that probably had the longest and largest printings were the Guide Books series by Whitman. Published only from 1940–43, they almost certainly were sold throughout the war. They numbered at least fifteen and all of them were marvelous. The illustrations were unforgettable and the narratives had just enough information for a young lad. It is safe to say that much of what young boys learned, they learned from these small, three-by-five-inch, sixty-page, hard-bound mini-books. They sold for a dime, fit easily into a knapsack or pant's pocket, and could take a lot of wear and tear. Popular then, they are just as popular now, and show up all the time on dealer toy soldier lists as recommended visual backgrounds

The six aircraft books in the Whitman Guide Books series included three prewar (c.1940) editions: *Warplanes of the World, Wonder Warplanes,* and *American Airplanes.* All were edited by John B. Walker.

for soldier collections. More often than about any other small military toy collectible, one hears comments about the Whitman Guides. "Hey, I remember these; they were terrific!"

There were six aircraft books in the Guide Books series, all soft cover and all edited by John B. Walker. The three prewar versions, all copyrighted in 1940, were titled *Warplanes of the World, Wonder Warplanes,* and *American Airplanes.* The prewar series included aircraft from such "air powerhouses" as Spain, Norway, Brazil, Romania, Yugoslavia, Sweden, Denmark, Turkey and the Netherlands! As the contents continuously were updated to reflect

new aircraft like the P-51 Mustang fighter, once the U.S. entered the war all such aircraft disappeared in future editions. The illustrator, who took pains to show appropriate insignia, was not given credit for the excellent color renditions. Each picture was accompanied by a full paragraph of data.

Whitman published two editions of both the *Navy* and *Army Guides* in 1942 and 1943. The illustrations—sepia and brown for the Army and light blue hues for the Navy book—formed the basis for many a cardboard soldier or toy vehicle produced during that period. The guides to Navy and Army insignia, uniforms and medals rank right

111

up there with the famous *National Geographic* issues that featured the same. Also found in this series were books on codes and signals, first aid, and civil defense. All of the Whitman Guides are still readily available at low prices.

Rand McNally published over a dozen small hard-cover books. Three in four-by-six-inch sizes were published in 1941 before Pearl Harbor: *America on Guard, Wings over America,* and *Guardians of America.* Each emphasized the national defense theme and, recognizing the rapid build up of our forces, each book's preface contained a caveat that the information was "subject to change and modification." These books were sold throughout the war. The author's copies have handwritten flyleaf notes that indicate they were given as Christmas presents in 1943 and 1944.

Two three-by-four-inch items by the same publisher, *America's Army* and *America's Navy,* had great covers and a number of neat comic book-like illustrations identical to

those on the "Horrors of War" bubble gum cards. Like the cards, the illustrations are copyrighted by Gum, Inc. Both books were published in 1941 and both incorrectly reported a series of U.S. "victories" such as an alleged sinking of forty-six Japanese ships in a battle at Java and an air battle in which three U.S. pilots took on 108 Jap bombers! Rand McNally published several similar books that were somewhat more accurate in nature.

Fighting Yanks was a full-sized, soft-cover war atlas published in 1942 that became dog-eared from use in many homes. In addition to the usual materials found in an atlas, this publication had a separate map of all the places where

Rand McNally's *America's Army* and *America's Navy* had comic book-like illustrations identical to those on the "Horrors of War" bubble gum cards. Like the cards, the illustrations are copyrighted by Gum, Inc.

U. S. Flier Strafes Jap Airdrome

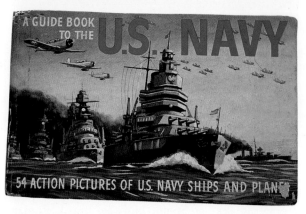

Whitman published a 1942 and a 1943 edition of *A Guide Book to the U.S. Navy.* Along with a similar guide to the U.S. Army, this book was the best and contained more hot poop than some books more than ten times its size.

Right.
Random House's wartime offerings for children ran the gamut: from baby animals to superman to war planes.

Below.
This atlas actually was used as a teaching aid in some classroom geography classes. Published by Rand McNally in 1942, it contained a map of all U.S. bases as well as a description of the customs and demographics of each country.

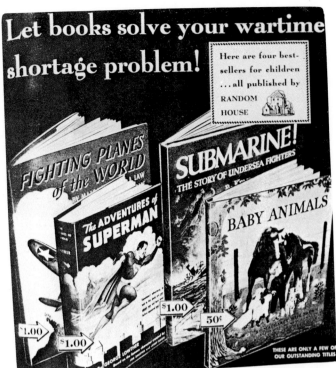

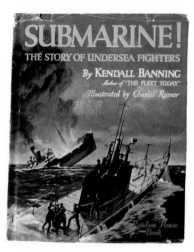

Above and below
Many of the nonfiction books for youth published during the war were authored by retired military officers.

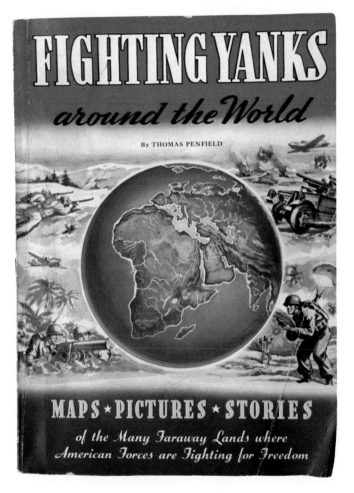

Several of these informational books feature text by Major Bernard Law and the colorful illustrations of Barry Bart. Bart's work also turned up frequently on posters and puzzles.

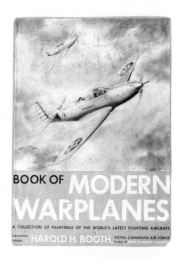

Like Random House and MacMillan and Company, Garden City Publishing produced an attractive line of children's nonfiction. While the entire line was advertised extensively in the trade press, the edition sporting a forward by famous air race celebrity Col. Roscoe Turner became particularly well known. Note the accurate drawings of the prototype P-39 (top) and the *Seagull* (bottom).

U.S. troops were stationed, including the chain of strategic Atlantic defense bases stretching from Greenland to Dutch Guiana, and a lengthy narrative description of the people, customs and demographics of each country.

Numerous large size (9½″×1½″) hard-bound picture books dealing with military subjects were published for boys. Those by Random House, Garden City Publishing, and MacMillan and Company were particularly attractive and informative. Random House published six in various editions between 1940 and 1943. The emphasis was on aircraft and the Air Force, clearly the most popular branch of the service. Several of these informational books feature text by Major Bernard Law and the colorful illustrations of Barry Bart. Bart's work also turned up frequently on posters and puzzles.

War in the Air (1940–1941) contained numerous black and white drawings illustrating bombing techniques and British air defenses. Illustrated chapters on parachute troops and airborne infantry from the successful German parachute attacks on Crete and Holland were included. The series was advertised in the trade press and also included *Submarines* and *Fighting Ships of the Navy. Playthings* ran a regular feature section on such books called "On the Playthings Bookshelf."

Garden City Publishing's line of large books was very similar and, in fact, somewhat more varied. Its *Book of Modern Airplanes*, published in 1940–41, had a forward by the famous air race celebrity of the twenties and thirties, Col. Roscoe Turner. Turner had a real promotional flair and his visage turned up on everything: the fact that he designed his own flashy uniforms and sometimes flew with a pet lion cub may have had something to do with his popularity.

Those who bought a two-year subscription to *Air Trails* magazine in 1942 received a copy of the *Book of Modern Warplanes*. It came in at least three editions. The 1940 red cover issue had a P-39 on the cover and the blue issue, a Navy observation plane. Both featured a full page on Germany's *Condor* 4-engine transport that set a 1938 Berlin to New York, nonstop speed record. (This article may have been responsible, in part, for stirring up all the fuss a few years later about possible air bombing raids on the East

Above and facing page. **Particularly in the early war years when maintaining home front morale was considered important, a good deal of editorial license was common in these "true stories" of heroes such as Generals Patton and MacArthur.** © 1943 DELL PUBLISHING COMPANY, INC.

Coast.) A 1941 version, updated from war developments, for some reason had the obsolete Curtis P-36 on the cover. All these books retailed at a dollar. For a dollar one could also buy portfolios containing five of the color prints "suitable for framing."

The best in the Garden City series was *A Book of Battles: From Troy to Bataan.* It was a beautifully illustrated record of sixteen great battles of history. Barry Bart did the full-page color illustrations and the drawings of weapons and uniforms for the margins. Other titles in the series included *Story of the U.S. Army Air Forces* (1945), *Fighting Ships of the U.S. Navy* (1941), and *Inside Story of the Flying Fortress.*

Grosset and Dunlap's large format Close-up series was well done and included *Our Navy's Striking Power, Mechanizing our Army,* and *What's New in the Air Force.* For eight to fourteen year olds, these books were unusual in that they emphasized how weapons worked and their scientific basis. Published right around Pearl Harbor, the Navy book has a cover with a *Stuka* being shot down by a U.S. ship. Significantly, instead of an insignia, the *Stuka* has green squares where swastikas would have been! This series also came in a soft-cover, comic book-style version with slightly different covers but the same drawings and text on the inside.

Defense for America and *Guardians of America* were interesting, substantially identical hard-cover books published by Rand McNally. Naturally they focused on the geographic aspects. They were edited by Thomas Penfred, editor of the *Fighting Yanks* atlas. Other offerings by major publishers included *First To Fight: U.S. Marine Corps* (David MacKay Company), *Battles: How They are Won* (Doubleday Doran & Company), *This is the Navy* (Dodd Mead), *Insignia of the Services* (Charles Scribner), *The U.S. Army* (Little Brown), *Famous Planes & Flights,* 1940 & 1943 eds. (Platt & Munk Co. Inc.), and *The Story of Our Navy* (McLoughlin Bros.).

Numerous large-format, patriotic comic books were published during the war. The War Heroes series by Dell Publishing featured General MacArthur in its inaugural 1942 issue. Other stories revolved around Capt. Colin Kelly Jr., "Butch" O'Hare (a Navy ace after whom O'Hare Field in Chicago is named), Royal Canadian Air Force aces in Europe, and the Battle of Midway.

Beginning in 1944, True Comics, Inc. published a similar series entitled *True Comics—U.S. Heroes.* These publications sold for a dime. Several other comic book-size paperbacks featuring generals such as MacArthur and Eisenhower were collected by kids. A ten-cent quarterly by Goodman called *USA at War—America on the Offensive* was particularly well done.

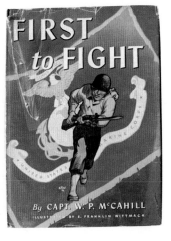

Above. **First to Fight is one of the few WWII books devoted exclusively to the Marines.**

Below. **Grosset and Dunlap's excellent series of early war "How They Work" books on weapons.**

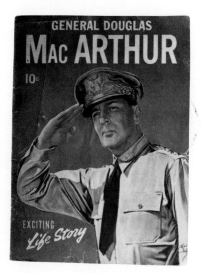

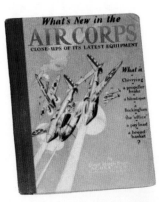

5

PUNCH, STICK, COLOR & GLUE

Connect the dot books have been popular for 100 years. WWII was no exception. Parents felt they aided in developing hand-to-eye coordination skills.

I F ONE CATEGORY OF TOYS had to be selected to exemplify the material availability, creativity, marketing and consumer attitudes of the WWII years, cardboard toys would be chosen. From coloring books to cut, paste and stick sets, the art work was uniquely suited to the mood of the times and the patriotic tastes of the young consumer. Even children initially dismayed by the lack of metal toys soon were won over by the skillful packaging and clever contents of the new cardboard and paper toys.

Dating at least to the middle of the last century, the U.S. manufacture of paper and cardboard soldiers and military toys has a venerable tradition. The first paper soldiers that can be dated with certainty were published in 1857 by McLoughlin Brothers of New York, a prominent and highly successful publisher of children's books, games, puzzles, blocks and paper dolls. McLoughlin's set of five cards, each bearing four or five soldier figures, was sold in an envelope bearing the legend "Home Amusement for Boys—PAPER SOLDIERS." During the next sixty-three years, McLoughlin Brothers published literally millions of paper soldiers in different formats. Most were printed in sheets of varying sizes for cutting but, by the turn of the century, McLoughlin had begun printing some of its soldiers on cardboard, stamping them out, fitting them with wooden bases, and selling them in attractive boxed sets. These were a forerunner of the WWII "punch-out" sets.

By the 1890s, McLoughlin's domination of the paper soldier market was being challenged by Parker Brothers, whose soldiers were sold in boxed sets as games, usually with some kind of popgun or small balls with which to knock over the soldiers. Early in the twentieth century, concentrating on boxed games of soldiers, Milton Bradley entered the market.

While these three companies were far and away the major manufacturers of paper soldiers, they by no means had the field to themselves. The Advance Company in New York published strips of soldiers, folded in booklet form, that were quite similar in appearance to the early McLoughlin

sets. A publisher in Cincinnati, Peter G. Thomson, manufactured much the same product, but soon sold out to McLoughlin. The New York firm of Clark and Sowdon produced several boxed sets of American soldiers and sailors entitled "Mimic War." J.H. Singer, another New York publisher, produced a number of boxed sets of fancifully designed and highly attractive foot soldiers and cavalry. Fletcher Toy Manufacturing Company made boxed sets of cardboard soldiers of various nations and soldiers for cutting out that were printed on cards. An especially elaborate set of cut-out soldiers published in 1915 by the Frederick A. Stokes Company of New York was entitled "The American Boy's Cut-Out Book of Soldiers. For the Defense of Our Country."

As the Second World War was to do some twenty years later, the First World War inspired many more publishers

Since many retailers made prominent use of window displays, Colorgraphic furnished point-of-sale items for this purpose and saved the small store, in particular, a lot of work. This rare Young Patriot display is made of heavy fiberboard and measures 26-by-27-by-10 inches. The toys and targets are actual models that came mounted on the display piece.

of "free" newspaper soldiers did not persist during WWII.

Four firms that published paper soldiers during the 1920s and 1930s are particularly noteworthy. J. Pressman, a New York company, published a variety of boxed sets of cardboard soldiers of very toy-like and colorful design. Its larger sets came with a cardboard fort and some type of cannon or rapid-fire gun. Platt & Nourse issued boxed sets of cut-out sheets entitled "Soldier Cut-outs—Cavalry" and "Infantry." These later were reissued by Platt & Munk as "Toy Army I Can Make." Samuel Gabriel Sons & Co., also of New York, published several particularly attractive sets of cut-out sheets of American infantry, cavalry, artillery, marines and sailors.

Other prewar sets included Wyandotte's boxed "U.S. Defense," which came in two sizes; "Forward March," a fiberboard fold-out set that contained heavy stock soldiers, officers and field pieces; and "Playtime on Parade," a set that contained a hundred tied-down figures.

In 1937, with the threat of war hanging over Europe, the Saalfield Publishing Co. of Akron, Ohio, which had made its reputation on children's books and paper dolls, entered the paper soldier arena briefly with punch-out sheets of U.S. soldiers and airmen complete with tanks, guns, and aircraft. Entitled "Army Cut-Outs," the seven punch-out sheets were sold in an attractive box. In 1941 Saalfield republished these figures in three punch-out boxed booklets entitled "Our Soldiers," "Field and Air Forces," and "Our Brave Defenders." Unlike later three-dimensional, boxed punch-out sets that had to be assembled, these early "equipment pieces" were flat and merely stood up when side tabs were folded. Saalfield continued actively in the field during the war years. Except for Parker Brothers and Milton Bradley, who only produced games during WWII, the other companies mentioned either failed to survive into the forties or stopped manufacturing toys.

Apart from the wide variety of commercial paper toy give-a-ways, paper and cardboard military toys of the WWII period fell into four major categories: punch-out sets, which were sold in boxes, envelopes and booklets; paper dolls, which were either cut-outs or punch-outs; cut, stick or paste sets; and coloring books. Punch-out sets constituted the largest, most varied, creative, colorful and popular category.

to offer American children toy soldiers made of paper. In 1918 Litho Novelty Company printed a dozen cut-out sheets of American soldiers and sailors and Allied commanders. McLoughlin, Parker Brothers, and Milton Bradley all had their versions of American and Allied soldiers. The opposing German army also was represented.

As early as the turn of the century, newspapers had been including sheets of paper soldiers among their Sunday Supplement offerings. The *Boston Sunday Post* ran series entitled "Armies of the World" and "Navies of the World." The latter consisted of warships and their crews of "Jackies," so-named for the British Navy's Jack Tar or Admiral of the Fleet, Lord "Jackie" Fisher who created the famed Dreadnought line of battleships. The *Journal of New York* issued a series of famous battles—Bunker Hill, New Orleans, Mobile Bay—in cut-out form, and the *Boston Sunday Herald* contributed "Boy Soldiers of All Nations—Cut-Out Series." One such Sunday Supplement consisted of a group of figures of Grand Army of the Republic veterans gathered around a flag-draped statue of Lincoln on Memorial Day; this item is now quite rare. These newspaper supplements continued during WWI but, for some reason, the tradition

PUNCH-OUT MODELS: THE WALLIS RIGBY STORY

THOUGH HIS "MODELS" were somewhat difficult to construct (they were definitely beyond the capacity of any normal child under the age of eight) any discussion of punch-out and cut-out paper toys that had to be folded, slotted, inserted, glued and strengthened, must begin with the godfather of such gems, the Englishman Wallis Rigby. By the late thirties, Rigby had been an advocate of paper construction toys for many years. After many years of experimentation, Rigby determined that for cut-out and punch-out models intended to be folded to the proper shape, good quality paper was better than thicker cardboard. While cardboard had area rigidity, it easily cracked on the fold and crumbled and bruised when subjected to use. Heavy stock paper, on the other hand, took a fold more easily and held up better to use. By the start of WWII his English company had produced upwards of six million models of various types of scale aviation and ship models and other models including a paper "cannon-car." The ships, made of high-grade, heavyweight paper, actually sailed well in water.

Rigby came to the States in the late 1930s and founded Rigby Models. The company primarily designed punch-out booklets for various companies. The earliest Rigby book in the author's collection is the "Marvel Model Book." It was published in 1939 by Robert Teller and Sons & Darner of New York City. Measuring fourteen-by-twenty inches and numbering thirty-six pages of heavy, high-quality paper stock, it contained fourteen models including the HMS *Mauritania* liner; a model of the famous, record-setting speed boat, the *Bluebird*; Army and Navy fighter planes; a two-story doll house with sets of furniture; a baby carriage; a balancing clown; and a "waddling Sea Lion." Rigby's book certainly had something for all age groups!

"Rigby's Book of Models," published by David McKay Co. of Philadelphia in 1941, was all military with the excep-

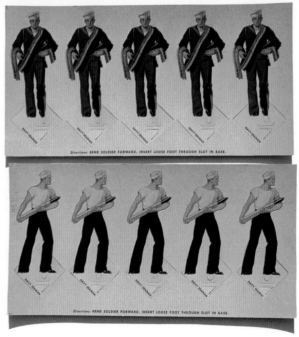

tion of the Cunard liner, *Queen Elizabeth*, and some Pennsylvania R.R. locomotives. While all Rigby books in good condition are quite pricey today, "Rigby's Book of Models" and the "Marvel Model Book" in particular are rare.

Rigby's models soon appeared in American newspaper inserts in the Sunday "Comic Weekly" section. While printed on lowquality newspaper stock, the dimensions, design and instructions were identical to the commercially sold booklet models.

As soon as war started, Rigby's regular *Playthings* column took on a decidedly martial air. In an interesting article written soon after Pearl Harbor entitled "How Models Were Used to Help Build the Totalitarian State," Rigby recounted seeing many German mechanical military toys exported at below-cost during the thirties to advertise Germany's might. The extensive model building activities of the Hitler Youth, in Rigby's view, were "war-mind builders." Perhaps he was suggesting the same tactic to the U.S. toy industry.

Rigby's wartime efforts were produced by the Garden City Publishing Co., Inc. of Long Island. His 1943 "Warplanes of the World," is a superb boxed set of thirty-three large Russian, British, Italian, German, and U.S. airplanes. Included were the experimental *Flying Wing* and little-

Right
This is a typical comic book advertisement for mail order toys.

The colorful pre-war figures in Wyandotte's "U.S. Defense" set wore 1920's and '30's uniforms.

known planes like the Russian 1-18 fighter and German Fokker D-21. The "2nd Series" version came in a large booklet and contained sixteen planes. Identical cover art on both sets shows a boy and his father making the models.

Rigby was unique in that he went to considerable length to explain to young modelers how to make his models. Two pages of detailed instructions were included along with extensive "how to" diagrams. Many common sense hints were given such as keeping a bowl of water handy ("away from your elbow") to wash glue off one's fingers and using a ruler

RIGBY'S
MODEL SUBMARINES
INCLUDES ALL PARTS FOR
2 GIANT MODELS
2 FAMOUS MIDGETS

ATOMIC 'USS NAUTILUS' OVER 30 INCHES LONG
24" MODEL 'SS' FAMOUS RAIDER 'USS FLASHER'
'USS HOLLAND' FIRST NAVY SUB, COMMISSIONED 1900
NEW MIDGET US NAVY SUB 'USS T-1', TARGET-TRAINER

EASY TO BUILD—SIMPLY PUNCH OUT PARTS AND ASSEMBLE

Rigby's model ships were made of high-grade heavyweight paper and part of the fun of building them was that they actually sailed.

This Rigby model book was indeed a "marvel." Published in 1939, its diverse contents assured fun for everyone: a doll house for girls, warplanes for military buffs, and a waddling sea lion for the very young.

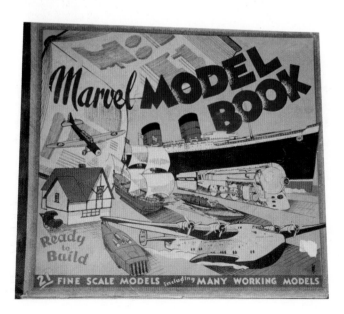

Marvel MODEL BOOK

Ready to Build

21 FINE SCALE MODELS *including* MANY WORKING MODELS

Rigby's BOOK OF MODELS

15 SCALE MODELS
READY CUT • READY CREASED • READY TO BUILD
Book No. 1

to crease or fold along dotted lines. His watchword was patience. "Proceed slowly and carefully to achieve a good end product," he encouraged the young model builder.

"[The models] can be assembled by any one," announced the booklet cover in large, red type. But just to make sure that everyone understood that these items were a cut above the average paper toy, the publisher also constantly reminded buyers: "These models are REAL ENGINEERING JOBS, NOT JUST MODEL CUT OUTS." "Rigby's Easy To Build Models of Naval Craft," published in 1944, proclaimed, "These are not just toys!" This set included a battleship, carrier, cruiser, PT boat, armed merchantman, and several types of invasion craft and convoy vessels.

While today's countless paper models of everything from cathedrals to entire villages are extremely precise and not for the impatient, young builder, Rigby truly can be said to have initiated their popularity. Although early on American toy manufacturers concluded that they had to simplify Rigby's models and building techniques considerably to appeal to a much broader age range, the basic assembly form of slotting, folding and gluing can be attributed to Rigby.

Roughly twenty American companies produced punch-out and cut-out wartime sets. While all were attractive in their own way, they differed considerably in quality and price. At the high end, selling for one dollar, were the very large sets of Pachter, Warren Paper Products, and Colorgraphic; at the low end were the twenty-five-cent bargains of Wyandotte and the cheap, ten-cent envelope packages of Reed and the Electric Corporation of America (ECA). In terms of variety and quality, the leading trade names were Bild-A-Set, Young Patriot, Built-Rite, Lowe, and Wyandotte.

OUR SOLDIERS

FIELD and AIR FORCES

OUR BRAVE DEFENDERS

HOME DEFENDERS

Above
These Saalfield booklets were among the few that pictured multifigure scenes and one-dimensional airplanes, ships and vehicles that stood up.

121

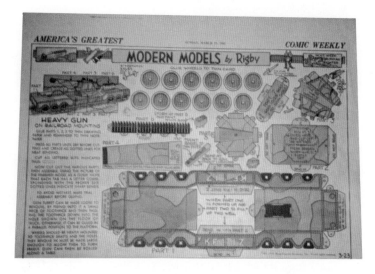

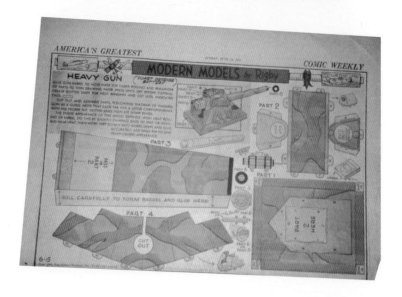

This page and facing page
American newspapers featured Rigby's models in the Sunday paper.
The examples shown here appeared in Baltimore, Maryland,
newspapers from January to June 1941. One rarely finds uncut
sheets in good condition.

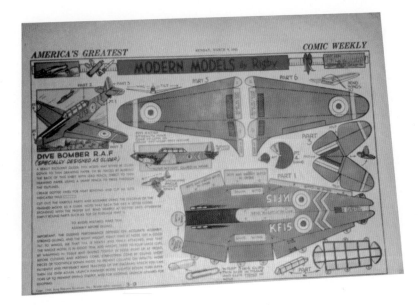

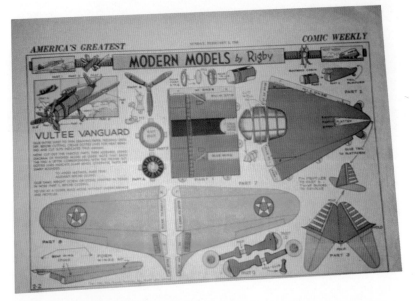

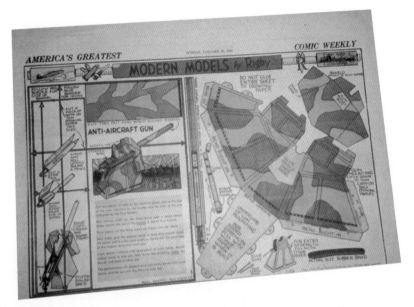

Above

Garden City published Rigby's "Supersonic Planes" in the mid 1950s. This booklet featured a twenty-five-inch-long North American F-100 interceptor. The 100 series was the mainstay of the West's domestic interceptor defense system during a full decade of the Cold War.

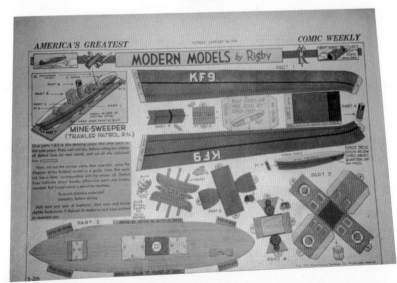

Above

By 1944 Rigby was including invasion craft and convoy vessels that related to Allied successes in North Africa and Italy.

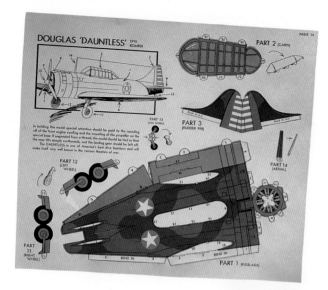

Garden City packaged as many as thirty-three airplanes in its Rigby sets. Care was the key to building these detailed models successfully. Today, less experienced modelers might find it helpful to practice on xerox copies of the originals; of course, this wasn't an option in the thirties and forties!

124

THE WYANDOTTE LINE

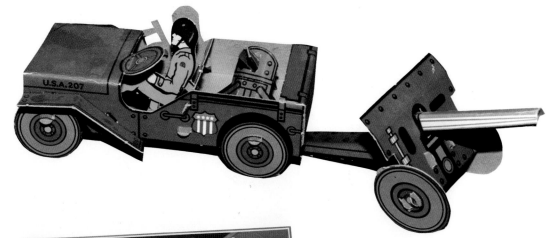

FOR YEARS THE All Metal Products Company of Wyandotte, Michigan, had produced a well-respected line of metal toys rivaling those of Unique Art, Wolverine and Marx. Pistols, popguns and toy vehicles were Wyandotte's specialties. But like other metal toy stalwarts, Wyandotte went off to war and by 1943 All Metal was busy making gun parts for the government. All new equipment had to be installed as none of the machines used for making toys could be used for this high-precision work. Thankfully, like some others in similar circumstances, the company kept its hand in the toy field by retaining one factory unit to turn out a line of die-cut cardboard toys and wooden playthings, most of which were military in nature. The latter included wooden clicker pistol and holster sets and boxed jeeps and airplanes.

The punch-out line that sold under the Wyandotte "Build-Your-Own" label, had a limited production and today they are difficult to find. They usually sold for twenty-five cents per boxed set. Standard Toy-Kraft Products also used the phrase "build-your-own" in its 1941 copyrighted sets, and Pachter's "Bild-A-Set" was a registered trademark, too. Everyone may have just ignored the legal niceties.

"Wyandotte toys are good and safe," mothers were told in large letters on the side of the box, as well as "interesting and educational." Among the Wyandotte sets produced were:

- Army Base Set (#522): One of the best, this set contained twenty-three pieces including a terrific barbed wire fence, a hospital tent, a nurse, and a stretcher-bearer team.
- Army Attack Squad Set: This set had eighteen pieces, with a dive bomber, armored car, tank and jeep.
- Navy Patrol Set: It contained a terrific twenty-four-inch destroyer, a submarine, PT Boat, admiral's barge, and several sailors.
- Toy Soldier Action Set: This set had five identical sheets of twelve different soldiers in action poses. Included was a two-piece heavy machine gun.

This page and next
The color, art work and animation of Wyandotte's figures, vehicles, and supporting pieces were unsurpassed and, unlike that of other manufacturers, Wyandotte's paper stock was sturdy, well slotted, easily assembled and held up well.

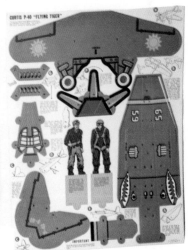

125

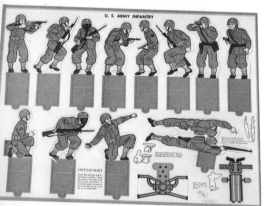

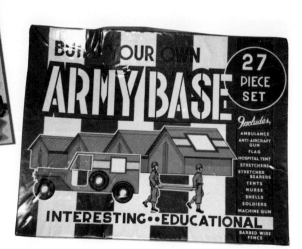

- Air Squadron Set (#526): This was a set of United Nations planes and is the toughest Wyandotte set to find today.
- American Commandos: This was a twenty piece invasion set.
- Anti-Aircraft Gun Set (#521)

The sets described above contained as many as twenty-nine different figures and twenty-five different larger pieces. Quite a bargain at twenty-five cents per set! All-Metal eased operations in 1956. What a shame!

YOUNG PATRIOTS (COLORGRAPHIC)

COLORGRAPHIC, INC. was a subsidiary of the Meyer-cord Company of Chicago, a major manufacturer of packing materials. Its wartime production of punch-out toys was a natural outgrowth of its primary business. Made of heavy fiberboard, Colorgraphic's toys were about the sturdiest of the punch-out class. Their boxes were very large, and the box art dramatic, varied, and colorful.

Colorgraphic marketed a line of combat sets of cardboard toys that worked. It prided itself on the mechanical features: the tanks, trucks and jeeps rolled on wheels and the planes dropped cardboard bombs. The only down side to the Young Patriot line was that its cardboard punch-out sheets tended to be a rather drab khaki and gray, a far cry from Wyandotte's authentic, multi-colored beauties. Its flag decals also left something to be desired in terms of authenticity—few if any real vehicles, planes and ships went through the war with the national ensign plastered all over them.

The entire Young Patriot line initially included different size boxed variations of the Army and Navy sets. Later it grew to include about ten different boxes, including the "Smash The Axis" target set and "Fighting Units," "Invasion," and "Army Combat." Retail prices ranged from a quarter to one dollar.

Colorgraphic's large caricatures of Hitler, Hirohito and Mussolini were a favorite wartime target. Like earlier Wolverine and Marx metal counterparts, these caricatures fell over when hit by a cannon projectile. Colorgraphic's line survived through the war and, in view of their advertising budget, one suspects that they maintained a healthy share of the market.

Three pieces at right

Boxed sets by Colorgraphic tended to have colorful, eye-catching artwork on the box—a contrast to the drab, monochrome color of the actual contents.

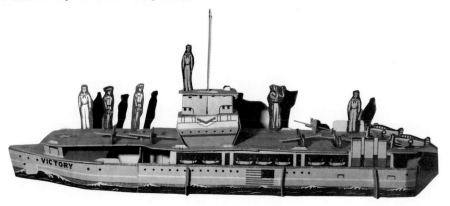

The Colorgraphic figures that accompanied its vehicles, ships and planes were not nearly as attractive as Wyandotte's.

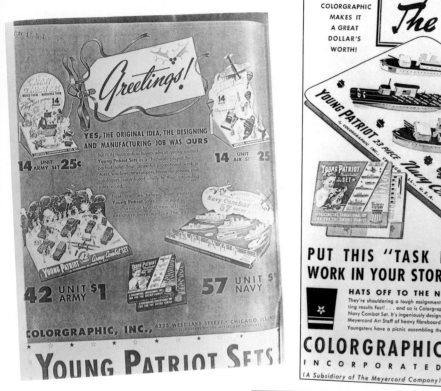

Above and below. **Colorgraphic's "Sculpture-ettes"** sets came in two sizes and received some good play in the trade press. "Decorate your room with these attractive, timely little sculpture-ettes," said the advertising. Made of cheap paper, these doll-like items were not very attractive, however, and it is difficult to know to whom they were intended to appeal.

Above
Colorgraphic made frequent use of the toy trade press to market its "Young Patriot" line. Their ads were expensive two-page spreads that often featured scenes of a child making the toy; in return the company received good magazine copy.

Right
Colorgraphic Inc. was a subsidiary of the Meyercord Company of Chicago, a major manufacturer of packing materials. The company prided itself on the mechanical features of its heavy cardboard tanks, trucks and jeeps.

AL-NU

According to Richard O'Brien, the Godfather of American toy soldier research, this small company was founded by a Frank Krupp in 1938. Just as Al-Nu was starting to produce an excellent line of metal soldiers that are quite pricey today due to their scarcity, wartime metal restrictions put an end to all such production. Krupp then designed, colored and published a series of cardboard soldiers of excellent quality. They probably are the most attractive and accurate of all of the paper soldiers of the period. Strangely enough, this line achieved

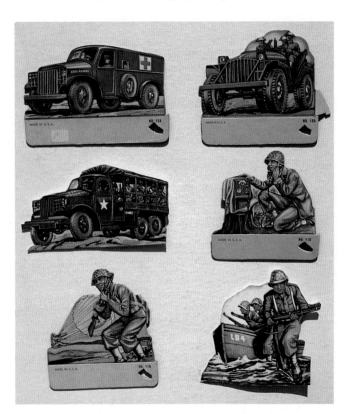

little success at the time. Today they are sought by dime-store collectors and have become perhaps the single priciest paper soldier collectible of the WWII period. Some five inches in height, they are totally out of scale with all of the cardboard vehicles, planes and ships, a fact that may account for their failure to sell well at the time of manufacture. Krupp produced some twenty-five soldiers and one nurse who are led by an accurate figure of General Mac-Arthur, plus a few one-dimensional vehicles in an extremely rare boxed set.

Al-Nu published probably the most attractive and accurate paper soldiers of the period. In the extremely rare set pictured here numerous soldiers and one nurse are led by a figure of General MacArthur. These are the hardest Al-Nu pieces to find.

129

BILD-A-SET

"IT'S EASY TO BUILD with Bild-A-Set," said D.A. Pachter & Company's advertising. "Build for Victory — all cut and ready to assemble — no tools needed, educational and entertaining, rolling, turning, moving, extra large realistic units with motion." That said it all. A youngster needed to know no more. Bild-A-Set also was among the best lines in terms of box art.

In April 1943, *Playthings* gave Pachter's new line a big send off in a full-page article published right after that year's Toy Fair. Credit for many of the new (nonstrategic material) toy developments, the writer said, rightfully belonged to Pachter. The company, it continued, had exhibited "an extraordinary display of ingenuity and had employed top-notch engineers and designers." In addition to numerous military sets, Pachter's Bild-A-Set line included a "Three-Ring Circus Carnival" set, a "Fast Freight and Streamline Flyer" set, and a "Constructor Kit" that allegedly made 1,001 different types of toys and buildings.

In August 1943, Pachter followed up *Playthings*' kudos by announcing a major national campaign for the fall utilizing major catalogs and children's magazines. The fall Bild-A-Set line included twenty-five-cent to one-dollar variations of two basic sets of Army and Navy pieces. High spots of the army sets included a large B-17 and M4 tank. The large "Navy Fighting Fleet" set boasted a 14½-inch aircraft carrier. Less sturdy than Colorgraphic's card stock, Bild-A-Set pieces visually were more attractive, accurate and colorful.

Bild-A-Set variations included "Army Fighting Forces" (79 units), "Action for American Youth" set (39 pieces), "Army Combat Units" (45 pieces), "Navy Fighting Fleet"

This and facing page **Like most toy companies, during the war D.A. Pachter & Company focused on military toys in its "Bild-A-Set" line. Ironically, their civilian pieces were more creative, particularly the carnival set with its revolving carousal and ferris wheel and the farm set with its revolving windmill.**

(69 units), "Junior Navy Fighting Fleet" (23 pieces), and a combined "Junior Army and Navy Fighting Forces" set (45 units). (A unit included a single soldier or sailor of whatever size. "Motorized" units averaged about eight per box.) Pachter's "Beautiful Girls in Uniform" boxed set, discussed more fully in the paper doll section, is the rarest of the company's sets today. Ad copy called it the "most beautiful box in the Bild-a-Set line," and they were right.

Below. **This set, a late war addition to the line, was Colorgraphic's most colorful. The large B-17 and tank destroyer were excellent models.**

Below
Like Colorgraphic, Pachter waged aggressive and expensive marketing campaigns. Its large, 24-by-18-by-18 inch, brightly colored counter and window displays were easily assembled by the retailer and made use of the actual toys.

BUILT-RITE
THE DIME STORE COLLECTOR'S FAVORITE

COLLECTING WWII-ERA paper military toys is becoming popular among metal figure collectors, particularly those who specialize in the so-called "dime store" soldiers manufactured by companies such as Barclay and Manoil. Currently the most popular paper soldier collectibles are those manufactured under the Built-Rite name by Warren Paper Products, Inc. of Lafayette, Indiana. Collectors pay quite a bit for the larger boxed fort sets in excellent condition and for individual cardboard tanks and trucks in mint condition. The reason for Built-Rite's current popularity eludes even the dime store expert;

extensive marketing during the war and fond memories of those collectors now over fifty may be responsible.

Of all the makers of cardboard toys, Built-Rite had a distinct sales advantage since the line was carried extensively throughout the war by Sears Roebuck and Montgomery Ward, the two giant retailers. Only a few other makers had access to such a large distribution network and then only on occasion.

Warren Paper Products began in 1922 as a manufacturer of cardboard boxes. As early as the mid-1930s it made a wide range of games

This page
The "Built-Rite" line by Warren Paper Products, Inc. was carried by Sears Roebuck and Montgomery Ward. Dealer catalogs indicate that sets were shipped two dozen to the box. Built-Rite currently is the most popular paper soldier collectible; wouldn't it be great to find an unopened carton of their boxed sets!

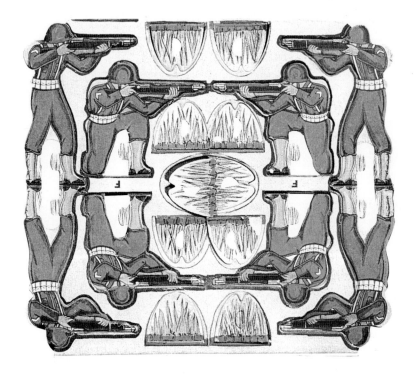

YOU'LL WANT THESE BUILT-RITE TOYS

Be sure you have a Built-Rite Fortress to protect your soldiers. It is sturdy and has three large towers and a runway to get your tanks on the upper floor.

Built-Rite Toy Soldiers have regulation uniforms and real insignia, indicating Privates, Corporals, Sergeants, Lieutenants and Captains. With each set is an instruction sheet, showing how to line them up in real military formations.

132

YOU'LL WANT THESE BUILT-RITE TOYS

For a Real Army Layout Get Set No. 100A Fortress, No. 201 Guardsman, No. 25A Fort, and No. 22 Army Outpost, as Illustrated Above.

Warren's magazine ads contained a coupon that allowed children to buy toys directly from the manufacturer if unavailable through local dealers. These ads continued to run for several years after the war ended.

"BUILT-RITE ARMY CAMP"

1 FORT
4 TRENCHES
6 PUP TENTS
108 SOLDIERS

NO CUTTING — NO PASTING

Left

Unlike later sets, Built-Rite's "Guardsman" not only came with detailed instructions but also suggestions for a number of games that could be played with the soldiers such as "Box Barrage" and "Trench Raider." The "Army Camp" set added a fort and tents to the Guardsman's contents. These sets rarely are found in the box today.

GUARDSMAN

A GAME OF
Action
Thrills
AND
Skill

SHOOTS
harmless
RUBBER
BANDS

133

This page and next
Over the years, Built-Rite produced some fifteen different boxed military sets. All but one, the "Navy Battle Fleet and Coast Artillery Gun (#60)," featured the Army.

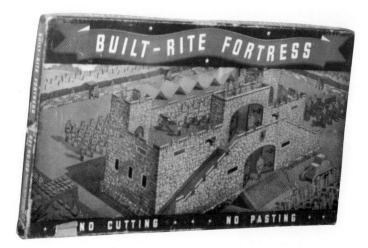

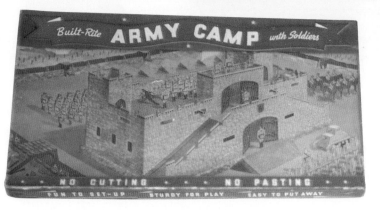

Right
Built-Rite produced eight different tanks, halftracks and other army vehicles, which were found in various boxed sets along with the usual soldiers, and often a fort. The individual vehicles, in mint condition, today sell for around thirty dollars.

and puzzles, cardboard doll houses complete with furniture, villages and train buildings and accessories in various scales. Their products were highly popular with both girls and boys. Warren continues to produce a wide range of products today. Notwithstanding repeated attempts by current collectors to induce them to reissue the WWII military line, the company appears to have no interest in doing so.

Built-Rite issued regular dealer catalogs of its line during and after the war, and it is easy to put together an almost complete listing of its military toys. Among its earliest sets, the "Guardsman (#2)" is the most difficult to find today. Unlike later sets, it not only came with detailed construction instructions but also a number of suggested games that could be played with the cardboard soldiers. Suggested trench and artillery games included "Box Barrage," "Big Bertha," and "Trench Raider." The games consisted of setting up the soldiers in various configurations and shooting at them with a rubber band-firing cardboard pistol or cannon. The equally rare, early "Built-Rite Army Camp" added a fort and tents to the Guardsman's contents. At least six

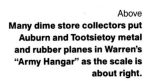

Above

Many dime store collectors put Auburn and Tootsietoy metal and rubber planes in Warren's "Army Hangar" as the scale is about right.

Above and below

With their civilian themes, these two Built-Rite municipal airport sets are most unusual.

fort and vehicle soldier sets still were being produced in the late forties and early fifties. The soldiers in these sets, however, were completely different from those made in the 1940s.

The largest Built-Rite set appears to be the "American Fighters" set of some one hundred pieces. It included an entire line of eight cardboard vehicles. It was advertised extensively by Montgomery Ward and appeared in just about all of their 1940's catalogs. It's not, however, the rarest set today; that distinction goes to the small "Army Hangar" set that, in spite of the fact that three colorful airplanes were shown on the box, consisted simply of a First Pursuit Group building.

OTHER COMPANIES

MORE THAN TWO DOZEN other companies, most of whom had not been in the toy business before the war, produced punch-out sets. Others like Fawcett, Lowe and Whitman were publishers of children's books. All capitalized on the surge of patriotism in the country by providing children with a means of recreating the battles raging overseas. In contrast with the prewar sets of paper soldiers, the sets offered by these relative newcomers to the trade were dominated by the paraphernalia of modern war—tanks, guns, airplanes ships, trucks and jeeps—with soldiers playing a supporting role.

The quality of these miscellaneous sets ranged from excellent to downright awful. While some were carefully designed and colored to resemble as closely as possible their real life prototypes, others were crudely stamped out monochrome silhouettes. Sadly, the box art on the poorer sets was usually quite dynamic and attractive in order to catch a kid's eye and quite often promised far more than the contents of the box delivered. What follows is a baker's dozen of these various manufacturers.

THE PAPER PRODUCTS DIVISION
OF ELECTRIC CORPORATION OF AMERICA

ELECTRIC CORPORATION of America's (ECA) main line of work was the production of electric fans, fluorescent lighting and other equipment and during the war years was a major war production company. ECA produced some of the worst paper toys of the period.

As was true of the packaging of several other companies, ECA's box art promised a lot and delivered little. Large type on the box of ECA's biggest set, the "Land-Sea-Air Super Battle Set," announced that the set contained 181 pieces. Buried in a lengthy description of the contents, however, much smaller lettering indicated that over half the pieces were monochrome soldiers; such contents contributed little in terms of aesthetics. Clearly, ECA's sales tactic was to boast the overall piece count. ECA advertised heavily in the trade press. In 1944 the "Land-Sea-Air Super Battle Set" was featured retailing for fifty cents on a full-page ad in *Playthings*.

Other ECA sets that sold in cheaper retail outlets for twenty-five and fifty cents included "Make Your own Battle Set" and "American Skyhawk Squadron—A Complete Action Airfield" (1943). Two cheaper sets produced in 1942, "Make Your Own Battle Set—Mechanized Force" and "Make Your Own Battle Set—Invasion Surprise Attack Fleet," were marketed under the Evans Novelty Co. name. In the same price range, "Surprise Attack Fleet Smash the Axis" produced in 1943 had the best caricatures of Tojo, Hitler, Mussolini of the war. The "Action Ace Plane Kit" (1944) contained two paper airplanes, the usual dialed aircraft identifier and sixty photos. A much larger companion piece with the same name was a combination of several sets. The airfield, for some reason, also contained the "Super Flat-Top!" Such inconsistencies didn't seem to bother kids. On a positive note, although the pieces for this set were ugly brown, blue and red colors, it did include pieces never included in other wartime U.S. sets such as a hangar and control tower, crash and oil trucks, and a catapult runway.

ECA's offerings were sold in large, extremely colorful paper envelopes and cheap cardboard folders. They were made of lightweight paper, however, and were flimsy, tore easily, and were difficult to stand up.

ECA made one of the longest WWII paper toys, the "Super Flat Top." Twenty inches in length, it had a cleverly designed rubber-band powered catapult that launched six small cardboard planes. Unfortunately, due to the flimsy construction, this toy seldom lasted long.

ECA produced an array of cardboard items that included a picture frame for a serviceman's picture, a charming "Puppet Parade" with five subjects, and a collapsible picnic box that could be used as a tray when opened. The latter was targeted for war workers, but one wonders if the flimsy piece stood up under any use.

ECA's "American Skyhawk Squadron" set contained many pieces never included in other wartime sets such as a hangar and control tower, crash and oil trucks, and a catapult runway. For some reason, it also contained the "Super Flat-Top"! The pieces were primarily brown, red and blue.

The "Land-Sea-Air Super Battle Set" was ECA's largest set. It retailed for fifty cents.

SAMUEL LOWE CO.

THE WAR TOYS of this long-time manufacturer of paper dolls were a mixed bag. Its two unique "U.S. Stand Up Soldiers" and "Sailors" pamphlets (#L-1063 and 1093) were excellent. An ingenious folder of ten, 7¼-inch-figures overlapped in ascending rank order from Buck Private to Warrant Officer with a four-star General added for symmetry, and in such a way that all were visible on the cover. When the booklet was turned over, the ranks of the same ten figures descend from General to Second Lieutenant. Interspersed among the figures were smaller soldiers, three young boys manning an anti-aircraft gun, guns, and a

138

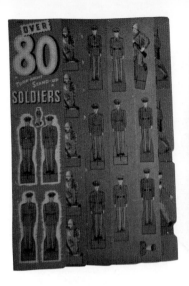
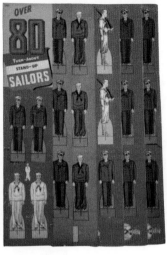

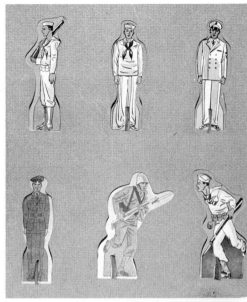

Top, left to right. **The quality of Samuel Lowe Co.'s paper doll folders varied from the interesting, sturdy figures included in its "U.S. Stand Up Soldiers" and "Sailors" booklets, to the flimsy pieces that came with the "Over 80 Turn-about Stand Up" booklets.**

tank and jeep. The sailor booklet of the same year is identical in format. Variety was introduced in the sailors and officers' uniforms by varying the uniform color from white to khaki. The six-page companion booklets entitled "Over 80 Turn-about Stand Up Soldiers and Sailors (#L-140 and L-141)" were printed on cheaper paper. Their slotted stands were terrible and it was very difficult to get these pieces to stand up. They are so light that a strong breath knocks them over.

Lowe's 1943 line included a set of five booklets printed on cheap paper, two boxed sets of punch-out tanks and planes, and a larger combination booklet entitled "U.S. Commandos (#1089)" that contained pieces from the other three. These sets rarely show up today without being torn and damaged in some way. Lowe's "Victory Punch-Outs, Tank, Soldiers, Sailors, Planes (#848)" is simply a combination of the contents of the booklet series in a larger format. "Service Kit of America's Armed Forces (#L-1265)" contained the one-dimensional, colorful, well-drawn tanks, ships, and planes from the earlier soldier and sailor sets. "Harry the Soldier, Dick the Sailor, Tom the Aviator (#L-1074)," a somewhat sissified paper doll set, completed the Lowe line.

Below. **The boxed "Junior Ranger Anti-Aircraft Gun" is a relatively sturdy catapult-type toy, obviously copied from Roman siege weapons. The toy works quite well.**

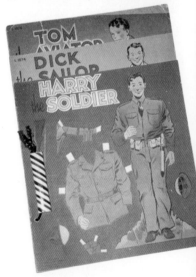

Above
Lowe's "Harry the Soldier, Dick the Sailor, Tom the Aviator" set is popular with paper doll collectors.

139

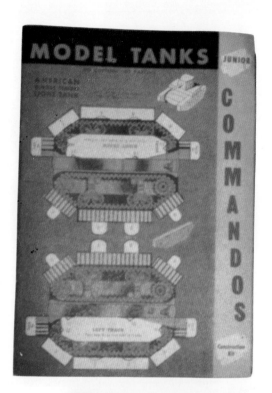

This and facing page
Lowe marketed a series of "construction kits" containing colorful, well-drawn models of various tanks, ships and planes. Larger sets also included soldiers and sailors.

WHITMAN PUBLISHING CO.

IN ADDITION TO its excellent line of WWII military picture books for children, Whitman tried its hand at paper soldier sets. Its three large eleven-by-fourteen-inch books, "American Defense Battles Punch-out Book," and two versions of the "100 Soldiers Punch-Out Book," had among the best covers and soldiers of all time. The soldier books had identical contents and contained absolutely authentic depictions of infantry in action and on sentry duty, machine gunners, engineers, signal corps, artillery officers, tank crews, aircraft armorers, military police and nurses. The only drawback was the built-in slotted stand intended to simplify for children the process of putting the troops on their feet. Usually it was not successful in preventing the figures from toppling over or leaning too far to one side.

Whitman's "30 Toy Solders—Sailors—Marines" (1943) set was a thirteen-inch box containing sailors with belts of .50 caliber machine gun ammo draped over their shoulders, sailors holding three-inch shells, and army soldiers and of-

Above, top right
These paper soldier sets by Whitman are well known by collectors for their exciting covers and authentically posed soldiers.

Left
Whitman was known for high-quality products. These punch-out airplane booklets were an exception: the paper was too flimsy for the large format and the coloring inappropriate.

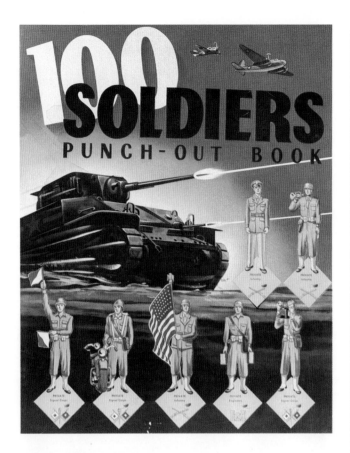

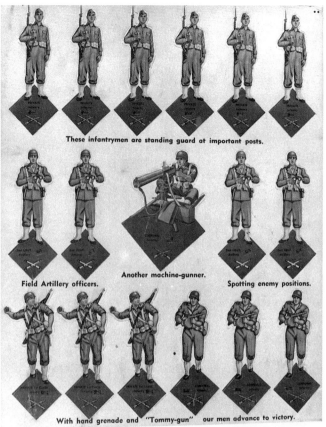

These infantrymen are standing guard at important posts.

Field Artillery officers.   Another machine-gunner.   Spotting enemy positions.

With hand grenade and "Tommy-gun" our men advance to victory.

ficers in various action poses. While well designed and printed on both sides, these large figures are way out of scale and, if the number found today is any indication, did not sell well. Whitman also sold a perfectly awful reproduction of a coastal air base, "Models of USA—Air Defense," that was printed on cheap paper.

Surprisingly, Whitman's two attempts in 1943 at punch-out airplanes were a quality failure. Though large in format, "Fighting Planes (#95)" and "Fighting Bombers (#961)" were printed on cheap stock and were ugly and flimsy. While an attempt at reproducing camouflage was made, the main body colors were similar to day-glow red, orange and green. Besides the fact that they did contain some planes that were not reproduced very often in toy books, such as the British Short *Stirling* bomber and the U.S. Bell *Airacobra* P-39, the only redeeming feature was the price—they only cost a dime.

143

VICTORY TOY COMPANY

T HIS APTLY NAMED Chicago manufacturer issued several boxed sets with various titles built around the theme of combat: "The Captain—Army-Navy Combat Set," "The Colonel—Army Combat Set," and "Junior Commander—Army-Navy Combat Units." Victory's line also included "Complete Set-Up for War Maneuvers" and a larger version (#400) with probably the longest box-art title of them all, "Junior Commander Army-Navy Combat Set Complete For Land, Sea and Air Maneuvers."

With one exception, box art was so-so and contents poor. It is little wonder that very few ads for this line are found. Only the 1943 "Sure-Fire Cannon" set wasn't bad. It was a larger toy and unusual in that it contained no soldiers, only a single cannon. A few years ago, several boxed sets showed up in mint condition at a small antique mall near Reading, Pennsylvania.

This and facing page **Victory Toy Company's punch-out line was at the bottom of the barrel in terms of quality. While the box art was inviting, the coloring of the contents was drab and the pieces were difficult to remove.**

Above
This early '40s Victory Toy's set had four sheets of airplanes.
COURTESY HAKE'S AMERICANA

Above
Victory Toy's "Sure Fire Cannon" was the best toy in its line.

145

Other Manufacturers

WHILE PROBABLY NOT complete, a listing of other manufacturers of punch-out sets follows. Some have familiar names and others were never to be heard from again:

These punch-out sets were manufactured by the less well-known companies of Advance Games, Inc. (below), and Dell Publishing (right).

- Advance Games, Inc.: They produced the "United for Liberty-Allied Soldiers—Together They Fight (#726)" set containing twelve figures of U.S. Marines.
- Concord Toy Co., New York, New York: Concord's "Fighting Soldiers with Jeep (#1502)" was a small box of poor quality soldiers and is one of the worst sets made during the war.

- Container Corporation of America, Chicago, Illinois: This company's ad in the March 1943 issue of *Playthings* magazine illustrates a set with the aggressive title "U.S. Fighters for All out War."
- Dell Publishing: "Our Soldiers Cut-Out Army Uniforms" was a large pamphlet containing four soldiers with uniforms. The set had a terrific cover drawn by Nat Folk and was published in 1941.
- Einson-Freeman Co., Inc., Long Island City, New York: Einson-Freeman advertised in the 1943 issues of *Playthings* and produced at least four sets. Its large, boxed "Self-Running Army Combat Models" was quite creative. While printed on stock a little too thin, it had quite accurate renditions of a jeep, tank, and ambulance. The colorful vehicles were mechanically powered by an accordion-folded, string-

Below
The E.F. Fairchild Corporation of Rochester, New York, produced two small sets under the "All-Fair" name. Consistent with All-Fair's line of board games, the quality of these twenty-soldier sets was fairly good. Apparently these were the only sets of soldiers that the company made.

Above
"Junior Bombardier" was another boxed set by Einson-Freeman.

Above
Einson-Freeman's "mystic motor" consisted of an accordion-folded, string-tied, cardboard spring. Pushing down forced the wheels forward or backward and caused the vehicle to run forward or backward several feet.

Left
This Einson-Freeman set used paper of inferior quality but was quite colorful. It retailed for twenty-nine cents.

147

tied, cardboard spring. Also included in the set was a dive bomber that dropped small marbles, a cannon, two pursuit planes, a large searchlight, and thirty-two excellent stand-up soldiers. Even though a large, four-page pamphlet of illustrated instructions accompanied the set, due to the so-called "mystic motor," this set was one of the more complicated to assemble.

Another great item was Einson-Freeman's "Pre-Flight Trainer, A Complete Cockpit." It came in a huge box and included a large cardboard instrument panel with neat decals, a wheel control, rudder pedals, a "shoot down

Left
Einson-Freeman's "Pre-Flight Trainer" was a bargain for a dollar. The authentic cockpit was based on the Air Force Link Trainer.

Below
Note the authentic tech-sergeant radioman in this set of sturdy, 3½-inch soldiers by J-Mar.

Fawcett Publishing put out two booklets on heavy stock with cover scenes of a boy and girl assembling the contents of either the "13 Toy Models, Warplane and Tank Punch-out" or "Nine Model Warplanes, 4 Model Tanks" set. The models appear to be quite similar to several Lowe sets.

148

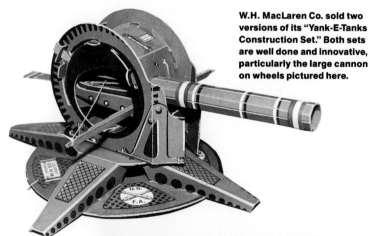

W.H. MacLaren Co. sold two versions of its "Yank-E-Tanks Construction Set." Both sets are well done and innovative, particularly the large cannon on wheels pictured here.

enemy planes" spinner wheel, and booklets. It is a most unusual and desirable WWII toy.

Also of an action nature were Einson-Freeman's cardboard target sets, "Sea Raiding Battleship" and "Secret Airplane Bombsight." The company also produced "18 Inch Mammoth Coastal Artillery Gun and 15 Tubular Soldiers." The company was still around in 1953 when it issued a set entitled "Junior Bombardier (#202)" that contained conventional three-inch action soldiers.

- J-Mar: This company produced a sturdy set of 3 ½-inch, wood-based soldiers entitled "Attack Force Soldier Set."
- Jay-Line Manufacturing Co.: An unusual boxed toy was Jay-Line Manufacturing Co.'s "Camouflage Defense Force." Produced in 1943, this set consisted of innocent-appearing farm buildings that quickly could be converted into ready-for-action gun emplacements, airplane hangars and other military facilities. Included in the set were figures that were soldiers on one side and farm animals on the other. A machine gunner in prone position, for example, turned into a pig when the figure was reversed. Surprisingly, this set turns up fairly often and is not very expensive.
- Hasbor: Single punch-out sets were produced by Hasenfeld Bros. (Hasbro) of Pawtucket, Rhode Island. Its "Combat Attack" set was unusual in that it included a bridge.
- American Toy Mfg. Co.: Picking up on the Jimmy Doolittle B-25 Tokyo raid of 1942, Chicago-based American

This creative "camouflage" toy by J-Line Manufacturing Company is the only one of its kind produced during the war.

149

Merrill Publishing's "American Defense Battles Punch-Out Book" was published in 1940 and designed by George Trimmer. Its colorful, one-dimensional, stand up Army, Navy and Air Force action scenes feature late-1930s soldiers and equipment. A number of the cheap dime store soldiers may have been copied from this book.

National's "Commandos Aircraft" set had a colorful, action-filled cover, but its one-dimensional contents were poorly designed and were difficult to stand.

Above. **National Handi-Kraft Toys out of Philadelphia made thirteen heavy duty envelope toys that utilized the accordion-pleat-axle device to make the toy roll. Subjects for the single-unit sets included a Navy seaplane and an invasion barge. Each retailed for a dime.**

Toy Mfg. Co. produced a "Tokio Raiders" set with a twenty-three-inch aircraft carrier and ten B-25 bombers. Whether the misspelling was intentional or not, if the actual USS *Hornet* had been painted in the same way as this carrier—light blue with bright red stripes—it never would have made it to its Pacific launch site! (Additionally, the three-inch cardboard bombers were bright red.) Printed in large letters in several places on the vessel was the phrase, "Shangri-La." This was a reference to the famous reply made

by President Roosevelt when asked by reporters where the Tokyo bombers had come from. "From Shangri-La, of course," Roosevelt slyly said. (Shangri-La was the mythical Tibetan mountain paradise of James Hilton's popular mid-1930 novel, *Lost Horizons*. The book was made into an award-winning movie directed by Frank Capra who later served as an Army Colonel in the Signal Corps and produced the famous "Why We Fight" documentaries.) A great way to get a feel for the patriotic mood of the times is to view these tapes.

A series of large, bulky, flimsy "Fold-A-Planes" that allegedly flew were sold by the Crestcraft Co. of Chicago. The envelope art was quite colorful but the items were inferior. Large ads for these appeared throughout the war in the trade press, however, so they must have sold well. Similar sets were advertised and produced by Fold-A-Toy Co., also of Chicago.

Other sets advertised in the Billy and Ruth catalogs include a fiberboard/cardboard fort set with twelve cardboard soldiers and a boxed set of twenty-one U.S., English and Russian soldiers with wooden stands. Their makers remain unidentified. Technically, they are not punch-outs.

One cannot leave a discussion of the punch-out line without mention of Chicago's ever-popular Dave Rapaport of Woodburn Mfg. Co. His "Rap-A-Jap" sets were definitely in the lower half of all such sets as far as quality is concerned, but Rapaport deserves a medal for marketing. "Buy U.S. War Bonds and Rap-A-Jap," was one of his popular slogans. He got a lot of trade press coverage on his line, spent a bunch of dough on advertising and produced some terrific point-of-sale displays for retailers.

Many of these "one-shot" toys were advertised as "A Reed Toy," and one suspects they were all marketed out of a single sales building and printed by one or more job printers in the area. But what great names some of these overnight companies came up with!

With all this activity, perhaps some of the companies that had stuck their toes in the water felt by this time that the paper toy field was getting a little crowded.

Doolittle was probably the oldest well-known hero of WWII. Another hero, Captain Eddie Rickenbacker, the leading WWI ace, survived twenty-four days in a raft in the Pacific after his plane went down.

Left
The low quality of these two ships by Reed Associates was typical of envelope punch-outs.

Above. **Zack Mosely, creator of the "Smilin Jack" comic strip, won the Air Medal for helping sink a submarine off the coast of Florida as a member of the Civil Air Patrol. Any collector would love to have a boxed set of "Smilin Jack's Victory Bombers."**

Persuasive advertising indicated that Crestcraft's planes were made of strenoflex, a paper "specially manufactured for flying purposes," and claimed they could fly, glide and land. In reality these planes were to bulky and flimsy to stay airborne.

In spite of their low price, some toys weren't worth the money. The "Jr. Yank's Wawky-Tawky String Phone," for example, included about half a penny's worth of string and cardboard—the purchaser had to supply his own tin cans!

152

When assembled, a few of the inexpensive envelope toys did exactly what the envelope said they would. J. L. Schilling's P-40 "Swing-A-Plane," for example, really could dogfight.

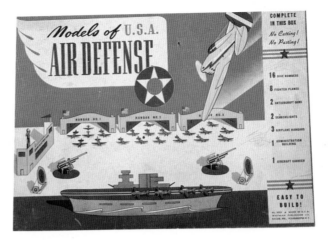

Whitman's "Models of U.S.A. Air Defense" was a perfectly awful reproduction of a coastal air base that was printed on cheap paper.

Einson-Freeman Co.'s "Coastal Artillery Gun" retailed for $1.00.

Above
Since many boxed sets sold for the same price, twenty-nine cents seems a lot for Artsheet Publishing's "Machine Gun."

"Secret Weapon Invasion Set," with its "mystery power tube" (a vacuum plunger that could sent a cardboard airplane fifty feet), an excellent "Uncle Sam Fighter Set," and "Soldier Set" with twelve, eight-inch figures of heavy board on wooden stands, are a sampling of punch-out games by unidentified manufacturers.

Cut, Paste and Stick Sets

THESE BOOKLETS were intended for the younger age groups. The child either cut out and pasted, or cut out, licked and stuck colorful, puzzle-like pieces onto an outlined scene. Few of these booklets were produced, and all the wartime ones were produced by the major paper doll companies. The best and most adult of the four shown was Merrill's "Our Army and Navy in Action," a cut, lick and stick book.

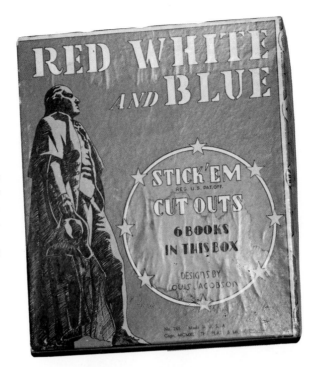

Above
The patriotic focus of these "stick-em" books is a far cry from today's lighthearted sticker books featuring children's TV heros such as Barney the Dinosaur and Walt Disney characters such as Beauty and the Beast.

Merrill's "Soldier-Sailor, Sticker Pictures to Make" book featured poor cartoons of children in uniforms flying planes, riding tanks, and so on. Big explosions with "Boom" and "Bang" were included, together with charming uniformed puppies riding cannons.

Left
This booklet by Merrill had more accurate drawings than most.

Lowe's ABC sticker book depicted children at war with scenes such as "D is for Dive Bomber" and "K is for K.P." The sticker for the "G is for General" page looked like an eight-year-old General MacArthur, four stars, scrambled eggs cap and all.

SOMETHING FOR GIRLS
MILITARY PAPER DOLLS

MOST OF THE military toys of the WWII era were targeted for boys. Girls were still relegated to the realms of dolls, doll houses and the like. When a service item for the ladies did appear, it usually involved the traditional role of nurse. The FAO Schwartz "Nurses Uniform" and "Nurses Kits" are two examples. The establishment of the uniformed services for women—Women's Air Corps (WAC), WAVES, SPARS, Women Marines, and the Women's Air Ferry Services (WAFS)—changed this somewhat. Nowhere was this change more apparent than in the paper doll industry. Was this the start of a women's liberation movement by the toy industry? Surely the defense industry played a role; for the first time, women in the millions took on jobs traditionally reserved for men and did them just as well, if not better, than men. Maybe the toy industry also played a role.

The earliest paper dolls from France and Germany date to around 1850 and were handmade and colored. In the nineteenth century they were used to promote commercial household products such as flour, stove polish and thread. They were not intended for children. This changed in the twentieth century, however, and by the time of the Depression, paper dolls were the biggest selling dime store toy. Paper doll historians estimate that about fifty different sets of WWII military paper dolls were produced between 1941 and 1944. Most WWII paper doll books are large eleven-by-fourteen-inch booklets and were produced by the four long time manufacturers: Lowe, Whitman, Saalfield and Merrill. These companies employed well-known doll artists and designers. All of the sets used the usual format, i.e., six to eight dolls, approximately six to ten inches tall, made of heavy stock and usually designed to be punched out from the front and back covers of the booklet. Inside were several pages of cut-out uniforms, hats, on-duty clothes and, occasionally, accoutrements of various kinds. This clothing was notable for its military authenticity, which was not always the case with the punch-out soldier sets of the time. Most books sold for a dime.

Some sets such as the early 1941 Lowe sets of servicemen Harry, Dick and Tom were designed to appeal to boys. These Lowe sets were of different sizes and were bound together with colored twine looped through a red, white and blue tube. The punch-out action scenes and weapons later were used in other Lowe sets. Like most paper dolls, the faces of the servicemen are very youthful. No one appears much over eighteen!

While some paper doll books were reprinted in the original form, others had fewer pages or a new title or artwork on the cover. In some instances, just one doll and costume were removed from an older book and a new book published.

Unlike the seventy-five punch-out sets discussed earlier, the four dozen paper doll books designed for girls are remarkably uniform in quality; overall they are quite good. The fact that the four major producers had been in the paper doll business for many years may account for the high quality and also may explain why their paper dolls are better than their punch-out soldiers in most cases.

Lowe produced some fourteen military paper doll sets:
• Babs the Ambulance Driver (#L-1048)
• Dick The Sailor (#L-1074), 1941
• Edith of the AWVS (#L-1048), 1941
• Eleanor of the OCD (#L-1048)
• Florence the Nurse (#L-1048)
• Girls in the War (#L-1028), 1943
• Girls in Uniform (#L-1048), 1942
• Harry The Soldier (#L-1074), 1941
• Pressed Board Doll (#L-1023), 1943
• Ruth of the Stage Door Canteen (#L-1048)

Samuel Lowe Co.'s "Girls In Uniform" set was an amalgamation of several others. It contained individual pages of civilian, civil defense and service dress for "Sybil of the Field Hospital" and for her several girlfriends. Apparently Sybil was also a USO entertainer during her off-duty hours. COURTESY MARY YOUNG

• Sybil of the Field Hospital (#L-1048)
• Tom The Aviator (#L-1074), 1941
• Victory Girls (#L-58), boxed set
• War Girls (#L-529), 1943
    Merrill had ten paper doll books. They were:
• Army Nurse and Doctor (#M-3425), 1942
• Bride and Groom Military Wedding Party, 1941
• Girl Pilots of the Ferry Command (#M-4852), 1943
• Liberty Belles (#M-3477), 1943
• Military Wedding Party (#M-3411), 1941
• Navy Girls and Marines (#M-4855), 1943
• Navy Scouts (#M-3428), 1942
• Paper Dolls Wedding (#M-385), 1943
• Soldiers and Sailors House Party (#M-3481), 1943
• Victory Volunteers (#M-3424), 1942

The "Army Nurse and Doctor" set had smaller dolls, some six inches high, but made up for it with eight pages of uniforms. The "Navy Girls and Marines" booklet was obviously well researched. Absolutely authentic uniforms and accessories for enlisted men and women and officers

Above
This book is a reprint of Samuel Lowe Co.'s "Girls in Uniforms." No publishing date is given. COURTESY MARY YOUNG

were laid out on colorful pages decorated with dozens of service insignia. Merrill's "Ferry Command" set featured the Women's Auxiliary Ferrying Squadron (WAFS). Founded by a famous aviatrix of the thirties, Jacqueline Cochran, these highly trained women pilots logged millions of hours of flying time ferrying everything from single-engine *Piper Cubs* to four engine B-17s in the U.S. and on dangerous cross-Atlantic flights to England. A number were killed in the process. Denied veteran status for many years, they finally were granted full veteran's benefits and wartime medals in the 1980s, mainly due to the efforts of Senator Barry Goldwater.

For a maker of paper dolls, Saalfield Publishing Co. had an interesting history. During Saalfield's existence, it became one of the largest publishers of its kind due, in part, to its printing of the *American Edition of the Encyclopedia Britannica* and *Webster's Dictionary*. Following its great success with the children's book, *Billy Whiskers*—some twenty different titles were published over the years—Saalfield produced a highly popular series of children's books sold through Woolworths and other low-budget stores. This led to its long-term production of paper dolls. This success was aided immeasurably by foresight in getting exclusive rights to Shirley Temple paper products in the 1930s. The company survived well into the eighties.

Saalfield's series of wartime paper dolls consisted of:

Below. This booklet mainly contained dolls and uniforms from other booklets. Saalfield often employed this money-saving tactic.

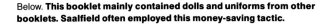

Above
Early in the war, with so many American men enlisting or being drafted into the armed services, Merrill's 1942 "Navy Scouts" booklet played up the romantic image of dating a man in uniform.
COURTESY MARY YOUNG

Left
This Merrill set paid tribute to the heroic efforts of the members of the Women's Auxiliary Ferrying Squadron (WAFS). PHOTOGRAPH COURTESY JEAN BIERMEISTER

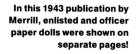

In this 1943 publication by Merrill, enlisted and officer paper dolls were shown on separate pages!

Above, below. **Living up to the adage, "All work and no play makes Jack a dull boy," many of the paper doll books that were military oriented included civilian clothing as well. In Merrill's "Army Nurse and Doctor" book, for example, half the items were evening gowns, nightdresses, and so on.**

- Air, Land and Sea (#5313), 1943
- Army and Navy Wedding Party (#S-2446), 1943
- Joan and Judy's Paper Dolls (#S-898), 1943, contained paper dolls from "Army and Navy Wedding Party" and "Stage Door Canteen"
- Junior Volunteers (#S-593), 1943, boxed set
- Military Wedding (#S-314), 1943
- Papers Dolls in Uniforms of the U.S.A (#S-592), 1943, boxed set
- Red, White and Blue (#S-321), 1943
- Stage Door Canteen (#S-2468), 1943
- Stage Door Canteen (#S-347), 1943
- Uncle Sam's Little Helpers (#S-2450), 1943
- United We Stand (#S-113), 1943
- Victory Paper Dolls (#S-2445), 1943

Above. **This attractive paper doll book cover reminds readers just how strong the wave of volunteerism was during WWII.**

Left
This smaller Saalfield booklet retailed for a nickel and contained marvelous "cartoon" like scenes of its characters at the top of each page.

Left
Dover Publications Inc. recently reprinted this Saalfield book from a 1943 original located in the Wentham, Massachusetts Museum.

The "Air, Land and Sea" and the "Victory Paper Dolls" sets mainly combined dolls and uniforms from each other. This often was done so as to produce a new book with a different cover while saving publishing costs; of all companies Saalfield appears to have published the most reprints. Note that all of their paper doll offerings were produced in 1943. No new military paper dolls were issued after 1943, and possibly due to the paper pinch felt by the industry later in the war, few new paper dolls of any kind are dated 1944 or 1945.

Whitman's line-up of wartime military doll sets contained:

- Our WAAC Joan, also called Mary of the WAACS (#W-3980), 1943
- Our Nurse Nancy (#W-3980), 1943, box or envelope
- Our Sailor Bob (#W-3980), 1943, box or envelope
- Our Soldier Jim (#W-3980), 1943
- Our WAVE Joan (#W-1012), 1943, box or envelope
- Our WAVE Patsy (#W-3980), 1943, box or envelope
- WACS and WAVES (#W-985), 1943

The "WACS and WAVES" book is one known as a "double cover" book; the four dolls to punch out are printed on the second, inside cover and their faces can be seen through cut-out stars.

During the 1930s paper doll books of movie stars and other celebrities became extremely popular. This continued during the war years. Thus, Bob Hope and Dorothy Lamour, both famous movie stars who did yeoman service entertaining the troops, often during difficult and dangerous wartime conditions, were pictured in paper doll books in uniforms and military accessories. One book features Bob Hope in an Army uniform.

Even comic strip characters got involved. A Blondie and Dagwood paper doll set has them dressed in Civil Defense uniforms and victory garden clothes. Many newspaper supplement comic strip paper dolls of the period such as "Boots and Her Buddies" and "Toots and Casper" occasionally had wartime motifs.

Children's magazines also featured cut-out military paper dolls and two of the most popular magazines, *Children's Play Mate* and *Jack and Jill* ran regular series of them. These beautiful dolls were well drawn, accurate, and in excellent color.

Above
This is one of two booklets with a wedding theme from Saalfield Publishing's paper doll line. Both sets were published in 1943.
COURTESY MARY YOUNG

Right
Designed by Margaret Voigt, "United We Stand" was a small book that sold for a nickel. Like Saalfield's "Uncle Sam's Little Helpers," its delightful figures were preschoolers playing grownup and performing military and home front tasks in military uniforms.

162

This set contained a single, ten-inch felt board doll and four pages of uniforms on glossy paper. Prior to Pearl Harbor, in early 1942, Whitman made a sixteen-inch wooden doll, "An American Nurse," that sold in a pocket with Army, Navy and Red Cross uniforms.

With national and regional clubs and newsletters, some devoted to the output of only one company, paper doll collecting is an extremely popular hobby today. Numerous conventions are held that include meetings for which the members dress up as paper dolls. WWII booklets with the dolls not punched out are difficult to find, and examples in mint condition are quite expensive. Like other fragile paper and cardboard toys, time has taken its toll. And, because there are more collectors of paper dolls than of similar soldier sets, wartime paper doll books garner higher prices.

Above. **Both *Children's Play Mate* and *Jack and Jill*
magazine occasionally featured colorful, well-drawn
cut-out paper dolls such as these.**

The paper dolls in image 1 are labeled:

Row 1: Informal Khaki, Field Uniform, Field Uniform, Trench Hat, Sergeant, Armored Force (Tanks), Tropical Shorts, Snowshoe Soldier, Parachutist

Row 2: Second Lieutenant, First Lieutenant, Captain, Major, Colonel, Brigadier General, Major General, Lieutenant General

Above. **Children's valentines marketed during the war often featured
small, cut-out military paper dolls. The Valentine Day sentiments
expressed were more patriotic than romantic.** COURTESY MARY YOUNG

WAC and WAVE
By Beth Henninger

Left. ***Jack and Jill*'s October 1943 offerings included a WAC and a WAVE
paper doll.** COURTESY MARY YOUNG

Left
The March 1944 issue of *Jack and Jill* magazine featured this romantic set entitled "A Wedding on Cherry Road." The groom is a Marine.

Below
Anticipating the war's end, "The Homecoming" was printed in the January 1945 issue of *Jack and Jill* magazine. COURTESY MARY YOUNG

Above, right
"Janet the WAVE," a punch-out paper doll, made *Children's Play Mate* magazine in September 1943, followed by "Betty the Marine" in October 1943. The July issue supplied "Jane a Nurse" and the August issue, "Ann a WAC."
COURTESY MARY YOUNG

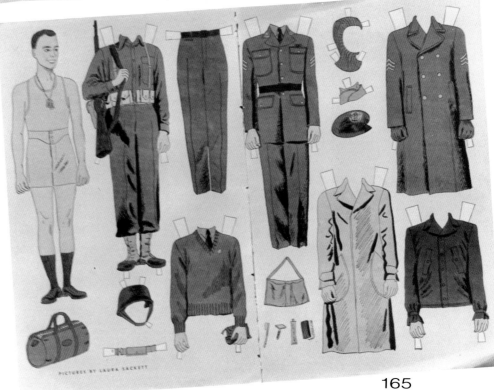

165

A Marine, in her summer work uniform of green and white seersucker, camouflages a model air field. The design will be used on a real air field.

Saalfield also printed small, eight-by-eleven-inch coloring books. Though Saalfield's sketches, on the whole, tended to be somewhat less detailed than Merrill's, they depicted the subject matter just as accurately.

Coloring books for older children tended to use adults in their drawings of military and civil defense scenes.

COLORING BOOKS
P-40S DON'T HAVE RED WINGS AND PURPLE TAILS!

COLORING BOOKS were the cheapest and most readily available of paper playthings during the war. In some ways, they are among the most interesting in their depiction of home front and battlefield scenes. Representing a relatively small fraction of those printed during the war, pictured here are over two dozen different books. Sometimes called "paint" books and consisting of anywhere from ten to one hundred pages, coloring books were printed on very cheap paper stock and usually measured fourteen-by-eleven inches. Customarily they sold for a dime. This was quite a bargain when one considers the countless hours of quiet fun they provided for a child.

While occasionally a coloring book turns up where the child stayed within the lines and used, by and large, the right colors, most of these young Rembrandts didn't know a P-40 pursuit plane from a pony cart, as far as correct colors went. B-17s with purple wings and orange tails abound, as do red mortars, purple tanks, green P-T boats, and blue and red searchlights and artillery pieces. If any proof is needed of the accuracy of marketing research on the appeal of primary colors to the very young toy user, it is found in the use of that spectrum in these books. This preference also accounts for the proliferation of wooden military toys painted red, yellow and green.

For the most part the coloring books of the period were published by the major paper doll makers and clearly were intended for two different age groups. Books for the six to ten year olds featured highly accurate sketches of military and civilian defense scenes. The soldiers, sailors, aviators, marines and home front workers were pictured as adults, not as children. The only truly identifiable series of such books was published by Merrill between 1942 and 1944.

This 1943 publication by Saalfield has an exceptional cover by artist H. Lupprian depicting two children in a P-39 pursuit ship steel pedal toy. This particular pedal toy was quite expensive at the time and today in restored condition costs several thousand dollars.

of a technical nature such as how a submachine gun worked.

Since most coloring books were used immediately after purchase, it is tough to find one in unused condition; typically unused books sell for about twice a used copy. One great buy of mint Merrill books come from a paper doll dealer who had bought several at an estate sale because "my husband said he had them as a child."

Saalfield's coloring books for older children included "Fighting Yanks," "America At War," "Uncle Sam at War," two versions of "Flying for Victory" and a giant, twenty-five-cent "Victory" book of 176 pages that combined most of the contents from the other books. Artist Russell Andrew Abbott, who also received credit for the cover, did many of Saalfield's books. On a sociohistorical note, "Fighting Yanks" had one portrayal of an American sentry entitled "An American Negro Soldier on Duty in Liberia." This is the only depiction of an African-American serviceman that the author has found in any WWII children's book.

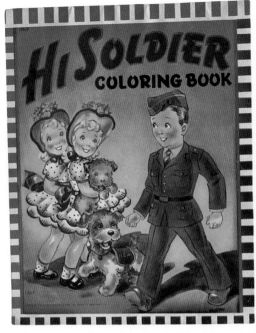

Above, left
"Kiddie" military coloring books such as these are not particularly collectible.

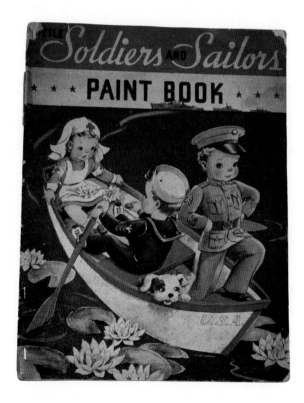

Featuring line drawings by artist Fredric C. Madan who got credit for his colorful covers, the first was "War Planes, Tanks and Jeeps (#3462)." Other titles included "Spot the Planes," "Flying Forts," "Rangers and Commandos," "Flying Cadets," "We Fly for the Navy," "Girls of the Army and Navy," "Submarine," "U.S. Marines," and "The Story of Guns." Few technical errors can be found. Educationally oriented, each sketch contained a short narrative description explaining the scene. These often contained an insert

This unlucky Jap tank-crew has run into a tank trap made of logs. They are now at the mercy of the Marines who are firing a 50-caliber machine gun.

This and facing page
This educationally oriented coloring book series was published by Merrill between 1942 and 1944. With many a repeat, this series featured well over a hundred excellent line drawings by Fredric C. Madan, as well as colorful covers by the same artist.

A number of Saalfield coloring books in mint condition became available from the archives of the public library in Saalfield's hometown of Akron, Ohio.

In 1942 Samuel Lowe published a fine "Crackerjack Paint Book" series. Many of Lowe's outline sketches were borrowed from its various soldier punch-out sets, an example of economics in the field of publishing at its best.

The second broad category of military coloring books were those obviously intended to appeal to the preschool and early primary school age groups. In these books both

the covers and contents might feature young children in uniforms. Many times, however, children in service uniforms were portrayed on the covers while the contents were primarily reprints of the usual animals, toys, boats, nursery rhymes and similar subjects. Two marvelous examples of wartime covers by Saalfield are "Snappy" (a big tough army sentry dog guards a dog house full of pups), and "Jeepers" (two helmeted puppies ride a bucking jeep).

Florence Winship, Saalfield's paper doll designer, did several of the charming children's covers including "Soldiers

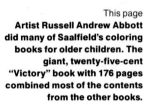

and Sailors Paint Book." This cover had all the right elements in bright colors: kids, uniforms, a cute puppy and a military scene. Inside, scenes showed six-year-olds flying bombers, riding jeeps, reviewing troops and standing in a chow line. H. Lupprian's "Soldier Coloring Book" for Saalfield has similar scenes.

In 1943 Lowe published a small, twelve-page, seven-by-nine-inch coloring ("paint") book entitled "The Bugle Call." This book was unusual in that on each page was a two-by-three-inch, full-color illustration that the child could copy

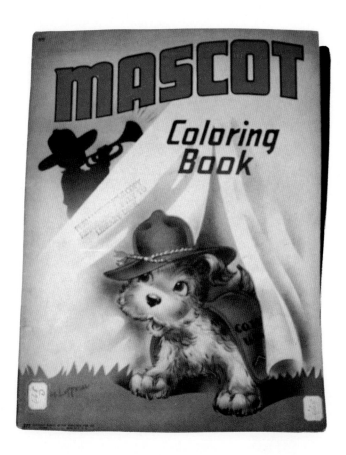

Illustrated here are a variety of paint, color, dot-to-dot, and trace books. Without fail the cover has a patriotic appeal.

in completing the larger, outlined sketch. Lowe also produced boxed sets of smaller coloring books.

"Connect the dots" books always have been popular. The only WWII military find is Merrill's 1943 "Boys and Girls" item. Some books in which tracing paper was interleaved throughout so that the younger child could copy the pre-existing objects had military covers. The touch of water made everything inside Saalfield's "Wet A Brush" book turn light blue and pink. This item definitely was intended for the under-six crowd.

Coloring books for younger children tended to have a wartime cover and standard children's contents such as animals and nursery rhymes. Pictured here are several published by Saalfield.

Even children's paint sets and crayon packages had military motifs as illustrated by American Crayon Company's "Army and Air Force Printing Set" and "Blendwel" crayons.

6
WOODEN TOYS

The best of early war wooden toys was this expensive air rifle, which left store shelves in 1943 when metal restrictions on supplying new ones took hold.

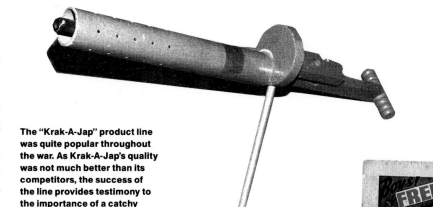

WHEN IT CAME to playing war with miniature tanks, planes, cannons and ships, children growing up during WWII wished to do things full scale. Playing army was serious business. Unfortunately, children could no longer purchase a Marx metal "G-men Tommy Gun," and those children who had a terrific Hubley pistol or marvelous Daisy air rifle broke their treasure sooner or later. Thus, wooden toys became very important.

U.S. soldiers had much the same problem in the early days of the defense buildup and the draft. Before the U.S. war machine was at work full speed, actual weapons were in very short supply, and draftees often trained with wooden guns and tanks. Newsreels of the day show them with painted wooden rifles and machine guns carved from two-by-fours.

But the man with the wood lathe came through. Countless small companies soon began making ingenious wooden toys, the overwhelming majority of which contained almost no strategic materials. The index to *Playthings* indicates that approximately fifty companies were advertising wooden toys in the magazine. Many more local and regional companies with little or no advertising budget probably existed —it seems every outfit with a few pieces of wood-turning and lathe equipment got into the act.

And what novel names these companies had! How about Knock on Wood Industries of Bloomfield, Iowa? Their big seller was "Repeater Junior Pistol" and "Commando Rifle." The "Krak-A-Jap" line of toys produced by New Enterprises of Winston-Salem, North Carolina, produced "Ranger," "Raider," "Commando," "Scout," and "Victory" machine guns and "Parade," "Invader Special," "Bango," and "Yankee Sniper" rifles. Let's not forget those all-time name favorites, the "Aveng-O-Matic" automatic rifle by Modern Crafts Company, St. Louis, Missouri, and the giant "Goon Gun" with its barrel measuring three inches

in diameter by Geo. Borgfeldt Corporation. Rapaport was also back in the act with a very lifelike "American Craft 50 .cal Raider" machine gun.

Wood traditionally had accounted for five percent of the toy volume. In early 1941 the trade press predicted that wood for toys was likely to become scarce. Lumber would be difficult to obtain and higher in price, particularly plywood, wallboard and manufactured lumber. All of these materials were needed for use in the tens of thousands of new military buildings, barracks and workhouses that were under construction. Veneers, also used in toys, were slated for use in certain types of training planes.

Reports throughout the war, however, are conflicting as to the actual effect on the production of wooden toys of the alleged scarcity of wood materials. In fact, notwithstanding the 1941 prediction, it was reported in June 1945 that while hardwood veneers and plywood production

had fallen sharply, these products had been available for all civilian and military needs so as to make government controls unnecessary. Soft wood plywood, on the other hand, ultimately was controlled rigidly.

Since many lumberjacks in the Pacific Northwest left the woods for higher paying jobs in nearby aircraft industry plants, wooden toys did become somewhat higher in price and took a little longer to get throughout the war. But no reports have been found of manufacturer cutbacks for wood toys or of very sharp increases in retail prices. Evidently, somehow, wood was found. The twenty major manufacturers of prewar wooden toys traditionally used approximately ten million board feet of lumber annually. This amount more than tripled during the war. Wood quickly began to dominate in the action toy category. In October 1942, *Playthings* had a three-page list of procurable toys, i.e., those which manufacturers could supply readily. Except for a few dolls, crayons and slate blackboards, all toys were made of wood or of paper/cardboard. The first requests for waivers on price ceilings made to the Office of Price Administration, with one exception, were for wooden toys. Those requests included two Springfield wooden rifles.

WWII wooden toys were creative but, for the most part, lacking in detail. Only a very few employed paper lithograph coverings such as were found on the wooden toys of the 1890–1915 era. And nothing made during WWII measured up to the marvelous, early lithographed wooden pull ships made by Reed, the buildings by Bliss, the blocks by Singer, or the soldiers by McGlothlin, Parker Bros. and Milton Bradley. These early toys were the real eye-catchers.

This page
Like most Hollywood war movies, even the Grade A productions, *Bataan* was a "back lot" production. Nonetheless, its closing scene in which Taylar fires a heavy machine gun directly at the camera lens for over a minute is marvelous and was repeated in many a backyard.

MOW 'EM DOWN

TOMMY GUNS and machine guns, particularly of the heavy variety, were featured in most of the early war films at the Saturday matinees and, not surprisingly, machine guns became the favorite full-scale wood toy. Toy machine guns in hand, children could fantasize about mowing down hundreds of the enemy just as Robert Taylor and his plucky troops did in the terrific early war movie, *Bataan*. Or what child could forget the two Prestons—Preston Foster and Robert Preston (later of *Music Man* fame)—mowing down the invading Japanese on the beaches in *Wake Island* or John Garfield shooting down a Zero with a hand-held .50 caliber MG. (The recoil, in real as opposed to "reel" life, would have broken his shoulder and sent him flying!) Thirty-caliber Browning water-cooled machine guns could do a lot of damage when

Machine guns were big sellers, especially those that made noises.

they didn't jam! Of course, in a child's fantasies he never ran out of ammo or had his gun jam!

Tommy guns did the trick for Errol Flynn in *Objective Burma*. Flynn plays an American paratrooper who single-handedly wins the second battle of Burma. (This film upset the British press somewhat since the Brits had done ninety-nine percent of the fighting in the China-Burma-India Theater.) Cowboy star Randolph Scott used a Tommy gun as he led Marine raiders in *Gung Ho*, Hollywood's version of Colonel Carlson's raid on Japanese facilities on Makin Island, the first real U.S. land offensive effort of the war. *Desperate Journey* with Flynn and Ronald Reagan, *Flying Leathernecks* with John Wayne, *Guadalcanal Diary*, *Purple Heart*, *Flying Tigers*, *Eagle Squadron*, *Thirty Seconds Over Tokyo*, *Bombardier*, and *Action in the North Atlantic* led the big-budget war films of the period.

Low-cost, hour-long B films were an important part of each matinee double feature. Too countless to mention, they

were watched eagerly each week. Many of the B flicks involved submarines. According to film historians, this kept costs down as production essentially involved only one set, the sub interior. The rest was done with models. Children didn't care, what was important was the view through the periscope of the enemy ship going down with the Rising Sun or swastika flag showing. There was no doubt as to who torpedoed whom, and this scene always got a cheer. All of these early war films were simplistic, frankly propagandistic, and clearly intended to boost home front morale. In turn, they set the tone for children's wargame fantasies.

The popular cliffhanger serials also adapted readily to wartime plots. The Canadian Mounties simply foiled Japanese and German spies instead of outlaw gangs. "Spy Smasher" finally caught up with the head of the German secret spy ring in the

Above
Most toy makers produced at least one machine gun. The most authentic looking was the twenty-six-inch long "Yank Raider" by C.L. Spoor Co. of Chicago.

Left
"Air Force" was the best of a number of grade-A war films by Warner Bros.

177

NOTHING ELSE LIKE IT . . .

CLAIMED BY BUYERS WHO REALLY KNOW MERCHANDISE TO BE

"The best new idea of a toy developed since Pearl Harbor —in the entire Toy Industry."

The New "HELL-RAISER"—constant firing patented double action (push-pull trigger action) is the All-American gun for 1945.

W. BOYCE AND COMPANY . . . *Direct Factory Selling Agent.*

"AMERICAN BOY" 3 IN 1 GUN

PATENT PENDING

Every Part Made With Care—Not Just Another Ordinary Gun Made by Cabinet Makers Skilled in Precision Work!

THE ONLY GUN WITH A CAMOUFLAGED SHIELD

* ABSOLUTELY HARMLESS
* SHIELD EASILY REMOVED
* CAN BE USED AS A TOMMY GUN, ANTI-TANK OR ANTI-AIRCRAFT GUN
* LOOKS AND SOUNDS LIKE THE REAL THING
* PISTOL GRIP

* MADE OF WOOD—NO CRITICAL MATERIALS USED
* ENAMEL FINISHED IN OLIVE DRAB—REGULATION ARMY COLOR
* FRONT AND REAR SIGHTS
* GUN SWINGS IN ANY DIRECTION
* 28" LONG — 20" HIGH, MOUNTED

Orders Now Being Booked For Early 1944 Delivery Write For Prices and Details

BALLANTYNE MANUFACTURING CO.
1947 HOWARD ST.   CHICAGO 26, ILL.

observation platform). Not too many fathers made their children fill in the home-town battlefields either. After all, Dad understood there was a war on.

The twenty-four-inch "Chattermatic" machine gun with red cylindrical magazine was made by the Daisy Air Rifle Company. Most likely it was purchased at Montgomery Ward or Sears where it sold for eight-four cents. Simple as it was, the "Chattermatic" remained popular throughout the war. Still shown in Ward's 1945 Christmas catalog, it was one of the few remaining military toys. In two years it had only gone up a nickel in price!

For minutiae fans, a check of toy industry trade press ads by type of wooden toy during 1942–45 shows thirteen rifles and pistols, five planes, nine tanks, ten cannons, twenty miscellaneous vehicles, twenty-one ships and twenty-two machine guns, mostly of the tripod type. Many of the machine guns had detachable guns that became a Tommy gun.

U.S. "Smilin' Jack" saved the island of Mandan and, in one of the best, "G-Men vs. the Black Dragon," Rod Cameron as agent Rex Bennet foils Hurachi, the Black Dragon Society's chieftain.

As might be expected, in summarizing the 1942 toy season and the effects of Order L-81 on production, *Playthings* reported that during the last half of 1942 buyers had paid particular attention to wood toys as replacement for metal toys and that military playthings—wood rifles and machine guns in particular—were popular.

Creating hideouts is what kids did in countless backyards, fields, woods and even trees (a terrific place for an

One of the best looking heavy machine guns produced was the colorful "Yank Raider" action machine gun by C.L. Spoor Co. of Chicago. Made of heavy cardboard and wood, it was big: twenty-six inches long and two feet high! The gun's magazine held eight wooden bullets that discharged through the barrel when the usual ratchet crank was turned. The gun also could be removed from the tripod and used as a Tommy gun. Individually boxed, at Pennsylvania's famous Black Angus Antique Mall it sold in 1988 for seventy-five dollars and at that price was a bargain!

The most accurate wooden guns were those made by the E.W. Boyce Co. of Ft. Wayne, Indiana. Boyce made gun stocks for the Army and used rejected stock of the famous carbine to produced a remarkable look alike, some three feet long, about the size of the actual weapon. Wholesaling for the odd price of $2.37 (minimum shipment three dozen) and retailing for $3.95, it was one of the few machine guns that did not use the rat-a-tat ratchet device. Ads announced that its trigger-operated noise maker made a sharp bullet-like sound, "not just a meek, mild click."

Boyce's "Hell-Raiser Tommy Gun" was the most lifelike of all. An exact duplicate of the clip-fed Thompson sub-machine gun, it came out in July 1945, just as the war was ending. This was a terrific piece, built to last with green, metal-like finish, stained stock, and heavy, olive drab shoulder straps. Boyce grandly called it "the best new idea of a toy developed since Pearl Harbor in the entire Toy Industry." While this may have been true, their timing was a little off — just one month later the atomic bomb was dropped on Hiroshima and Nagasaki and it was soon back to bikes, trains and dolls.

Undaunted, McGuire Industries came out with a similar Thompson in December 1945. Evidently, McGuire had bought up surplus Thompson stock pieces; its ads indicated that these choppers were made of hardwood and "turned out on the same machines that fashioned the original guns." If their timing had been better, the guns probably would have been real money makers; McGuire undoubtedly got the rejects dirt cheap. It would be interesting to know how these toys sold in the early months of peace when the marketing emphasis had shifted almost overnight to civilian toys. As neither the Boyce or the McGuire Tommy guns ever appear on the collector's market, it is unlikely that many were manufactured.

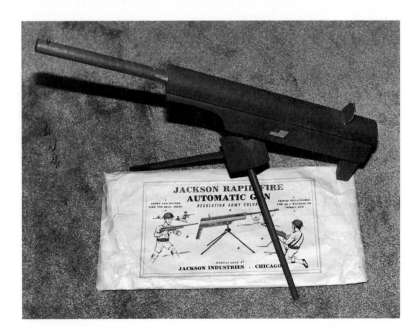

Jackson Industries' "Rapid-Fire Automatic Gun" was typical of toy guns that could be used as either a machine gun or a Tommy gun. ("Double play appeal" said the ads.) Its packaging was rather unusual; it came in a heavy paper envelope that depicted its dual use.

WAR TOYS WITH INSTANT APPEAL!
NIFTY NEW GUNS GO OVER WITH A "BANG"

The Avenger 30 cal.

"INVADER SPECIAL"
24 inches overall—3 colors

"AVENGER TOMMY GUN"
24 inches overall—4 colors

THE 1944 MODEL 30 CALIBRE

All wood construction, put up in individual envelope . . . Well made and finished . . . Plenty of eye appeal and easy to sell. Write us immediately.

The INVADER SPECIAL

HARMLESS

MODEL 45 TOMMY GUN   Simulates Sound of Firing

YES! . . . EASTER RABBITS

Made in two sizes: 20 and 27 inches long.
Constructed of plywood; 5-inch red wheel.
Nicely finished in four colors.
Packed six to a carton.

Order Now for Easter Delivery

•

THE MODERN CRAFTS CO.

This page
To simulate the sound of firing, most toy Tommy guns had a crank-turned ratchet device. The marvelous Rockefeller Colonial Museum in Williamsburg, Virginia, contains a major collection of eighteenth century homemade, wooden toys, many of which employ the ratchet noise-making device.

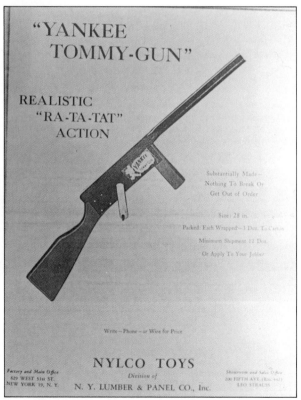

"YANKEE TOMMY-GUN"

REALISTIC "RA-TA-TAT" ACTION

Substantially Made—
Nothing To Break Or
Get Out of Order

Size: 28 in.

Packed: Each Wrapped—3 Doz. To Carton

Minimum Shipment 12 Doz.

Or Apply To Your Jobber

Write – Phone – or Wire for Price

NYLCO TOYS
Division of

Factory and Main Office
629 WEST 51st ST.
NEW YORK 19, N.Y.

Showroom and Sales Office
200 FIFTH AVE. (Rm. 442)
LEO STRAUS

N. Y. LUMBER & PANEL CO., Inc.

Left
NYLCO Toys, the maker of the "Yankee," was a division of the N.Y. Lumber and Pancel Co. Many wood companies made toy guns with their small scrap lumber pieces.

GEO. BORGFELDT CORPORATION
44-60 EAST 23rd STREET   NEW YORK, N.Y.
Phone: GRamercy 7-0400

WORKRITE
MACHINE GUNS
TOMMY GUNS
ANTI-AIRCRAFT GUNS

STRONG - DURABLE
CAREFULLY DESIGNED

•

NO. 10

NO. 20

NO. 30

SEE
OUR NEW No. 2 BOMBER
OUR NEW No. 4 AIRLINER

The Ratchet Connection

With one or two exceptions such as the Boyce carbine, toy machine guns, Tommy guns, and rifles made during the war employed a centuries-old noise-making device. As early as colonial times, toy makers knew that young children like noisy toys. Long employed in pull toys and still widely used today, the simple water-wheel-shaped ratchet device was turned against a wooden flange by a crank or a wheel and axle combination. This mechanism worked beautifully for wartime toys. For weapons, the noise-making mechanism was the crank; in the tank, truck, plane and ship toys, the wheel and axle did the job. So, whether it was a "Yankee Tommy Gun" or a "Victory Tommy Gun Repeater," almost all of the toy assault weapons had some form of crank sticking out the right-hand side. Lefties had to make do the best they could.

Advertisers tried hard to outdo each other in describing the sound these toys made. Our toy, said the propaganda, "simulates the sound of firing," "sounds like the real thing," "sounds like the ack-ack," and "makes a noise like a machine gun." (New Enterprise even went so far as to claim that it had patented the noise-making device on its

"Krak-A-Jap" #20 machine gun.) The truth was, all these toys sounded exactly alike. They made the same clickety-click sound that ratchet toys had been making for generations.

As time went on, some manufacturers tried to get a jump on the competition by becoming more innovative. Bullet-firing guns started showing up in 1944 and 1945. Typical were Rose City Novelty's model 500 "Tripod Machine Gun" that spit "small paper bullets all over the place." It used the same spring-action mechanism in its model 200 "Invasion Cannon" and model 400 "Ack-Ack." These bullets supposedly were hurled fifteen to twenty feet! C.L. Bradford Associates advertised two versions, the 77mm "Defender Gun" (a funny caliber for a machine gun), and its .45 caliber pistol. Each had five rapid-firing wooden bullets. Its "Commando" machine gun allegedly shot seven bullets in one loading. A. Robineau & Co. produced the "Yankee Sniper Bow Rifle." This hardwood rifle shot ten dowel bullets and came in an attractive, heavy paper sleeve case.

The Oscar For Achievement in Noise Effects in the Hand-Held Weapons Category must go to the "Bango Rifle" and "Bango Pistol." Manufactured by Air Arms Manufacturing Co. of Grand Rapids, Michigan, both toys involved the age-old cork popgun principle. In a jab at the bullet-firing toys of its competitors, Air Arms claimed that "Bango" was harmless to children since the cork was attached by a string. (Most likely its safety depended on how close brother stood to little sister when he popped the cork!) Retailing for eight-nine and fifty-nine cents respectively, these popguns allegedly "swept the country" two years running and "sold like hotcakes." Avid collectors, however, report that they have never chanced upon either.

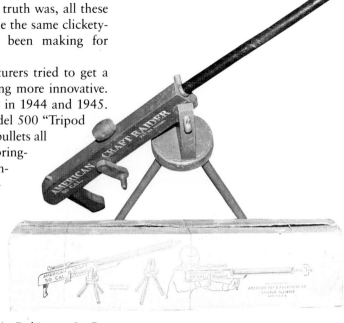

This page
Ads for the "American Craft 50 Cal Raider" tripod machine gun claimed that its explosions were "amazingly realistic."

50-Caliber American Raider Machine Gun, mounted on Tripod. Has telescopic sight, revolving, and up and down motion, realistic crank-ratchet explosive action. Can be removed from tripod and used as a Tommy Gun. Sturdy wood construction, Olive Drab finish, portable, and easily assembled. Stands 17 inches high, overall length 31 inches. Individually packed.
No. 53N39. Per dozen.................................**16.00**

RIFLES

I T'S EASY TO SEE why Tommy guns outsold rifles two-and-a-half to one. In the early stages of the war, in 1942 when metal parts were already in the pipeline and toy metal raw stock not yet depleted, some terrific rifles were made with all-metal sliding bolt actions. The best was the "Daisy Defender," a thousand shot repeater BB gun. Like its counterpart, the famous "Red Ryder Cowboy Carbine Special," it was an absolute favorite and very expensive; it retailed for five dollars. It was also a rather unusual rifle in that it had both a bolt and carbine action. The bolt served only as a safety, the carbine fired the BBs. It also used a lot of metal.

A lot of children, however, weren't allowed to have BB guns. For these children, next best by far were the cadets of the America Trainer Rifles series made by the Paris Manufacturing Co. of Savannah, Tennessee. Action types

seemed to have been their best seller. The cadets were quite sturdy with high-quality, hardwood stocks and steel barrels, triggers, pump levers and sling-clips. The label on one of the larger pieces indicated that cadets are courteous and reverent and devoted to loyalty and honor. Paris' best piece is its large version of the Model 1903 Springfield with heavy bolt action and a full-size golden bullet in the breach. Measuring about three feet, in the hands of a few lucky kids this sturdy rifle lasted throughout the war. Cadets show up regularly today in good shape and sell in the thirty- to fifty-dollar range.

After the metal restrictions went into effect, however, the toy rifles that were produced were comparatively unin-

Right
Armed with wooden guns and wearing tin helmets, three boys scale a barrier in a Junior Commando drill at the Detroit Boys Club playground.
NATIONAL ARCHIVES

Below
Measuring about three feet in length, in the hands of a few lucky kids this sturdy rifle by the Paris Manufacturing Company lasted throughout the war.

teresting. Most had no moving parts and were simply one or two piece pattern cut-outs. Their price reflected their generally cheap quality; most sold in the one- to two-dollar range. To hype the product, most had colorful patriotic decals on the gun butt and came with pamphlets illustrating the *Manual of Arms*.

PISTOLS

The toy pistols made of nonstrategic materials were awful. The industry tried everything—composition, compressed wood pulp, fiberboard, wood and even cardboard—but they were all extremely poor imitations of the prewar product. Disillusioned with such offerings, children continued to use their Hubley and other cowboy revolvers and automatics until they broke, in spite of the fact that they weren't military weapons. They did fire caps, and this was a big advantage. Perhaps toy makers knew that their products were inferior; pistols were very lightly advertised.

Often pistols came in cardboard holsters fastened on cardboard belts as part of cheap uniform sets. Sometimes not more than a quarter-inch thick, they easily could be snapped in half. One can imagine how long these articles held up under rough play or in the rain.

Cowboy pistol sets were easily modified for military usage. Well Made Doll and Toy Co. retailed a boxed holster of genuine cowhide with a "Purple Sage Colt .45" made of composition materials. Cowboy Colt revolvers were modified as army pieces by the use of appropriate embossments. One is engraved U.S. Army and General MacArthur USA on the butt. Their cardboard holsters also pay homage to the Defender of the Philippines. Leaving no stone unturned, they are engraved as well with tanks, AA guns, officers' insignia, and the words "Mech. Tank Div.," which one assumes stands for Mechanized Tank Division. The Sears pistol set also contained a overseas cap trimmed in

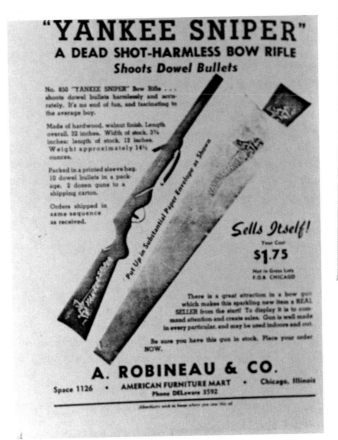

Late in the war, toy gun manufacturers added another popular feature: guns now fired wooden bullets. One suspects that every mother's concern that Johnny would put little sister Susie's eye out with such a toy kept sales of such items low. In any event, they only appear once in the trade press.

"Bango" popguns allegedly "swept the country" and "sold like hotcakes" for two years running. Avid collectors, however, report that they have never chanced upon either the rifle or the pistol.

yellow, all four pieces sold for eighty-nine cents. The only good feature of these cheap holster and pistol sets was the canvas web bullet belts with several wooden bullets.

General MacArthur was used once more to save a pistol line in an attractive boxed set with a full-color action scene whose contents were labeled inaccurately, "U.S. Army Outfit." The "outfit" consisted of another cardboard holster set that was a modified version of the "Mech. Tank Div." piece. The pistol cradle on this holster depicted a B-17 dropping bombs on a Japanese battleship with the words "U.S. Army Air Corps" engraved. This probably came out around the time of Captain Colin Kelly's alleged sinking of the battleship *Hurana*, which historians now know never happened.

The ads show two other pistols made from nonstrategic materials. One, a composition Army .45 automatic, is somewhat realistic; the other, an "American Ranger" automatic with ratchet action, looks more like a Star Trek phaser. These items retailed for only fifteen to twenty-five cents so if they broke easily or melted in the rain, a youngster always could get another without cutting too deeply into his allowance. Five dollars will buy one today.

"Official" lettering or engravings of tanks, antiaircraft guns, insignia, and the like, turned prewar revolvers into army ordnance.

TANKS AND OTHER WAR VEHICLES

Lucky was the child whose all-metal .45 caliber pistol with simulated white pearl handle survived through the war years. It easily fit into an open, cowboy-type holster.

CHILDREN LOVED TANKS then, and children and adults love tanks now. During the war tank toys and kits were very popular, today plastic tank kits continue to be best sellers. In terms of realism, however, the toy industry during WWII totally failed. As a group, tanks were probably the crudest of the wartime wooden toys, and were, by any standard, ugly! Five of the nine advertised in the trade press are shown here.

Most of the tank toys were wheeled and some added a noise-maker. Again, copyrighters were quite creative when it came to describing the ratchet sound. The machine guns were said to make a "realistic" Tommy gun sound; ads for the identical ratchet in the "Victory Tank" manufactured by Richard Appel of New York City, said it reproduced the "noise of cannon fire." This similarity certainly would have surprised any infantrymen who heard both! But only the most knowledgeable and critical of kids cared about such niceties—the point was it made a noise! Like many toys of the day, the "Victory Tank" came in lively red and yellow colors in addition to olive drab or military green. Sears sold it for forty-three cents in 1943. (Toy manufacturers have long known that bright primary colors, particularly red and

The oddest tank produced was one by Noma Toys, an outstanding and long-established toy company. Its 1945 issue "Heavy Tank" was made of composition and wood and, for some strange reason, had a four-inch wooden peg sticking out of the upper tank body over which one slipped the gun turret.

yellow, aid sales with children. Red, yellow and blue had long been a normal color combination on tinplate toys.)

Trade press ads illustrate about three dozen miscellaneous wooden toys, including planes, but since the very small companies seldom advertised nationally, there were no doubt many more wooden toys produced. If one ignores the fact that they came in red, blue and yellow colors, jeeps, cannon and landing craft toys were more realistic than the tanks.

Leading the list of wooden toy manufacturers was the famous Buddy L Co. founded in 1925 by Fred Lundahl,

Left

Two fairly good reproductions of actual ordnance were Woodburn's "T-44 Armored Combat Tank" (actually a late-war tank destroyer), and Wood Commodity Corp.'s "1261-M5 USA."

Appel also made a "Victory Tank" pull toy. It had extra decals and sold at Sears for forty-three cents in 1943.

Left

The Morse code for "V" (dot-dot-dot-dash) is printed on the side of the box for the push along "Victory Tank" produced by Richard Appel. A good number of these tanks, for some reason, can be found at toy shows still in the box.

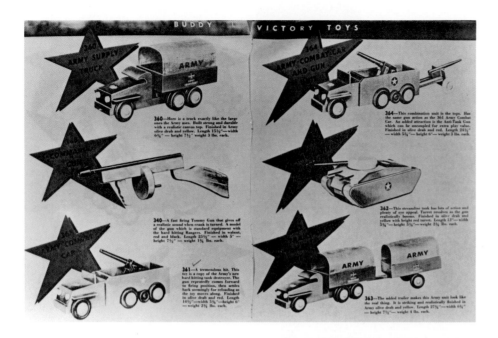

Buddy L published a five-page catalog in 1943 featuring its line of "Victory Toys." The line was described as "unsurpassed in design, finest in workmanship, and richly colored"; in truth the quality of the soft pine wood was poor.

A.I. Root's line of wooden military toys was fairly crude and was priced accordingly.

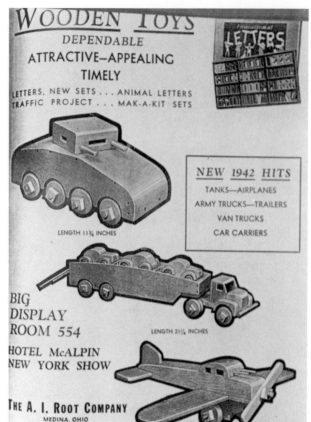

the owner of Moline Pressed Steel Co., a maker of auto parts. Buddy L's pressed steel toys were and are among the finest American toys ever produced. Richard O'Brien, author of the definitive *The Story of American Toys*, calls Buddy L one of the most prestigious toy firms in America.

Buddy L, so-named for Lundahl's son, got caught by the war's metal ban and, like most others, the company went to war. *Playthings'* list of war work by toy companies doesn't describe what Buddy L made, maybe the company did top-secret work. In any event, its entire steel working plant was used for military production. The company, however, did stay in the toy game; pine wood came to the rescue.

According to O'Brien, Buddy L set up a small plant in Glens Falls, New York, and produced a line of wooden war and civilian toys. The company's ad for their new line trumpeted, "Steel toys have gone to war! But Buddy L carries on the tradition with Buddy L Victory Toys."

Consistent with Buddy L's long-time emphasis on size, its wartime line of wooden toys contained some of the biggest items made during the period. Of the twenty toys featured, nine were military. The best was the "Army Combat Car (#367)," which looked like an eight-wheeled White scout car with a 75mm cannon in an open-top rear compartment. As the fifteen-inch car/truck was pushed along,

In this *Playthings*' ad, Wood Commondities brags that its Commando series outsold all other military toys in 1943. The line included the invasion barge, jeep and cannon pictured here.

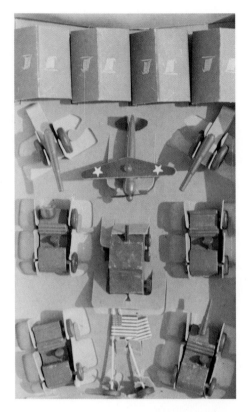

the cannon came forward to a firing position and then settled back "seemingly for reloading," according to the catalog. The red cannon and yellow hubcaps and headlights were another sacrifice of realism for eye appeal. One of the best things about these toys was the great sticker on the side. In good condition this label adds considerably to today's price for these collectibles. In mint condition, they are the highest priced WWII wooden toy antiques.

In addition to Buddy L, New Enterprises' "Krak-A-Jap" toys and Wood Commodities' "Commando Toy" line were at the top of an otherwise sorry lot of miscellaneous toys. The Commando 1200 series sold well throughout the war; in fact the company claimed it outsold all other military toys in 1943. The series included a "General Grant M-5 Tank," a foot-long red jeep, a "new improved" elevating 75mm mobile gun with a push-along ratchet noise-maker, and a M-3 "Invasion Barge" with a let-down gate and small tanks inside. The barge came in bright blue/red and olive drab versions.

Krak-A-Jap's line was quite similar. Its jeep came in two color versions and had luminous headlights. An eighteen-inch long 75mm cannon was sold as a companion piece. It had large wheels with painted spokes and a peg in back that allowed it to be hooked to the jeep. These toys came in individual red, white and blue boxes. New Enterprises claimed it sold over a half million #20 "Krak-A-Jap Machine Guns." A few quite ugly six-inch vehicles of composition materials and spray painted in a light khaki finish also were sold. All of Krak-A-Jap's stock rolling toys can be found today for about thirty dollars.

Only a few large wooden wagons with seats or doodlebug military toys surfaced during the war. US Traveler, the inventor of the famous patented steel doodlebug toys, produced four large, wooden riding toys with military themes. They were designed for two-and-a-half- to ten-year-olds. All were made of kiln-dried hardwoods and looked remarkably like their prewar steel counterparts. The creative addition of a

wooden antiaircraft gun here and a military name and emblem there serviced the military craze; red bodies, wheels and white striping, however, remained. With such modifications a civilian toy became the "USA Patrol" toy of US Traveler's 1943 Victory Line. These toys were expensive; the "USA Patrol" with gun went for $15.95.

Another big toy was Mann-Riley Co.'s "Jumbo Victory Zephyr Five Piece Ordnance Train." Over five feet long, a small child could ride on the locomotive. The train consisted of three cars, an engine and two flat cars, one with an AA gun that looked more like a modern rocket launcher and the other with a wooden tank. Both the gun and the tank were removable and equipped with a ratchet noise-maker. This military train was painted bright red and had yellow trim—perhaps a new form of home front camouflage?

Scandia of Los Angeles, another longtime quality toy maker, produced an interesting series of very large toys in 1942. Its cannon was large enough for a child to ride on and shot wooden bullets. The company hastened to assure mothers that the bullets "moved so slowly that even at close range a window glass will not be broken." Accompanying the forty-two-inch cannon was an ammunition cart with a long pull handle called the "Dragon Wagon." It was designed to store small toys and the cannon bullets. Scandia's "U.S. Coaster Patrol" was a simple style scooter that

Above
The contents of the large Midgie toy set made into a nice army camp scene. A bargain for 98¢.

Right
Krak-A-Jap's eighteen-inch long cannon had a peg in the back that allowed it to be hooked to a jeep.

had ball bearing wheels. (Since the line came out early in 1942, Scandia probably was using prewar ball bearing stock since ball bearings later became impossible to obtain for toy production.) Though painted in olive drab, all items had bright red wheels and large red, white and blue stars and stripes shield decals.

N.D. Cass Toys, a company that had been around for half a century, joined the parade with the only military toy it advertised during the war years. The "USN Invasion Barge" was a wheeled pull toy with twelve clothespin soldiers. It was very childlike and obviously designed for children under six.

The wooden giants prize for military toys goes to Stengaard Co. Its Christmas 1944 military line was huge. Its toys, big enough for a good-sized eight-year-old to ride on, included a sub, battleship, jeep, plane, tank, plane, scout car, and an AA gun that ejected wooden shells. Designed to be ridden like a scooter, they could be steered and had ratchet guns that pivoted. The bodies were made

of masonite wood and the wheels of hard, dehydrated maple. They were extremely expensive for the times. The AA gun cost forty dollars (a week's salary for some adults) with the others ranging from twenty to forty dollars. Toy buyers reportedly like them so much they jumped the Christmas season and sold them early and "as fast as they could get them," particularly in toy-starved stores near major war industries.

Preassembled wooden toy planes (as opposed to plane kits) were few and far between. Airtronics Development Corp. of Dayton, Ohio, listed only once in *Playthings* or *Toys and Novelties*, advertised a line of solid maple airplane pull toys. These toy planes had crude Plexiglass disks intended to represent spinning propellers and canopies and noses of the same material. Included were a P-39, a B-17 and something labeled an A-21 twin bomber. Designed for the preschooler, these pull toys were not cheap: the fourteen-inch B-17 retailed at three dollars. The Harry T. Buck company of Massachusetts produced a small airplane pull toy that looked remarkably like a P-40. Mr. Buck was probably typical of the very small, but often quite good woodworker-turned-toy-entrepreneur who sprang up during the war.

This preassembled wooden toy plane of extremely simple design probably was made by Wood Commodities.

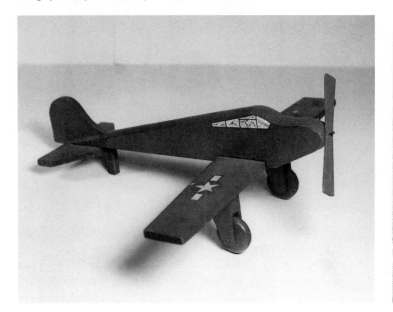

A few quite ugly six-inch vehicles of composition materials were manufactured by Krak-A-Jap. They were spray painted in a light khaki finish.

Small wooden toys, such as these by Keystone, were manufactured by several companies. They retailed for about a dime.

retailed at Montgomery Ward for ninety-eight cents in 1943. Today it costs sixty dollars at a toy show.

Keystone, the major ship and fort maker, and various other companies made wood land toys in the three- to six-inch range. Most sold for about a dime, now they go for five to twenty dollars. The top-turret armored car illustrated was one of five military vehicles included in a series of fourteen small wood toys for preschoolers that was sold by Ward. At twenty-five cents it doesn't seem to be much of a bargain for a five-inch block of wood.

Two companies produced "peg" assembly sets, unusual but creative additions to the wood lines. Airline Manufacturing Co. of Indianapolis did both an Army and Navy version. Consisting of a bunch of die-cut wooden parts, they were assembled by plugging wooden dowels, i.e., "pegs" into pre-cut holes. Airline's "Six Toy Navy Kit" contained a carrier, PT boat, and landing barge; its "Army Set" had the usual grouping of vehicles, cannon and aircraft. At

FROM BIG TO LITTLE

S URPRISINGLY, VERY FEW small-scale wood military vehicles were made during the war. Jaymar Specialty Co.'s "Midgie" boxed sets seemed to have been the most popular. They were featured in several wholesale catalogs and, more importantly, were sold by the major retailers. All of Montgomery Ward's wartime catalogs featured them. Their box art was among the best. Midgie sets come in various sizes containing different combinations of two- to three-inch jeeps, trucks, tanks, airplanes along with great cardboard tents and wooden flagpoles. One large set

Midgies are perhaps the most charming of the small boxed sets produced during WWII. The variety of pieces allowed a youngster to design his own battle scene or camp.

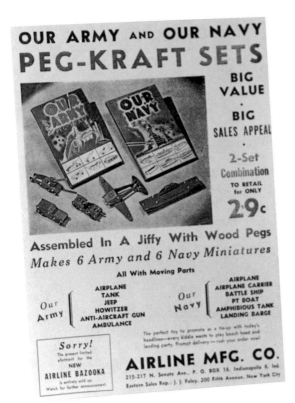

Like the familiar Tinkertoy, "peg" assembly sets appealed to parents who wanted their children to play with toys that encourage a child to be creative. Peg sets were produced by Airline Mfg. Co. and Toycraft.

twenty-nine cents, these sets were a good value. Toycraft's similar peg gun set emphasized making several gun models from the same parts. Its ad said the toy was so simple that even a child of four could handle it. Today these sets rarely show up in decent shape.

Various other odds and ends included Toycraft's wooden army periscope in red, white and blue, and an airplane hangar complete with canvas wind sock. Toyco's boxed "Victory Cannon" had, in addition to the standard spring-fired cannon, a set of cardboard enemy soldiers on wood pedestals. Its ad shows the cannon shell knocking a dagger right out of the hand of the usual ugly, grinning, buck-toothed "Jap." Nice shot though it seems a bit much to waste a cannon shell on a lousy knife!

HERE COMES THE NAVY

ONE MIGHT HAVE THOUGHT that toy ships would have been at the top of the toy "Hit Parade" during the war, but they weren't. Apart from Keystone, the king of wooden ships, and the Tillicum sets of Milton Bradley, surprisingly few boats were produced. Unlike the big assist the early war year movies gave to machine guns and military vehicles, the film industry didn't help the cause of ships much. Apart from the cheaply made submarine flicks, precious few Navy films were made by U.S. studios. Only three Navy movies were made by major studios in the first two years of the war and two of them were about submarine heroes. Cary Grant sailed to *Destination Tokyo* in 1943 and Marine Lt. Tyrone Power (playing a submarine Navy officer) *Crash Dive*[d] in the same year. The only other major film of note, Humphrey Bogart's *Action In The North Atlantic*, involved the Merchant

Marine. The best of the lot, John Wayne's *They Were Expendable,* a film revolving around a PT boat crew, wasn't released until four months after the war ended. Children weren't motivated to buy boats and ships by what they saw at the Saturday matinee.

Keystone had been around since the early 1920s and did some nice work during the war. Starting out small in a shop in Malden, Massachusetts, it gained a reputation for sturdy, quality toys, including wooden ships and forts as well as toy movie projectors. Keystone's line was carried by all the larger wholesalers. As early as 1942, the Butler Brothers' catalog pictured Keystone's PT boats, submarines, aircraft carriers and battleships. Its ships were large; the battleship, for example, was almost sixteen inches long. And these toys did things! The sub spring-fired wooden torpedoes, and the aircraft carrier launched a plane. Using a decades-old mechanical feature, set #217 featured a submarine that fired at a spring-loaded circular target on a battleship. The battleship then exploded. This was accomplished by having the deck turrets and funnels loosely assembled so they easily flew apart upon impact. This feature is found in toy sets of many nations. In 1915 the A. Schoenhut Co. made a floating steel battleship that exploded, broke into pieces, and sank to the bottom when hit by a sub-fired self-propelled torpedo made by the Walbert Mfg. Co.

The top of the Keystone line was its "Victory Battle Fleet (#617)" featuring all seven of its naval line packed in one giant box. Larger Keystone ships in excellent condition and in their individual boxes now sell in the seventy-five- to hundred-dollar range. It is difficult to predict what the entire "Victory Battle Fleet" would sell for today if it were to show up in the box and in mint condition!

About the most charming of WWII wooden toys are the five- to seven-inch-long ships in Milton Bradley's delightful "Tillicum" line. "Little Boats for Little Folks," was Bradley's catchy, box top slogan. Designed for table, tub or floor play, they were great favorites with younger children and parents alike. Wartime sets included "National Defense (#T-106)," "Convoy (#T-104)," and "Junior Harbor." The colorful pop art boxes gave the young buyer a really good idea of their contents.

Expensive, but of excellent quality, Keystone's line was the best in the ships category. They are still readily obtainable.

Above. **The forward turret of Keystone's sixteen-inch battleship fired two five-inch projectiles almost as big as the barrels of the guns themselves.**

Prewar, before its purchase by Milton Bradley, Tillicum made the "Battle Fleet (#115)" set. It came with a marvelous floating target and a lighthouse.

Below. **Despite their modest appearance, Milton Bradley's "Tillicum" sets were not cheap. They hit the pinnacle of retail exposure on the shelves of FAO Schwartz in New York where they retailed for $4.50. Still often available at toy shows, they sell in the seventy-five-dollar range and are usually found, box and all, in very good condition. Yes, they really do float!**

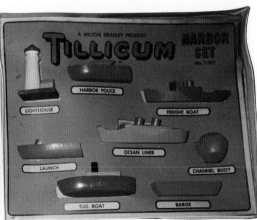

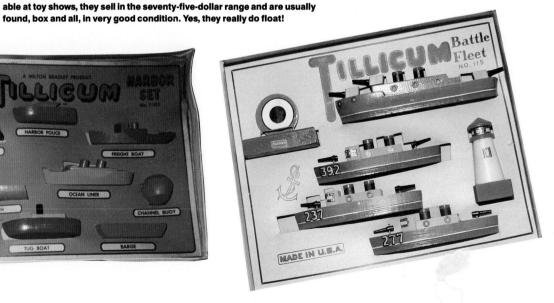

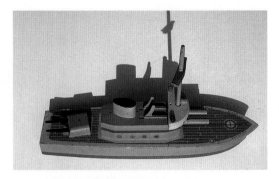
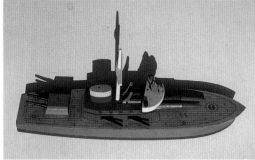
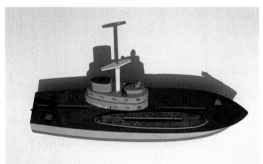
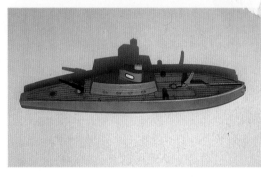

Victory Toy continued its ugly composition line with three medium-sized items, a PT boat, a destroyer, and a submarine.

Keystone's giant "Victory Battle Fleet" in the box in mint condition would be a rare find indeed.

Tillicum Toys Inc., also known as Tillicum Sales Corp., originated in Tacoma, Washington, and made larger naval vessels in its early years. One, a heavy, hardwood, enameled seventeen-inch battleship, probably dating from the early thirties, and must be considered quite rare.

Tudor Button and Novelty Co.'s "Little Admiral" boat set was a cheaper version of the Tillicum line. Cruder in appearance, it included two life rafts (a blue square with a hole in the middle) that were two-thirds the size of the set's three-inch destroyer.

It seems that most of the small wooden ships were not made until the last year of the war. The marketing rationale for this is unclear. The U.S. had been winning major sea battles like Midway long before then, so a lack of victories at sea had little to do with it. The frequency of trade press ads certainly supports the conclusion that ships just weren't as popular. There were only about a dozen different ads for toy ships during all of the war years.

In any event, several ship lines and sets surfaced in late 1944 and 1945. Dell-Harbor Manufacturing Co. had the biggest fleet, some twenty-one in all. They did it simply with only three hull shapes named "Raider," "Stinger," and "Torpedo." Designed for the preschool set, the colors red, green, yellow and blue were featured prominently. Dell did make one quite accurate product, a nice PT boat retailing for $1.29, which it proudly touted as "Not a war baby—prewar quality."

Clark Manufacturing's Kentline Toy Division picked up on the exploding target theme with its 1945 "Sea Battle" set. It was designed to be "assembled and used by very young children ... [to develop their] motor skills, mental alertness, and inventiveness." Kentline obviously had a child psychologist advising the marketing department! Psychology aside, the September 1945 release date probably had an adverse effect on sales.

Sidico Toys (Simon Distributing Corp. of Hagerstown, Maryland), released a thirty-inch carrier pull toy in July 1945 designed for five year olds. It had metal wheels (since the metal squeeze was off) and a metal-faced hull and flight deck along with twelve plastic airplanes. This toy is a great example of a late-war toy made of various nonstrategic as well as of materials formerly classed as strategic.

Baldwin created a smashing twenty-one-inch wood and cardboard carrier that deck-catapulted a small airplane. This was one of Baldwin's few wartime toys. Three airplanes came in the box. Aptly named the "Victory," it was a few years ahead of its time with a closed fo'c's'le and was a bargain at $1.09.

MOM, MY SOLDIERS ARE ALL MUSH!

COMPARED WITH EUROPE, America never had much of a quality metal toy soldier industry. A lot of companies tried and a few such as Barclay and Manoil succeeded for a while, but unlike the long tradition of outstanding European makers such as Mignot of France, Heyde of Germany, and Britains of England, the U.S. market never really caught on.

In the last fifteen years or so, however, a small but rapidly increasing group of American researchers and collectors led by Richard O'Brien and Don Peilin have done yeoman service in unearthing the history of the American toy soldier. Even though some of our European and Canadian friends still refer to prewar U.S. toy soldiers as the "American Uglies," the story of the varied output of these small-time U.S. entrepreneurs is a fascinating one and their products have become quite popular with collectors. The story has been told in great detail in O'Brien's excellent book, *Collecting Toys*, now in its fifth edition, and in his more recent magnum opus, *Collecting Toy Soldiers*. Two excellent periodicals specialize in continuing research: "Old Toy Soldier Newsletter," started by a group of dedicated Chicago-area collectors as a labor of love; and "Toy Soldier Review," a more recent and also worthy addition.

Right before the war, Barclay and Manoil, the major manufacturers of toy soldiers were at their peak. Barclay at one time employed over four hundred workers and sold about twenty million figures a year. Manoil started production a few years later in 1935 and came along slowly. When it ceased production for a time in April 1942, it was turning out eighty thousand figures a day.

Two other companies are worthy of note. Gray Iron, the first to make "dimestore" U.S. toy soldier makers, so-called because they were sold in the five-and-dime chains of the era such as Kresge and Woolworth, sold tons of cast-iron figures through the cheap retail outlets. Auburn Rubber of Auburn, Indiana, which started out, not surprisingly, as a tire manufacturer, competed for the business of the parent who worried about "harmful" heavy metal figures. Auburn emphasized the safety of its toys in all of its advertising; allegedly its lacquer paints were made of pure vegetable dyes. Unlike the slush, hollow-cast, and solid-cast soldiers of Barclay, Manoil and Gray Iron, Auburn hit the big time when its lines were sold by two major retailers, Montgomery Ward and Sears.

The 1942 metal and rubber restrictions brought the production lines of metal toy soldiers to a screeching halt. Barclay, Auburn and Gray Iron went to war. For some reason Manoil failed to line up any war work, even as a subcontractor, and after trying a number of things to stay afloat, including using its plant as a chicken hatchery, simply shut down for the duration.

What was left for the production of toys were the infamous nonstrategic materials. Paper and cardboard came through and produced countless colorful, two-dimensional

Crude composition and clay dimestore soldiers sold well after existing supplies of metal figures were exhausted.

in part to the fact that they were the same size as the prewar three-inch, metal figures.

Notwithstanding their obvious deficiencies, in the absence of any real competition these toys sold quite well. Molded's president said that distributors took everything they had to offer. Butler Bros. featured them prominently. Its 1942 catalog showed Playwood's entire line sold wholesale in different lots, depending on the complexity of the figures. The action machine and AA gunners sold for ninety-two cents a dozen, the lot with the motorcycle was four cents higher, and the simpler standing figures were seventy-two cents a dozen. Like metal soldiers had been, the composition figures were sold separately in bins at the five-and-ten-cent store. Apparently Playwood, using the sales name Toy Creations, also offered boxed sets of ten figures labeled "American Soldiers" and "American Sailors." According to an ad in the *Playthings* in July of '42, the sets retailed for $1.25.

cut-out and punch-out figures of varying degrees of artistic merit and quality. In the fully round, three-dimensional area, however, kids were left with next to nothing.

Three companies moved in to fill the gap. Molded Products opened its plant a week before Pearl Harbor. Anticipating upcoming metal shortages, its founders hired a toy soldier sculptor from the competition and using extruding equipment to produce so-called "composition" figures, hit pay dirt immediately as the metal soldier competition went to war. Molded Product's soldiers were made from wood, flour, water and starch. This substance went through a series of manufacturing steps to emerge from the molds as whitened soldiers. The figures then were dipped in ugly brown paint and detail, such as it was, was added on the production line.

A year later Transogram's Playwood Plastics division came out with its own version of the composition soldier. Playwood should get a gold medal for nonstrategic material use. In addition to using Twenty Mule Team Borax as an ingredient, the company used flour that had been turned down by government food inspectors. Neither of these companies was very big. At their heyday, they together employed only about 150 workers.

Although both company's products were crude and bulky, Playwood's were somewhat the better. It had some reasonably decent action figures including a motorcycler, a duplex figure machine gun team, and an AA gunner. Molded Products tended to put out marching figures. Its mounted officers probably were the ugliest U.S. toy soldiers ever made. Nonetheless, these figures had some appeal due

Auburn rubber figures were sold in early wartime while supplies lasted. They are hard to find in mint condition.

In very good condition (they are often faded), U.S. composition figures sell for about eight to twelve dollars a piece. They are readily available and a complete collection can be assembled rather quickly. Considering their fragile nature, it's amazing that so many survived. They broke rather easily, and horror stories of the effects of water abound. If a child was called for supper and forgot and left his composition figures in the sandbox overnight in the rain, he had Twenty Mule Team mush in the morning. And, unlike with a broken Barclay or Manoil soldiers, he couldn't stuff a firecracker down the body and blow the soldier to smithereens, all the time, of course, pretending they were "dirty Japs" or "nasty Nazis."

The excellent German composition figures made by Elastolin and Lineol had the same problem with moisture. Made with an internal wire armature and a higher quality compressed sawdust and glue, then meticulously hand painted, in all other respects they were a thousand times better than their American counterparts. Today they are very expensive.

In 1944 Manoil tried a brief experiment with even cruder figures. Made of a form of sulfite clay, they were extremely brittle. O'Brien, whose memory for such things seems to have held up better than most of his peers, recalls seeing them in the stores, buying a few, and breaking them almost immediately. This short-lived line consisted of only five items. Since they didn't survive much play, bad as they were, in mint condition they now cost a collector about from fifty to sixty dollars a piece.

Top right
Boxed sets of dimestore figures are rare.

Right
This late-war set of plastic ships is an example of the occasional toy use of this relatively new material.

197

One toy soldier company actually thrived during the war. Beton (Bergen Toy and Novelty Co.) started and stayed small with about ten employees. It used Tenate, an acetate form of early plastic, and its line of approximately two dozen soldiers and cadets was much more realistic than its composition competition. It soldiers and other figures were sold by major retailers in sets of eight and came packed in a small cardboard fort for eight-nine cents. They also sold in the usual local retail outlet bins for ten cents each. Even though its product easily survived if left in the rain, Beton didn't overwhelm its competition for a number of reasons. First, it neither produced nor distributed its figures, but only designed them. Second, unlike Barclay and Manoil, it made no vehicles or airplanes. Finally, its soldiers were slightly undersized.

One other maker of WWII plastic soldiers is known. Plastic Toys Inc. was founded in 1944 by a former Beton employee, possibly with the permission of the latter's owners. Its wartime line of about nine different poses was identical to Beton's with the exception of the bases.

Plastic Toys' were integral and round, while Beton's were oblong and detachable. Apart from a few ads in *Toys and Novelties* during 1944, the only other reference to this line is in Mayer's late-war wholesale catalog where the figures sold for $9.60 a gross. Plastic toy soldiers produced during WWII today cost collectors about three dollars each.

Wooden and composition-board forts were plentiful during the war years. Rich Mfg. Co. of Iowa and Keystone were the major manufacturers. Unlike their Elastolin and Lineol counterparts, which were quite authentic "westwall" fortifications, those by Rich and Keystone were not based on WWI or WWII forts but on castles and had a fantasy-like appearance. (Historically, of course, castles doubled as fortifications and dwellings.) The illustrations show numerous examples of such offerings, as well as forts made specially for FAO Schwartz. These forts had average dimensions of 11"(h)×20"(w)×8" (l) and sold in the two- to five-dollar range. Two of the Keystone variations were entitled "Exploding Fort."

Below
Beton's plastic soldiers were made from Tenate, an acetate form of early plastic, and were much more realistic than figures made of composition materials.

Right and facing page
Forts made by Rich Mfg. Co. and Keystone Mfg. Co. were sturdy and are relatively easy to find today. The "defense forts" by Keystone, however, often are missing small pieces such as swivel cannon and catapult airplanes.

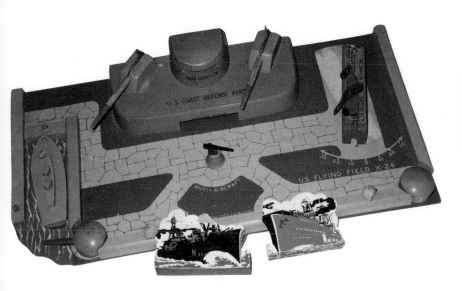

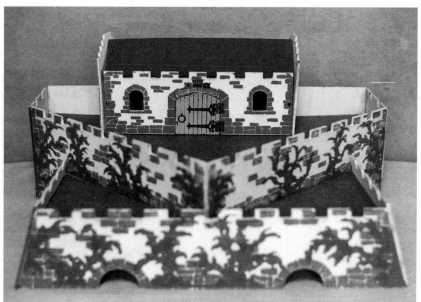

199

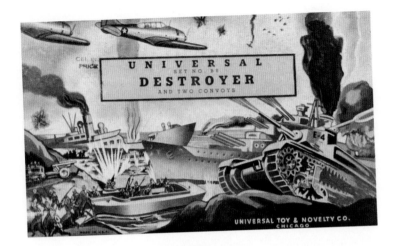

The Universal kits made up into somewhat crude ships.

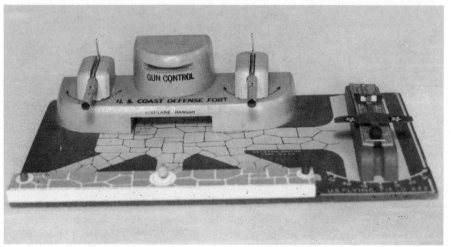

More forts by Keystone and Rich.

WARTIME MODEL KITS

IN THE AGE OF MODERN plastics and the molding machines and techniques that make possible the super accurate and pricy plastic model kits of today, it is sometimes difficult to remember how much tougher it was to make a wooden model fifty years ago. Nonetheless, balsa wood ("solid") and wood and tissue paper ("flying") kits were probably the biggest selling toys of the thirties and forties. Hardly an American kid over six didn't at least try to make one. Some children became incredibly good at it. Ship model kits, of course, had been around for decades. Starting with the advent of popular aviation in the late twenties, airplane model kits soon were sold by every toy retail outlet in the country. The variety was seemingly endless. Both *Playthings* and *Toys and Novelties* magazines soon had a multipage section in each issue devoted exclusively to craft and model making.

One of the pioneer retail and mail order outlets in the sale of kits was Polk's Hobby House of New York City. Operated by brothers Nat and Irwin, Polk's occupied its own building at 314 Fifth Avenue in Manhattan. Since it also imported and sold toy soldiers and other miniatures, Polk's was, for generations of American collectors, the mecca of the hobby. Its catalogs were crammed full of kits, parts and hobby accessories. The Polk brothers were also very active in wartime toy industry activities, including the Toy Knights and various war bond and aid to serviceman efforts.

Of the two basic types of kits, the wood and paper "flying" models were the most difficult to build. Among the most difficult tasks to learn was to properly cut, stretch, glue and dope the thin tissue paper that covered the planes skeletal structure. Tightening the tissue paper prior to applying several coats of paint or dope involved a delicate process of wetting the paper. A small water spray gun did the

best job. Many a first-timer tore a lot of paper, got a lot of glue on his hands and sprayed many a hole in the paper before getting the process down pat. As Wallis Rigby reminded young modelers, patience was the key.

Many companies produced flying models. Among the best were Joe Ott, Comet, and Bild-A-Set. The wind-up propellers were powered by a rubber band placed inside the model's fuselage. (After rationing went into effect, advertisements for models warned: "Rubber band not included.") When built correctly, wound tightly and launched from a decent height, these beautiful models flew a considerable distance. Sadly, they were somewhat fragile and generally survived only a few flights. Then it was time to set them on fire prior to launching and to pretend they represented enemy planes like the hated Messerschmitt Bf-109.

Solid kits, made primarily from soft woods like balsa, were much more varied. Kits for all sorts of ships, cannon, antiaircraft guns, searchlights, tanks and other vehicles were produced. Polk's scale model catalog for 1945 contained over fifty pages of solid kits in varying scale.

During the war, safe and educational flying models were probably the most popular present for boy eight years and older. Note that Bild-A-Set, wishing to capture as young of a market as possible, stressed on the box that their kits were easy to assemble and went together "in less than one-third the time."

In their most basic form, solid models originally contained many parts that were simply blocks of balsa wood such as the plane fuselage. By utilizing the paper templates supplied with the model kit, the young modeler used an x-acto or other sharp knife to whittle the block to the correct shape. Then, with repeated sand papering, a smooth and accurate part was obtained. This was more difficult than it sounds and many youngsters were never able to master the technique. Later on, most kit makers simplified the process by providing major parts pre-cast to shape, some parts even sanded. Still, adding the correct detail, proper paint schemes, and the appropriate insignia required skill. Polk's catalog had two pages of step-by-step instructions for building solid models; forty-four separate steps were listed.

Among the most popular solid kits were those made by Mod-AC Manufacturing Co. of Los Angeles, Austin Craft, Rogers, Comet, Marvel Mfg. Co., E.Z. Craft, and Testors. The leader, however, was certainly Strombecker Mfg Co. (Strom Becker) of Moline, Illinois. Strom Becker kits were featured by name by all the major retailers including Sears, Montgomery Ward, FAO Schwartz, and Polk's.

While most kits were sold separately, FAO Schwartz combined kits by various manufacturers into sets of different types. In 1942 it featured the "Tank Construction Set" consisting of eight solid model tanks by Amsco, Liberty and Williams. Its "Air-O-Trainer" assembly kit featured a non-flying model with an open cockpit and wire-controlled flying surfaces designed to teach a child how an airplane flew. Kit prices ranged from thirty-five cents for the simplest to $7.50 for a large "DeLuxe B-17 Flying Fortress."

Comet, Testors, and Rogers were among the big names in model kits. Kit prices ranged from thirty-five cents for the simplest to $7.50 for the large "DeLuxe B-17 Flying Fortress."

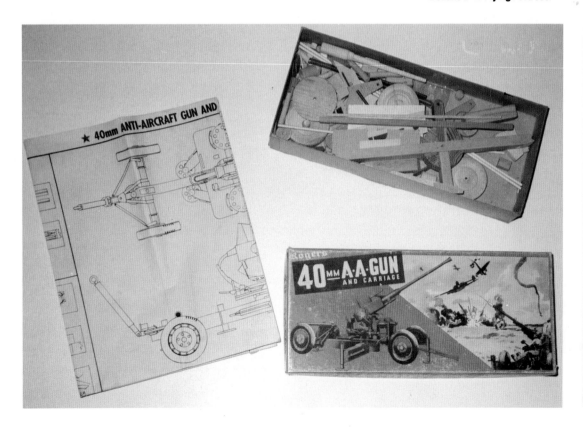

Above, right
Producing authentic, well-designed kits, Strombecker was a leader in the model kit industry during WWII.

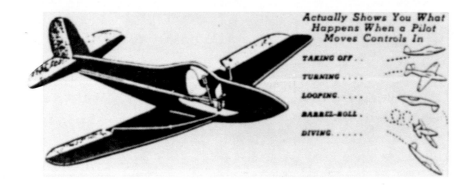

The "Air-O-Trainer" assembly kit marketed by FAO Schwartz featured a non-flying model with an open cockpit and wire-controlled flying surfaces designed to teach a child how an airplane flew.

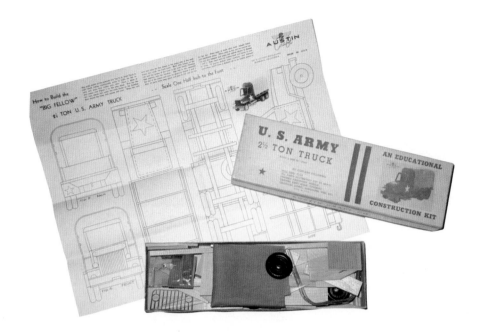

This page
Vehicle kits, while not as popular as plane items, sold briskly. Listed by Polk's as "military models," unlike aircraft they did not rate a separate catalog of their own.

The fall catalogs featured every conceivable kit and every airplane ever built. Special decals of insignia for both WWI and WWII Allied and enemy ordnance allowed young model builders to do all their models in a highly authentic fashion.

206

Air Recognition Models

R ECOGNITION OF ALLIED and enemy aircraft was a major wartime training effort for civil defense and armed forces alike. Junior and senior high school students in industrial and shop classes learned to make solid aviation models for use by the military in gunnery and pilot training. These models were made to precise government specifications and painted black when completed. Quality control was strict, so it was a proud student and class when a model was accepted for military use. Tens of thousands of such models were produced.

In addition to privately made recognition models, the government had many produced commercially by toy companies that had shifted to war work. Made in varying scales, these hard plastic models were marvelously authentic. Toward the end of the war Polk's bought up a large quantity from the government's huge surplus and marketed 138 different types under the "Aristocraft" name at prices ranging from one dollar to thirteen for the huge Japanese "Kawanishi 97 Flying Boat." Polk's sales pitch predicted they ultimately would become "priceless treasures." Indeed they are sought after today, particularly by collectors of aircraft and plane memorabilia.

Polk's also bought and marketed many miniature, solid metal recognition ships in 1/1200 scale that had been made for the military by Long Island's Comet Metal Products, Inc., the prewar maker of popular 54mm toy soldiers. The waterline "Authenticast" miniatures were detailed right down to the torpedo tubes. Authenticast vehicle recognition models in 1/108 scale were equally authentic. They are just as collectible today, particularly if found in their wooden armed forces cases.

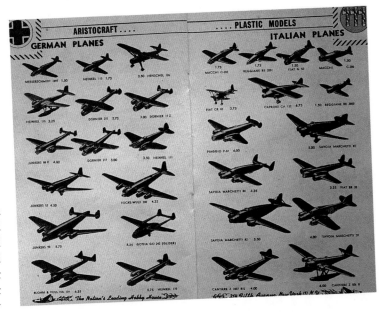

Polk's Hobby House sold 138 government surplus, plastic recognition models after the war. The huge Japanese "Kawanishi 97 Flying Boat" model went for the unheard of price of thirteen dollars!

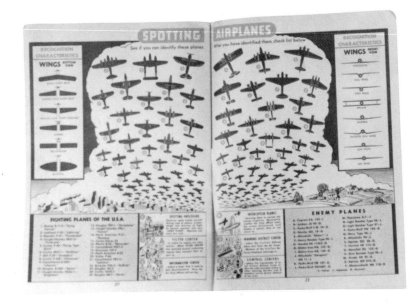

207

7
Box Tops & Dimes

Comic book ads promoted dozens of neat premiums, often of super hero patriotic clubs. Unlike giveaways, this stuff usually cost a dime.

IN ADDITION TO military toys, children played with and collected a lot of other items during World War II. Some of it they got for free, well . . . almost free. Many of these commercial giveaway items and premiums were among the neatest toys of all. To collectors a "giveaway" is technically an item that is handed out at no charge and no purchase is required. A "premium," on the other hand, is offered only in return for a nominal cost payment or for the submission of box tops or product seals; a purchase of a product is required.

Children received great giveaways from bread companies, the corner hardware store, gas stations, and in newspapers. All of these businesses seemed to love handing out blotters and pamphlets regarding uniforms and insignia. It was the relatively new medium of radio, continuing its 1930's pattern of sponsor premium items, however, that contributed many marvelous and now rare pieces to the wartime toy box. Radio premium collecting is a growing hobby today, due in part to the general growth in "nostalgia" collectibles. While not a large hobby by overall standards—there are estimated to be only about one thousand serious premium collectors—it is perhaps one of the top hobbies in terms of fun and memories. And, since so much of this memorabilia was produced during WWII, even the occasional collector can strike pay dirt with a little diligence.

A large number of premiums were created, designed and marketed to advertisers by the Gold Company of Chicago. Sam Gold, company owner, got a good write-up on his efforts in a 1949 *Life* magazine article. In the thirties, metal premiums were made mostly in the East and then shipped to the product companies in Battle Creek and elsewhere for delivery. Thus, the aggravating and interminable "allow six to eight weeks for delivery" phrase was necessary. The Einson-Freeman Company, maker of wartime paper punch-out toys, made most of the paper premiums in the thirties. It thus was positioned to become the leader in the field during WWII. The very same Sam Gold joined the Einson-

Freeman company as a vice president in 1942 to spearhead this effort.

Two excellent books and guides have been written on the general subject of radio giveaways and premiums. The first, *Jim Harmon's Nostalgia Catalog*, contains a lengthy chapter on such items with neat photographs of premiums and advertisements from the 1930s and 1940s. The author's delightful writing style makes it a really terrific read. In his engrossing style, Harmon sums up what collecting is all about:

> Collectors save things. They speak of *saving* comic books, *saving* matchbooks from the 1939 World's Fair and the Stork Club, *saving* movie star photographs. They *save* things because they can't protect the past they loved from the rush of the present or from the looming engulfment of the future. Collectors are not necessarily political conservatives—they are *conservationists* conserving the best of the past for themselves and others.

Editions of Tom Tumbusch's *Illustrated Radio Premium Catalog and Price Guide* written between 1979 and 1991 contain much useful information. They deal with radio premiums, and more recently, cereal box collectibles. Much of the knowledge of this area of collecting comes from the pioneering works of these two gentlemen.

While there are many part-time dealers in premium collectibles, the major source for all such collectibles seems to be Ted Hake's auction house. His descriptions of the condition of auction items are excellent.

By the attack on Pearl Harbor, radio giveaways had been around at least as long as 1919 when a photograph of Amos & Andy was given away. Commencing in the early thirties with Tom Mix and Orphan Annie, sponsors of such fifteen-minute radio shows gave away handouts by the hundreds. The giveaways were very popular. Today, due to the heavy cost of radio and television advertising, very few programs are sponsored by one company in their entirety; the viewer is deluged by dozens of thirty- and sixty-second spots. Once upon a time, however, the words "and now an important word from our sponsor" was a phrase eagerly awaited by

This excellent toy set reflects the outstanding contributions made by the uniformed women's services in WWII.

millions of American children because it usually meant that an "exciting new [premium] offer" was about to be made. (Often the script of preceding episodes gave a clue that something was up.)

Many of these radio shows featured comic book or comic strip characters. Some like the cowboy hero Tom Mix were based on the exploits of popular film stars. Others like the Lone Ranger were based on popular fiction, and a few such as Jack Armstrong, the All American Boy, were created solely for radio. But whatever their origin, the exploits of Buck Rogers in the Twenty-Fifth Century, Captain Midnight, Dick Tracy, Jack Armstrong, Orphan Annie, the Lone Ranger, Superman, Tom Mix, Chandu the Magician, Gangbusters, the Green Hornet, Terry and the Pirates and many others, kept youngsters eating certain kinds of cereal and bread and drinking various beverages.

For obvious reasons relating to the fragility of the material, paper premiums are among the rarest of wartime finds. The majority of paper premiums were created by the Gold Company team of Fred Voger and Wally Weist of Chicago. Voger, according to some observers, ranks up there with Wallis Rigby as a "paper engineer." He cut his teeth designing pop-up children's books for his father's paperboard printing and die-cutting company. His best wartime achievement was probably the rare Orphan Annie/Captain Sparks' "Airplane Pilot Cockpit Trainer."

During the war one had to buy, beg, borrow or steal

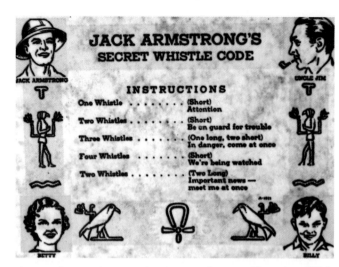

the product or its container to get that terrific prize. With great anticipation, a child ripped off the box tops, addressed the envelope, enclosed his money and sent the order on its way. Then the waiting began. Fortunately, the prize usually was returned quickly.

"Life itself often depended on box top gifts," says Jim Harmon. What he meant was that in a favorite program the secret ring or the magic whistle often saved a hero's life. But the quality of a child's life in those days, to some degree, depended on receiving a continuing supply of giveaways or premiums. During the Depression they often were the only toys a child had.

The majority of the 1930's premiums from the popular radio shows were made of metal; mostly they were badges, rings, whistles and decoders, all "secret" of course. Due to Order L81 and general wartime shortages, metal premiums disappeared almost totally during the war years, and the overall number of premiums was greatly reduced. The military related premiums that were produced, however, were terrific—in some ways even better than many store-bought toys because they so directly tied in with the wartime adventures of the radio heroes.

The largest breakfast cereal companies, General Mills, Quaker, Kellogg's, Post, and Ralston-Purina, were the major sponsors of these programs. These companies used radio as a major marketing tool for new products. General Mills'

leading brand, Wheaties, for example, had been around for some sixteen years when, in 1941 and 1942, the company used a national radio campaign built around news programs to persuade Americans to buy its new Cheri-Oats (Cheerios) cereal. The campaign sold 1.8 million cases of Cheri-Oats, an amount equal to two-thirds the sales volume of Wheaties.

Magazine ads built around war themes were used extensively. Cereal companies advocated "fighting breakfasts" for war workers. In one early wartime ad, a welder yells, "Take that, Mr. Hitler. I ate my fighting cereal this morning!" General Mills hasn't forgotten these days. Its charming, multicolored, third-quarter 1991 report to stockholders had a five-page section on the fiftieth anniversary of Cheerios that contained an excellent summary of its involvement with radio premium shows and numerous color photographs of premiums and vintage cereal boxes.

Jack Armstrong, the All American Boy, sponsored by Wheaties, then and now the "Breakfast of Champions," was one of the longest running radio adventure serials and, along with Tom Mix and Little Orphan Annie, the most prolific dispenser of premiums. During the war Jack and his gang fought spies and saboteurs and aided in all manner of home front activities. Its 1944 series of "Tru-Flite Fighter Models" is probably the most famous and common wartime premium. These terrific cardboard sheets made up into very realistic three-dimensional, multicolored copies of the real thing. Once a penny was glued inside the nose for balance, they flew a long ways.

Large point-of-sale ads such as the three-foot-long store poster pictured are rare today. Ads also appeared in comic books, newspapers and other periodicals, and they are worth framing. The text says that the planes flew seventy-five feet and, when rigged for G-line forays, would "zoom, dive, climb and hedge-hop—under your control." The best part was that for two box tops one received two airplanes! These planes were issued in seven sets of two each and didn't cost anything. Said General Mills, "Send no money—put your dimes in war stamps." Tru-Flite Models of Roseville, Michigan, has reproduced these Wheaties model sheets with great fidelity, and they have been sold at the Smithsonian Air and Space Museum gift shop. General Mills concurrently published "Jack Armstrong Tru-Moves" featur-

ing reports of flying contests with the airplane premiums and, in 1945, put out an envelope kit containing a "How to Fly Manual," "Pre-Flight Trainer Model," pilot corps transfers and like items. One rarely finds this complete item today.

Other Armstrong wartime premiums included a rare 1942 "Secret Bombsite" with three bombs and a "Write a Fighter Corps Manual." In mint condition the bombsight runs $350 today and is a regular item on premium collectors' "most wanted" lists.

Radio Orphan Annie, which first broadcast in 1931, picked up on the rise in patriotism in 1940 with a manual describing its new "Speed-O-Matic Double Track Decoding Machine." The illustrations combined symbols such as the American Eagle, the Red White and Blue Shield, and the flag. The sponsor for Ovaltine attempted to geometrically increase the sales of this chocolate-flavored "nutritional" drink in this way: A child got three friends to sign a pledge to drink Ovaltine regularly, got their parents to co-sign the pledge (a total of six adult signatures!), sent in three foil seals from under the lids, and enclosed ten cents with each one. Then, and only then, he received "absolutely free" an official red, white and blue "Code Cap and Belt" with a "Victory Metal Buckle" based on the U.S. Army's Garrison belt buckle. With all of these requirements it's no wonder there aren't many of these around today and that they cost a small fortune when found!

Wheaties 1944 series of "Tru-Flite Fighter Models" is probably the most famous and common wartime premium. These terrific cardboard copies flew a long ways if a penny was glued inside the nose for balance.

There were many Lone Ranger wartime premiums, often dealing with civilian defense themes.

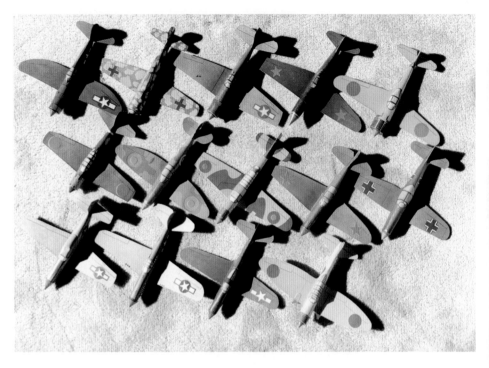

This page
**Most "Tru-Flite" sets contained
one Allied and one enemy
model such as a Curtiss P-40
and a Mitsubishi Zero.**

Soon after this promotion Annie lost her sponsor, Ovaltine, to Captain Midnight, certainly one of the all-time best children's action radio programs. Annie, however, still didn't ignore World War II. On the contrary, her new sponsor, Quaker's Sparkling Puffed Wheat and Rice, changed Annie's long standing Secret Society into the Safety Guard. The Orphan's new sidekick and the Safety Guard's Commander in Chief, the handsome, mustachioed Captain Sparks (he looked a lot like Errol Flynn), and the Guard's wartime activities led to a host of war-related promotional items in 1941 and 1942. Safety Guard emblem glow rings, initial rings, magnifying rings, nurse outfits, insignia caps, "Detecto Kits," "Whirl-O-Matic Decoders" made of cardboard, and "Tri-Tone Signal Badges" thrilled many a listener. The membership kit for the Guard contained numerous paper items.

It seems that many children really didn't like Orphan Annie and, although mothers thought it was good for them, hated Ovaltine. One writer called it the "brown sludge."

In any event, Annie's radio show peaked in 1941–1942, but Captain Midnight kept youngsters drinking the "brown sludge" for years to come. The Captain specialized in metal badges and code devices, usually called "Code-O-Graphs." For this reason, his offerings were greatly reduced in 1943. All Captain Midnight premiums can be considered military collectibles. The 1944's "Service Ribbon Pin Folder" and "Service Insignia Shoulder Patch" and chart, for example, are all based on World War II items.

Using a string and stick G-line two children could stage dog fights, but who wanted to be the enemy? Children tossed for it, with the loser taking his turn as the Nazi fighter pilot.

The Terry and the Pirates comic strip by Milton Caniff went all military during the war. Terry joined up and rose through Air Force ranks. The radio program was very similar to the strip and had all of the same characters. Highly popular, it didn't offer many giveaways, only one in 1941 and four between 1942 and 1948. Only one, the "Victory Airplane Spotter," falls in the military category, but it is one of the best. Featuring colorful drawings of all of the leading strip characters, it was large and utilized the same circular rotating device described in earlier chapters. It came in a colorful envelope. Like many paper items, today it's devilishly hard to find and expensive.

Superman, who was prevented from doing active service by flunking the draft physical when his X-ray vision went

Annie was only a Lieutenant Commander in the Safety Guard while Sparks was the Commander in Chief. Was this due to a sexist conspiracy at Ovaltine headquarters?

213

into the next examining room and read the wrong eye chart, got a late start in radio. The Mutual Network delivered the Man of Steel in 1940. In spite of his 4-F status, Superman fought Nazis, spies, and saboteurs throughout the war and gave away tons of premiums, mostly in packages of Kellogg's Pep cereal (no sending in required). Between 1942 and 1945, the sponsor handed out forty-four different metal pins of military squadron insignia or planes (the eight latter are somewhat larger), thirty-three balsa wood airplanes, and forty cardboard box-top planes together with a box series of "Know These Planes" ID sheets. The highly popular "Model War Planes" series came in a six-by-five-inch die-cut sheet right in the Pep cereal package. They are very collectible and pricy today. Assembled by slotting, they were not three-dimensional "flying" models like the Wheaties "Tru-Flite Fighter Models" but were intended to be used for silhouette identification. Due in part to the large number, Superman premiums are among the most popular and obtainable of collectibles today. The Pep pins are some of the harder to find and more expensive items in that line.

Superman's owners launched a highly successful marketing campaign with national bread companies in the early forties. Superman Bread contained inserts that made a child eligible for membership in the Superman Junior Defense League of America. Bread companies furnished local grocery stores with large window posters and cardboard stand-up signs urging League membership. Initially, Superman

Captain Midnight's Secret Squadron "Service Insignia Shoulder Patch" and chart was offered by Ovaltine in 1944.

premiums were not usually connected to the Superman radio program. In 1944 the Superman program gave away a heavy paper "Walkie Talkie" that also is now rare. Like many Pep premiums, this one didn't feature the superhero himself, but you did have to send away for it.

Radio programs featuring three cowboy heroes, one real, two fictional, had a few World War II prizes. Tom Mix, probably the most popular Hollywood cowboy star ever, was on the air for seventeen years and offered the greatest number of premiums. Ralston's Straight Shooters' Club featured the usual metal badges, secret rings, decoders, magnifying glasses and compasses, but its were more varied than any those of any other program. The war's metal ban brought a halt to these great prizes and between 1942 and 1944 youngsters were left with only "Tom Mix Commando" comic books.

The Lone Ranger, on the air for twenty-two years, did pretty well for U.S. wartime collectors. His National Defenders Club handed out the "Danger Warning Siren" in 1941. Club membership made you eligible for "a dozen pieces of special equipment." This club gave away the only membership booklet that listed all the available premiums, a tremendous aid to collectors. The war years saw Lone Ranger Victory Corps tabs and manuals, a paper "Blackout Kit" that glowed in the dark and, best of all, a secret compartment ring that came in four versions with one's choice of Army, Navy, Air Force or Marine Corps insignia. When one slid aside the insignia panel on the ring, a photo of the Lone Ranger and his horse, Silver, were revealed.

Captain America, another comic book hero who is still popular, fought the Nazis and the Japanese throughout the war. Its premiums for the Sentinels of Liberty Club were advertised in the comic books and included bronze and copper badges that soon fell prey to the metal ban.

Captain Marvel ("SHAZAM") didn't have a radio program but, nevertheless, was immensely popular and advertised many premiums in its Fawcett Publication comic books. Wartime items included embroidered and iron-on patches. When the Captain Marvel Club had to forego its monthly membership bulletin during the war due to paper shortages, an explanatory note to all members from the red-uniformed superhero explained he was doing it in an "all out effort to defeat the Axis."

The Junior Justice Society of America, which featured Wonder Woman, Hawkman, the Green Lantern, and the Flash among other superheroes, offered membership certificates, decals and cards. Would be members of the Justice Society signed a lengthy pledge not only to keep America united "in the face of enemy attempts to make we Americans think we are all different" and in so doing to defeat Axis propaganda, but also to buy every issue of All Star Comics!

Hop Harrigan, flying hero

215

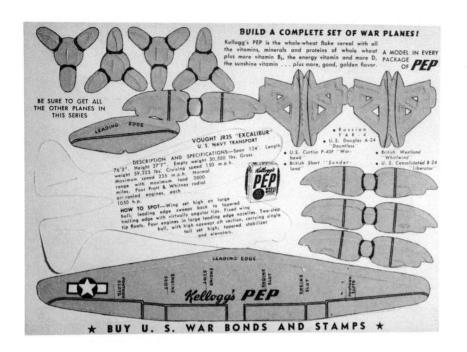

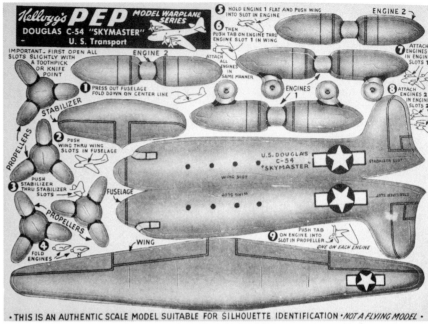

· THIS IS AN AUTHENTIC SCALE MODEL SUITABLE FOR SILHOUETTE IDENTIFICATION ·*NOT A FLYING MODEL*·

This page
Kellogg's line of warplane models included odd birds such as the British Westland *Whirlwind* and the Russian *Masco* fighters, hardly among the great performers of the Allied air forces. It also included aviation greats such as the Douglas C-54 *Skymaster* transport, which performed so well that a civilian version, the D-6, was constructed and became the mainstay of civilian aviation after the war.

of a relatively short-lived wartime radio serial, had, nevertheless, some of the most creative premiums. Most were advertised in the comics. Harrigan's fifteen-inch "B-29 Bombsight and Target Game" (ten cents and a box top from Grape Nuts Flakes) and "Para-Plane" premiums were better than most paper offerings.

A number of World War II military premiums were not connected with a particular radio program, but came in the cereal box or were promoted on it. General Mills, sponsor of the Lone Ranger, used its cereal product, Kix, to issue one of the rare, extended paper giveaway collectibles, the "Kix Airbase." This premium is among the best paper giveaways of the war years. It had the best box art, best point-of-sale ads, best graphics, and was the most fun. For ten cents and a Kix box coupon, one received a two-sided 26½-by-40-inch paper island airbase, plus ten cutouts of two-inch vehicles, buildings, control tower, and planes. Printed on the base runway were rules for playing "Kix Tag" (the usual squares game where a headquarters was captured); on the reverse side were instructions on how to get additional planes and tons of illustrated information on aircraft carrier landing signals, radio communication terms, airbase operation, and basic and de-

fensive flying principles and fighting tactics. That wasn't all! The inside of Kix boxes in this series contained three to four additional cut-out planes, tanks, and artillery to go with the airbase. Moreover, the air base was configured in such a way that it interlocked. Conceivably one could, by sending in more dimes, have an airbase that ran across the room, out the door, and down the street to a chum's house! Kix thoughtfully provided a multicolored "Kix-Top Spinner" on the box top with which to play the games. To make it into a top one simply "punched a stubby pencil" through the center.

Other General Mills premiums included a rare set of twenty 1/432 scale plastic Army and Navy planes including the late-war B-29. These planes were obtained by mail. Another premium was the "Victory Battles War Stamp Album" depicting eight large, colorful paintings of American victories ranging from the Doolittle Tokyo raid to the Battle of the Philippine Sea.

The final category of premiums are those that were part of the product container itself, usually the back of the cereal box. Cut-out planes, games, aircraft and ID information, cut-out paintings of tanks, planes and like items were among the

This page
Makers of Superman Bread furnished local grocery stores with large window posters and cardboard stand-up signs urging League membership. Members pledged to aid Superman in national defense. This membership, in turn, spawned a number of now rare giveaways, mostly paper items.

offerings. Kellogg's Pep Whole Wheat Flakes contained a simple, declarative sentence order: "Cut out and save these handy plane spotter cards." A series called "Fun at the Breakfast Table" contained pictorial quizzes on rank, insignia, badges, medals, headgear, uniforms, and military history. The colorful "Wings of Victory" series is also illustrative. Because sponsors kept coming out with all this stuff, children kept buying scrapbooks and glue.

Forerunners in the mid- to late-thirties were the Kellogg's Corn Flakes 1939 "Wings Over America" series and its somewhat earlier "Kellogg's Adventurer" set in which military topics such as airplane carriers, a new development in those days, and Army acrobatics were featured.

Children were enticed by enough military premiums during the war years to keep them eating their cereal without too much complaining.

Above
Red Ryder, a fictional radio and movie serial cowboy hero, was featured on the "V Patrol Rodeomatic Radio Decoder."

Below
Until 1943 Sentinel members were able to pin on their badges and "help fight spies and traitors to the U.S." After that, Captain America's metal badges fell prey to the metal ban.

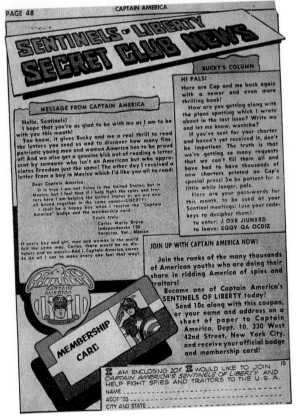

Above
Naturally, due to the sexist standards of 1942, Wonder Woman, as the only female superhero member of The Junior Justice Society, was the club's secretary!

218

Above, below
Hop Harrigan offered some of the war's most creative premiums. His colorful cloth Observation Corps patches adorned many a youngster's jacket.

Top right, bottom
The "Kix Airbase" came with two dozen cut-outs of different airplanes, airbase buildings and weapons. While not nearly as rare as the Lone Ranger's paper "Frontier Town," which can sell for upwards of one thousand dollars, a complete "Kix Airbase" is difficult to assemble and worth a lot of money.

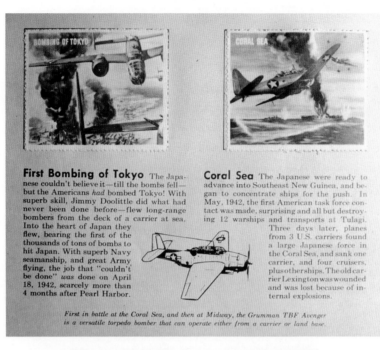

First Bombing of Tokyo The Japanese couldn't believe it—till the bombs fell—but the Americans *had* bombed Tokyo! With superb skill, Jimmy Doolittle did what had never been done before—flew long-range bombers from the deck of a carrier at sea. Into the heart of Japan they flew, bearing the first of the thousands of tons of bombs to hit Japan. With superb Navy seamanship, and great Army flying, the job that "couldn't be done" *was* done on April 18, 1942, scarcely more than 4 months after Pearl Harbor.

Coral Sea The Japanese were ready to advance into Southeast New Guinea, and began to concentrate ships for the push. In May, 1942, the first American task force contact was made, surprising and all but destroying 12 warships and transports at Tulagi. Three days later, planes from 3 U.S. carriers found a large Japanese force in the Coral Sea, and sank one carrier, and four cruisers, plus other ships. The old carrier Lexington was wounded and was lost because of internal explosions.

First in battle at the Coral Sea, and then at Midway, the Grumman TBF Avenger is a versatile torpedo bomber that can operate either from a carrier or land base.

FUN *AT THE* **BREAKFAST TABLE!** NO. 32

THERE ARE **20** THINGS WRONG WITH THIS SOLDIER'S UNIFORM & EQUIPMENT. CAN YOU FIND ALL 20 MISTAKES?

1. Wrong insignia on cap.
2. No visor on cap.
3. Incorrect salute.
4. No necktie.
5. Captain's bars on shoulder.
6. Sergeant's chevrons upside down.
7. Naval officer's stripes on cuff of coat.
8. Service bars on wrong breast.
9. No pocket on right breast.
10. Bayonet on wrong side.
11. Dress instead of web belt.
12. Sling loose on rifle.
13. Coat longer on one side.
14. Stripe on trousers.
15. One legging on, one off.
16. Fountain pen showing.
17. No insignia on lapels.
18. Coat unbuttoned.
19. No pockets on skirt of coat.
20. Cuff on trousers.

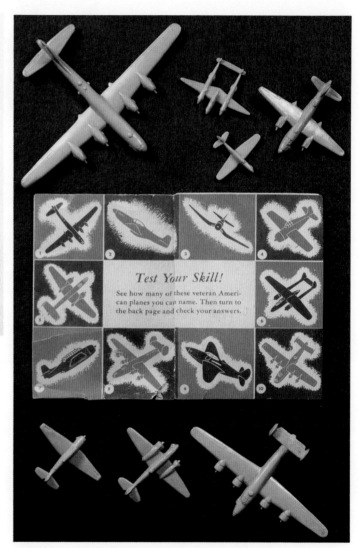

Test Your Skill!
See how many of these veteran American planes you can name. Then turn to the back page and check your answers.

This page
Capitalizing on the public's interest in the war, Kellogg's featured activities such as these on their products during WWII. Cereal manufacturers continue to use puzzles, mazes and other games on the back of the box as a ploy to entice consumers to purchase their cereal.

The "Kix Airbase," like many premiums, had a "bounce back" feature that enticed children to send away for yet another prize.

Left
Kellogg's featured the "Wings over America" series during the mid to late thirties. Collectors of box tops, the latest collectible craze, try to complete airplane series such as this and will pay top dollar for scarce items.

Left
Other examples of box cutout items. Today's cereal boxes have brought back this marketing device and feature TV cartoon characters.

Commercial Giveaways

IT SEEMED everywhere you turned during the war years—grocery store, drug store, gas station, magazine and newspaper stand—some merchandiser was giving away a patriotic item or something connected with the war. Laundries even printed soldiers on cardboard shirt inserts. These items numbered many thousands if matchbook covers, cigarette cards, Dixie Cup ice cream container covers, and the like are included.

Youngsters saved these items, traded them, and learned from them. Collections were kept in shoe boxes, bedroom bureau drawers and scrapbooks. Quite often, when one purchases odds and ends of this kind, it is obvious that the seller has pried it loose from a scrapbook found in an attic trove.

War stamp books were very popular with kids, many of whom already collected regular postage stamps. Outfits such as Disney designed the books for commercial companies that then marketed the books locally simply by imprinting, in the space provided, the name or logo of the company with which the giveaway was to be identified. A good example is the large paper album entitled "Combat Insignia Stamps of the United States Army & Navy Air Corps." Produced in 1942, this sixteen-page delight was designed to hold fifty colorful, gummed stamps of Disney-designed aircraft insignia. The series was produced for and copyrighted by Hearst Publications, the largest newspaper chain of the time. A kid received the album and the initial and succeeding weeks set of two to four stamps by clipping a coupon out of the paper and then taking it to a grocery store printed on the back of the coupon. Recently an album was auctioned at Hake's; it had been distributed by the Detroit Times.

The Los Angeles Times designed its own stamp album in 1942. "The Spirit of '42" stamp album had a place where the kid could insert his own name and address as an indicia of ownership. The booklet was crammed with information on army insignia, medals, and units. The marvelous stamps combined a unit insignia with an exciting action scene.

McLaurin-James Company of New York, a major defense contractor, issued a series of three very high quality insignia stamp booklets containing seventy-two stamps with Navy aircraft and ship insignia. They were issued free at the plants but cost twenty-five cents to obtain by mail. Going the Los Angeles Times one better, McLaurin-James advised the collector: "To guard against the loss of this valuable collection, we suggest you write your name and address in the space below." Since, fifty years later they are worth fifty dollars, maybe that wasn't such a bad idea!

Richland Gasoline Company issued a stamp album solely of airplanes in 1941. Hart, Schafner & Marx, the national men's clothing manufacturer, published a twenty-page "War Birds of the USA" album for use by local clothiers. In this case, the planes, laid out in sheets in a card format, were cut out and pasted in the album.

A fine example of a specially produced stamp album is "Our Navy," an outstanding series of art work done for a New York area bakery chain called Krugs. This large pamphlet is of the highest quality and obviously was expensive to produce. The company commissioned well-known marine artist Fred J. Hoertz to paint a series of thirty-six pictures of naval vessels. Some of the best military art ever, one appeared each week in the company's bulletin and then, as a stamp for the album. One wonders where it and Krugs—the patriotic bakery that urged its patrons, some fifty years ago, not to forget to order fruit cakes for American troops in Australia—are now.

General, informative, military booklets were passed out routinely by various retailers. Grocery, drug, and five-and-dimestores, and gas stations were typical outlets. Some booklets for the larger chains were prepared and imprinted specially. Others were wholesaled so that the local retailer could insert his store's name and address in the proper place.

J.C. Penney's full-color "Our Army and Navy" booklet is an excellent example of the former. Illustrated in comic

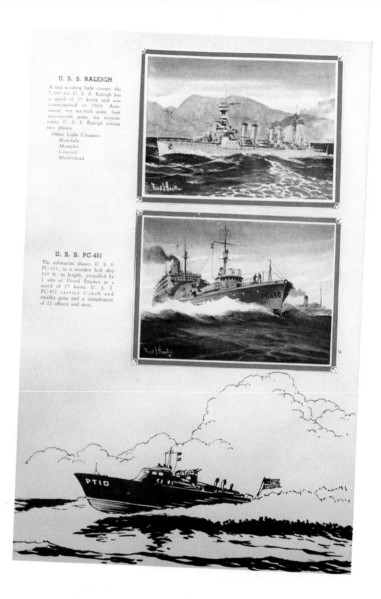

book style by Tom Hickey, it was highly accurate and contained fifty pages of just about everything a child needed to know about the armed forces. Unusual is its five-page section on the Medical Corps that included a page on flying ambulances, a very new development at the time. The text indicated that "girls" (nurses) could even rise to the rank of major and "are allowed to play . . . but . . . must not associate with anyone less than a Lieutenant." One rare-

ly sees so much contained so well in such a small package. The watercolor drawings are so good, they would make charming backgrounds for a collection of antique U.S. soldiers. Mr. J.C. Penney himself signed a message to the boys and girls of America, telling them that if their families wanted to economize in wartime, the place to shop was Penney's. A sales pitch was little enough to pay for such a neat handout.

This page
Both large and small companies distributed war stamp books to their customers. Often the colorful stamps of squadron insignia, battle scenes, aircraft and the like were pasted in and around an informative text.

An unmarked pamphlet, "Onward to Victory," is also illustrative. Printed on very cheap paper and in only three colors, it nevertheless has very good comic book style drawings.

Oil and gasoline companies often passed out illustrated booklets on insignia, rank and medal/ribbons right at the pump after the car owner had filled up. As more and more men and women entered the forces, everyone wanted to be able to identify the hundreds of mystifying patches that their family, friends and neighbors now wore, and the public couldn't get enough of these small, two-by-four-inch booklets. The photographs illustrate typical items produced by Shell Oil Company and Hammond Publishing, a printer of wartime maps and world atlas books.

A much sought after wartime paper collectible by collectors of Planters Peanuts' memorabilia (a big-bucks hobby specialty) is Planters' "Our Fighting Forces" book. Produced for Planters by Rand McNally, in addition to the usual pictures of weapons, uniforms, war scenes, maps and the like, the first page had three blank tabulations called "Watch those Axis Losses Grow" with which the reader was encouraged to keep his own record of enemy "men killed or captured [as] retribution comes to Germany and Japan." By today's standards that hyperbole would be considered a little blood thirsty, but in 1943 it didn't raise an eyebrow and thousands of people probably did keep score. This booklet is as sought after as Coke's "Spotter" booklet.

BLOTTERS

Next to matchbook covers, probably the easiest obtainable point-of-sale freebies were blotters. Everybody used them. They were cheap and light and easy to stamp with a local retailer's name. They also fit very well in food packages such as bakery goods. Illustrated here are several typical examples. The insignia and arms and aircraft blotters shown are early wartime vintage and were produced by the same company for local retailers who imprinted their company name in the red-lined box provided.

Wampole's Creo-Terpin Syrup for coughs and colds and its companion "tonic and stimulant for all ages in all seasons" urged users to "keep fit and win the war." It's not known how effective these tonics were, but the blotters were very accurate and are collected enthusiastically by military and medal enthusiasts. Note also the marvelous Air Force blotter sponsored by the Sanitary Family Laundry of York, Pennsylvania. Among blotter collectors (don't laugh—there are a lot of them), the Bond Bread aircraft series is a highly sought after group as it falls into two categories of collectibles, aviation as well as blotters, and as it is an identifiable series.

Other popular commercial giveaways included dial devices showing insignia, warships, and planes. These often were sponsored by bread companies. Marvels cigarettes passed out a paper billfold so you wouldn't lose your ration card.

Gum cards and cigarette cards, a distinct category of collectibles, will receive only a passing reference here. Gum card sets issued right before Pearl Harbor included "Don't Let it Happen Here" and "Defending America." Later card sets included "The Second World War," "Army, Navy and Air Corps," "Generals and Their Flags," "Heroes of the Sea," and a terrific set of battle paintings entitled "America

All types of cards made popular giveaway items. Coke's playing cards and bridge score pads featured an attractive female spotter, an image reproduced in 1991 along with a WWII Coke bottle. © THE COCA-COLA COMPANY

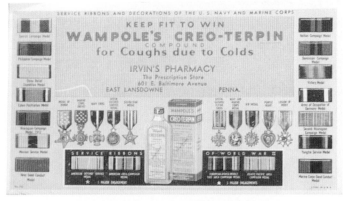

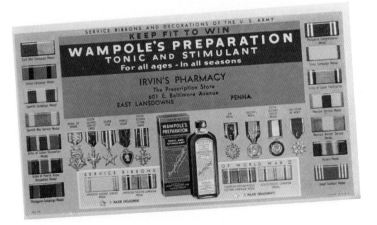

Attacks." Each card had a small Minuteman Buy War Bonds and Stamps logo in the upper right-hand corner. Illustrated cigarette cards, while not nearly as popular in the U.S. as they were in England, were another scrapbook war years collectible.

Cracker Jack had been putting small prizes in its colorful boxes since around 1890. It, too, ran afoul of the wartime metal ban. Cracker Jack's wartime paper card prizes, however, had some of the better illustrations. Scenes show-

ing heroes such as winners of the Victoria Cross, England's highest decoration for valor, and airplane spotter cards, were produced. There were twenty-four Cracker Jack airplane cards. If a child couldn't get all twenty-four out of the box, Cracker Jack offered to send the entire series for only three box wrappers and a nickel.

Dixie Cups, an ice cream confection that sold in a small paper cup for a nickel, switched to military picture lids during the war. While sought after by many paper ephemera collectors, they are not nearly as popular as the lids featuring photos of movie stars and sports heroes that dominated their offerings in the thirties. In any event, like all these freebies, they, too, went into many a scrapbook or desk drawer.

This page
A grouping of commercial giveaway and radio premiums. The Planter's Peanuts booklet is highly sought after by collectors of products of that popular snack.

Below
These identical aircraft paintings show up on cigarette cards and Cracker Jack's prizes, as well as on the pages of books and on posters.

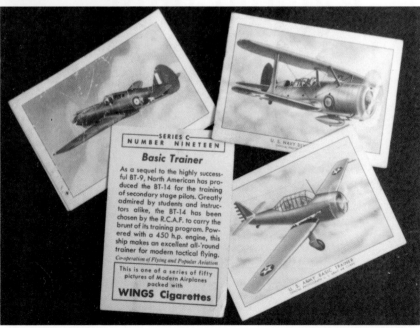

TOYS & PROPAGANDA

This large, remarkable coin-operated toy was made for retail stores; it took just one penny to "poison" Hitler! Now in Ken Fleck's outstanding collection of WWII propaganda collectibles, it is quite rare and worth well over $2,000.

COURTESY OF KEN FLECK

FOR THE DURATION of World War II, Americans truly hated their enemies. Abiding prejudice toward Japan and dread of the "yellow peril" had built up strongly during the 1930s as the "Horrors of War" gum cards gave witness. The hatred built somewhat slower toward Germany, but air attacks on popular England beginning in 1939 strengthened negative feelings toward Hitler's Germany.

The attack on Pearl Harbor fanned the simmering embers into flames. Japan had made a big mistake in attacking the United States, but to make it a surprise attack compounded the error many fold. The previous journalistic shadow of the Japanese as a scheming, devious and slant-eyed people was now fully justified in most people's minds. Even the responsible national media confirmed this negative stereotype. A national magazine that had prided itself on its long-standing liberal approach to Asian affairs now ran an article on "How to Tell Your [Chinese] Friends From the Japs." The Japanese, Americans were told, were heavier, thicker in torso, dogmatic, and arrogant. A sister publication ran large photographs of average Chinese and Japanese males accompanied by a recitation of their racial makeup and differences. Adjectives used to describe the Japanese male included squat, flat-headed, pig-eyed, yellow-skinned, and heavy bearded.

This hatred continued throughout the war. Two years after Pearl Harbor a Gallop poll was released that indicated that sixty-seven percent of Americans felt that they could get along much better with Germany than Japan after the war. Citizens applied the following adjectives to "the Japs": barbaric, evil, brutal, dirty, treacherous, sneaky, fanatical, savage, inhuman, bestial, uncivilized, un-Christian, and thoroughly untrustworthy. Other terms, added the pollster, were unprintable.

President Roosevelt's administration took the official position that the war had no racial aspects, but this stance did not prevent the War Production Board from approving

Adhesive patriotic stickers were immensely popular. They usually sold for a penny and adorned bikes, wagons, school bags and bedroom mirrors.

an early wartime advertisement that called for "extermination of the Japanese rats." The relocation of loyal Japanese-Americans from the West Coast to the concentration camps in the interior U.S., easily the most infamous violation of civil rights in the country's history, is well known. Furthermore, hostility toward the Japanese was reinforced continually by government released reports of Japanese cruelty during the Philippine campaign, the infamous Bataan death march, and like incidents. Less public was the national animosity toward all things Japanese generated by the surprise attack of December 7. Two days later, on December 9, 1941, the strong feelings were exemplified by an unknown culprit who chopped down a number of the Japanese cherry trees at the Washington Tidal Basin; the trees had been given in an earlier gesture of Sino-American friendship.

The vitriol against American-born Japanese was not restricted to the uneducated. "Japs live like rats, breed like rats, and act like rats," said Idaho's Governor Clark. Restaurants hung signs in their windows that read, "This restaurant poisons both rats and Japs," and barbershops advertised "Japs shaved; not responsible for accidents!"

Toys, books, and comics passed along this message to America's young people. One of the earliest and perhaps most propagandistic of such items was a booklet produced by Action Playbooks Inc. of New York City in 1942. This colorful, twenty-page, pop-up booklet was entitled "American in Action on Land, at Sea, in the Air—the Patriotic Action Play Book." If a collector wanted to obtain one piece illustrative of the mood of the times, this would be it. Some fourteen by ten inches and made of heavy cardboard, it's crammed with patriotic, jingoistic material. This was stuff to make every American kid's red blood boil with martial fever. Right off the bat, on the first page, one reads of the exploits of ace war correspondent Casey Roberts. In commenting on the Pearl Harbor attack, the fictional Casey tells readers that only last week he had interviewed the "grinning and slant-eyed traitor" who assured him that Japan sought only peace. More than a little historical license was taken when General MacArthur's gallant defenders allegedly repelled an attack in Subic Bay in the Philippines by "barges of slant-eyed little yellow men who were sucked screaming into the waters."

An ad in *Playthings* in July 1942, said the playbook "was crammed with exciting surprises" and contained numerous playthings and "many educational features." A modern reader may have some misgivings about the latter claim, particularly when intrepid reporter Casey Roberts states that after sinking an enemy convoy, the PT boat crews "lit-

The intensity of the American public's negative feelings toward Japan was reflected in commercial advertising as well as government printed materials.

This graphic bubblegum card is about the size of a playing card. It was one of a series of hundreds produced by Gum Inc.

up [their] cigarettes . . . puffs came like sighs of relief"! In any case, for one dollar a child acquired pilot wings, and was able to aim paper machine gunsights, collect postage stamps (a packet was included), build a paper B-17, use a code dial for secret messages, memorize airplane ID charts, study colorful insignia charts, and learn about world maps, Navy navigation and time zone differences.

Comic strips in particular contributed to the view of the Asian enemy as a barbaric subhuman species, all tooth and spectacles, and, contrary to facts in the first year or so of the war, no match for our heroic, gallant American boys. An examination of the early wartime comic books paint a marvelous picture of the images imposed on the minds of those under fifteen. Reflecting extreme fantasies that could not find their way into commercial ads or government-printed posters, the cover art of comics between 1940 and 1945 is actually the cultural propaganda pop art of the time.

The comic superhero was supreme. Historians speculate

that the rise of the superhero a few years prior to America's entry into World War II was a reaction to America's failure to deal directly with increasingly hostile fascism threats. In other words, if the country wasn't going to battle evil directly, the country could at least fight evil with fantasy. Hence, as the threat of evil multiplied throughout the world, the number of fictional heroes fighting it grew exponentially. Prior to Pearl Harbor publishers were leery of offending and, thus, though enemy weapons, helmets, planes, insignia, language, and even skin color looked awfully familiar, none of the foes are identified. With but a few superhero exceptions such as the "Human Torch" and "Sub Mariner," the terms "Nazi" or "Jap" were not used in the prewar era no matter how horrific the comic story line. After the sneak attack on December 7, however, all bets were off. Virtually every comic book and publisher portrayed and identified the evil Japs.

What fantastic names the fictional superheroes had! Names such as the American Avenger, Anchors Away, Bittlebattle, Blackhawk, Blue Beetle, Blade, Blaze, Bolt, Circle, Diamond, Eagle Crusader, Flame, Fire, Spyfight, and Streak were commonplace. Boy champions, commandos, heroes and over three dozen different captains used the names Courage, Midnight, Power, Redblazer, Triumph, Truth, Valor, Victory, Wings, Yank, Commando Cubs, Ranger and Yank, Human Bomb, Magnet, Nuclear, Top and Torch, Liberty Bell, Guards and Scouts, Mr. America, Atom, Hazard, Justice and Liberty, Skyfighter, Victory Boys, War Aces, and Birds and Nurses. There were ten different kinds of Yanks including the ever popular Doodle. The color red, however, seems to hold the all time record. A published list of characters shows forty-four "reds" including "Red Torpedo" and a can't miss character named "Red, White and Blue."

The evil enemies had equally evil names. How about Captain Nazi, Nippon or Swastika? There was the infamous Drs. Foo, Fu Manchu, Fury, Nemesis, and Pain. And the name of Jap Devil Dragon should get some kind

of prize. The Claw, Iron Jaw, and Iron Skull were probably the most famous, long lasting and evil-looking demonic wartime comic adversaries.

Comic covers gave a good idea of how many children viewed the enemy during World War II, and plots were every bit as wild. Clearly, as bad as the Germans were portrayed, the Japanese got the worst of the deal. Reflecting the overall national mood, this genre was a small but important form of national culture during the 1942–43 period. An interesting tabular study of the market percentage of the various types of comics during the "golden age" (superheroes, adventures and jungles, science fiction, etc.) has been done.

Comics embraced the defense
effort wholeheartedly, not to
mention that entire lines such
as "For Defense of Democracy"
and "Our Flag" were created in
response to the surge of
patriotism. Note, too, the
names of the characters: Miss
Victory, Red Cross, "Ace"
Reynolds and Captain Flight.

232

Superheroes went from thirty-three percent of the market share in 1919 to fifty-four percent in 1942, followed by a gradual decline in 1946 to twenty-eight percent as the war ended. Perhaps these results are an affirmation that everyone, including kids, finally gets sick of killing and war.

While caricatures of the enemy didn't overwhelm toys, they appeared often enough to demonstrate the prevailing approach of the children's print media. David Rapaport, for example, used a clever play on words to market his line of punch-out military toy sets. His "Rap-A-Jap" box covers featured a sketch of a G.I. socking a "Jap" in the jaw with his rifle butt. Though not particularly well done, these covers certainly conveyed the message. Electric Corporation of America (ECA) went so far as to modify the envelope of its inexpensive punch-out toy, "Make Your Own Invasion Battle Set." The new envelope's caricatures of Hitler (rat-like), Tojo (exaggerated buck teeth and slant eyes), and Mussolini (fat, frowning and heavy bearded) were found on hundreds of wartime items ranging from salt and pepper shakers to pin cushions and pocket puzzles. Otherwise, the contents were identical.

One of the most extreme depictions of the Japanese was the "Set the Son [of a bitch]" dart board produced in 1943. The advertisements in the trade press were even more ex-

233

plicit than the name. "All of us would really like to fire a round at the yellow 'Sons of Heaven.' Here's a game that gives . . . the same satisfying pleasure our boys in the Pacific feel each time they score!"

Dart boards, according to Hollywood, also appealed to the Germans. In the movie *They Came to Blow Up America*, the Gestapo chief brutally interrogates George Sanders' girlfriend while throwing darts into a target bearing a bulldog likeness of Winston Churchill!

The first place trophy for the most expressive anti-Axis game, however, must go to Carrom Games' "Hang the Tyrants" target set. Similar to a bowling alley game, a player rolled his marble up onto a board in an attempt to hit "enemy key objectives." One received the highest score for rolling his marble into a "tyrant rat hole" and hanging a spring-held Hitler, Mussolini or Tojo. An ad in *Playthings* said that the game afforded the public a safe "outlet for their pent up emotions" and helped to "promote grim determination to send the Axis tyrants spinning to destruction

This clever insert in the *Philadelphia Inquirer*'s Sunday Supplement was meant to be mounted on a piece of corkboard and used as a dart board.
COURTESY OF KEN FLECK

SET THE SUN – – —!

Above
Billed as the perfect way to let off steam, dart boards were a natural for propaganda pieces.
COURTESY OF KEN FLECK

Right
Even kid's stationery used a propaganda appeal. This is typical of anti-axis "comic" writing paper of the period.

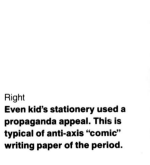

235

236

Depictions of Hitler, Mussolini and Hirohito such as are featured on this item became commonplace.

Far left, left
The standard party game, "Pin the Tail on the Donkey," was modified several times to fit public sentiments.
COURTESY OF KEN FLECK

237

Hang It On His Nose

Hang It On His Nose

Above
A Mussolini "Hang it on its Nose" piece completes this set.

on their own axis." "Everybody wants to HANG THE TYRANTS," Carrom assured toy store owners. The game's five-dollar price tag was very high for the times.

Colorgraphic's Young Patriots "Smashed the Axis" target set featured an almost identical Axis trio. The tip-over target was the highlight of this boxed set that included a heavy cardboard, punch-out cannon that fired a wooden dowel projectile. Also illustrated here is the cardboard toss-toy, "Hang It On His Nose." This toy enabled one to "bomb" Hitler and Hirohito.

Novelty toys and items that held the Axis leaders up to ridicule were very popular throughout the war with both youngsters and adults and graced many a bedroom dresser. Johnson Smith & Co., a Detroit novelty retailer, specialized in such items. Its mammoth catalogs sold for a quarter and were a kid's delight. For many years these catalogs were famous for their gag jokes and magic tricks: rubber snakes for a dime, the amazing Siberian chain escape trick, and hand held windup "shakers." In wartime they were full of stereotypical anti-Axis pieces. The "Hitler-the-Squealing-Pig Bank," for example, sold for fifty-nine cents. The fat, yellow pig had the face of Hitler, "the biggest pig of all,"

Right
This fall-over target is from the rare Colorgraphic Smash the Axis set.

238

Above
**Johnson Smith's motto was "We're in Business for Fun."
Hard-bound versions also were available for slightly
more. They are next to impossible to locate now.**

Above
**The Hitler pig bank reportedly
held enough coins to purchase
a war bond. With box, it is
among the rarest of
propaganda collectibles.**
COURTESY OF KEN FLECK

239

and was engraved with a Save for Victory slogan. "Holds enough to buy a war bond!" said the ad copy.

"The Hitler Pin Cushion," still very popular at collectible shows, gave one a chance (for sixty-nine cents) to stick a pin in Hitler's behind. President Roosevelt was said to keep one on his desk. A companion pin cushion featured a two-faced rat (Hirohito and Hitler). Another expensive knickknack featured "Hitler the Skunk—Der Phew-rer" ("shows Hitler as he really is!"); it retailed at eighty-nine cents. Finally, for a nickel one could "show your patriotism" and "razz the Axis" by wearing the large button emblazoned "Eliminate These Three Rats." The button had caricatures of "Musso," Hitler and Tojo. This button is very rare today and highly sought after by period and historic button collectors.

Hollywood, with the active assistance of the Office of War Information (OWI), the agency that approved all films, helped to perpetuate this portrait of the enemy. In an attempt by Hollywood to turn early defeats into moral victories, the plots of most action films made during the war were based in the Pacific. Japanese troops were portrayed as savage, uncivilized beasts that tortured and killed civilians and women and violated all the precepts of civilized warfare. The grinning Japanese interrogator in the film *Purple Heart* is a prime example; he tortures and ultimately beheads downed American flyers. American forces, on the other hand, were portrayed as multi-ethnic squads or platoons that were courageous and martyrs to the cause.

Above
Retailing for eighty-nine cents, this was not an inexpensive knickknack!

These are typical examples of poster and song sheet caricatures of "the enemy."

Some of the best films of the Pacific theatre still make terrific viewing, films such as *Wake Island, Guadalcanal Diary, Bataan, Cry Havoc, Gung Ho, Salute To The Marines,* and *30 Seconds Over Tokyo.* When John Wayne told us in *Fighting Seabees* that we were "fighting Tojo and his bugged-eyed pals," he summed up the attitude of his young fans. Observed his sidekick, "We're not fighting men anymore, we're fighting animals." Some critics and observers have called these films "animated recruitment posters [with] contrived heroics." Maybe they were, but kids loved every one of them.

These films may not inspire some of present-day "embarrassed" critics, but they sure inspired children back then.

The "Blast the Axis" target is from an unidentified game, and one wonders why Mussolini has the "X" when the other two were despised much more. "Put Hitler in the Dog House" is a simple, hand-held puzzle that sold for ten cents. Most popular was the Hitler pin cushion; President Roosevelt was said to keep one on his desk.

Sadistic torture scenes, particularly involving women, were commonplace in the Grade B flicks.

Several hundred such buttons were sold or given away. They make an attractive collection that can be displayed easily and takes up little room, two important considerations for collectors.

The Marine recruiting office knew their value; when a popular film about Marines was shown in a big city, the Corps set up a special recruiting office within a few blocks of the theatre. The films clearly inspired enlistments: *Guadalcanal Diary* was said to have inspired twelve thousand Marine enlistments. The Navy, too, made out. After seeing a terrific Naval war film, boys from the farmland who never had seen the ocean, signed up in droves. Children couldn't enlist but these films affected their play and, while no statistics are available, the local toy and department stores most likely had a run on war toys after each new war film opened!

Films about the early war in Europe, produced before American troop involvement, tended to be more inspirational in nature. Although it didn't really appeal to youngsters, the Academy Award winning *Mrs. Minniver* was typical. The propaganda features were still there—in the final scene the pastor preaches in a bombed out, roofless church and the congregation sings "Onward Christian Soldiers" as British planes fly past on their way to fire bomb German cities.

241

9

TOYS OF
FRIEND & FOE

An example of the outstanding
German children's board
games of the period, this
boxtop shows "walking out"
uniforms of the three armed
forces. The similarity of layout,
box art and method of play
of Allied and enemy games
is striking.

As in America, the use of metal for nonstrategic purposes was banned or severely restricted in Allied and belligerent countries during the war. Paper toys, particularly soldiers, however, originated in and had a long history in Europe. Thus it is not at all unusual to find many of the same kinds of wartime soldiers, punchout and cut-out items, games and books as in the U.S.

Paper cut-out soldiers, popular in continental European countries, were printed on large sheets. These colorful cut-out figures also included military encampments, battles and parades.

France in particular had a long-standing love affair with the paper soldier. The first commercially produced paper soldiers originated in France in the late eighteenth century. Following the French Revolution, the firm of Pellerin of Epinal and other similar firms produced a series of sheets depicting the various troops of the First Empire under Napoleon. Hundreds of thousands of sheets detailing an enormous variety of military subjects were produced right up to and during World War II. Also produced in sheet form were "Grande Construction" paper sheets that required folding to make a toy such as a soldier or a rocking horse. Nearby continental countries such as Belgium, Denmark, Spain and Italy produced similar paper toys.

Germany's sheets of cut-out paper soldiers had long been among the best and since the rise of militarism under Hitler from 1934 onward, the military offerings became better and better.

The several hundred different sheets by these famous printers covered all aspects of the German armed forces and the Nazi regime's "political" arms such as the SA and SS. While quite difficult to find in good condition, they are not particularly popular among modern German military collectors, except as an occasional framed wall hanging.

In Germany, and in many other Europen countries where the paper soldier was king, it was quite common to cut out the figures and to mount them on some form of sturdy backing, inserted in a slotted wooden base. Thus, these soldiers often turn up today mounted in such a way. Many were obviously first glued on a thin piece of wood and then cut out with a jigsaw or some other tool.

In addition to sheet soldiers, many German companies produced excellent embossed, heavy cardboard figures in various scenes, in addition to military parade types. Often they showed both sides of the figure. Coming in various sizes, they not only were in action but in "behind the line" camp scenes carrying firewood, ladling out food, etc.

Many wartime paper soldier sheets were rapidly produced as countries were liberated following D-Day, particularly in France, Belgium and Denmark. Paper sheets published anywhere *during* the German occupation are quite rare.

While not generally produced in Germany, punchout booklets were quite popular in British and Commonwealth nations. My collection includes items from England, Canada, Australia and New Zealand. Canadian products included a 25-inch "Commando Machine Gun" made of heavy stock cardboard, and three punchout booklets of wartime soldiers and a foot-long battleship. A mint cache of these recently surfaced and promptly found its way to ephemera shows.

Early on, Hitler Youth were compared to English-speaking nations' Boy and Girl Scouts. This changed as war approached. Military model making in Germany was so popular, a postage stamp was issued to promote it.

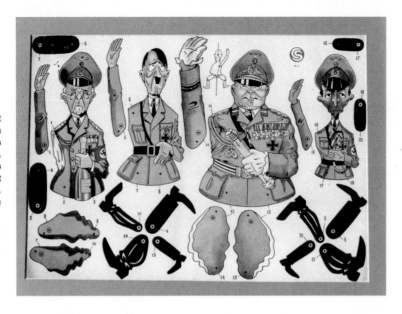

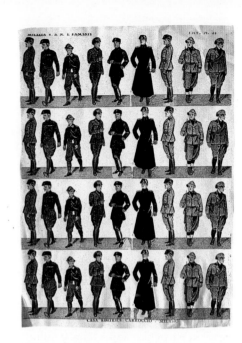

A highly unusual Canadian punchout toy was the boxed "Ach-Ach-Down a Nazi Dive Bomber." It made into a fourteen-inch-high tower in which a salt-fed chute fed a series of rotating enemy planes that one could shoot at with metal pellets. Each player could shoot as long as the salt-fed hopper rotated the targets. This amazing and intricate toy took a few hours to assemble and has to be quite rare today.

Australia sold a heavy cardboard large pamphlet "Spitfire and Bomber Squadron" by ACE Products, including Bren AA Carriers, ambulance, searchlights and a whole page of sandbags.

Dean and Son of England published a colorful "Victory" fourteen-by-thirteen-inch cutout book shortly after V-E Day. Five pages of marching troops—Empire and Allies—a Crusader tank towing a field piece and a scenic parade passing a background of Westminster Abbey and "Big Ben" were included.

Games, we can assume, were just as popular with the young people of our enemies and allies as they were in the States and probably for the same wartime gas rationing, travel restriction, and propaganda reasons. Two examples from Canada are quite interesting. "Bomb the Axis" was by Capp Clark Co. Ltd. of Toronto. The cover, unfortu-

nately, promised far more than the contents. It was played like a reverse type bingo. The massive Canadian bilingual "War Game" ("Jen de Guerre") by Playthings Company had a game board two feet by three feet. In a most unusual marketing device, the box art was identical to the board, a feature not seen in any other wartime game.

In Sydney, Australia, MetalWood Repetitions Co. made a cue-stick target game called "Navy Bobs," where in a clever use of non-strategic glass, wood and cardboard material "hits" were scored on printed ships. The company also made other wartime games such as "Target for Tonight," "Tactics" and "Bomb 'Em." An unidentified English toy maker produced an "exploding target" toy board game entitled "River Plate: The Greatest Naval Game Ever Known." The game was based on one of the first British naval victories of World War II, one sorely needed for morale purposes. In the game, hits made on the "exploding" ship were measured on a game board. First player to score 100 was the victor.

German children had a huge range of highly attractive and creative games to choose from in the mid to late thirties and during the war years. Some, among the rarest were tied to Hitler Youth activities, as were many other wartime cut-out toys and books. Games titles included "Tanks

My A.B.C. of the Royal Air Force and *My A.B.C. of the Navy.*

In the fictional line, the British equivalent of Dave Dawson and Lucky Terrell was the "Biggles" series. Other popular wartime heroes were "Gimlet of the Commandos" and the first girls wartime fictional heroine, Flight Officer Joan Worrelson of the WAAFS ("WORRAHS"). Red Fox Publishing is reissuing a series of Biggles reprints today and a major film and audio cassette have been made.

Germany's publishing industry produced a number of books and pamphlets tied directly to membership in the Hitler Youth, which had a number of components for both boys and girls. Service in the Hitler Youth was compulsory for boys, ages fifteen to eighteen.

Weekly and monthly picture booklets specifically targeted for German youth with excellent full-color covers and line drawings were published containing tales of German military greatness and exhortation for clean living and service to the Fatherland. Fictional hardback novels were quite

A rare Elastolin "picture" box for a tinplate motorcycle toy.
Very few have survived.

Forward," "Without a Propeller," "Bombs Over England," and "We Sail Against England—The New Game of Our U-Boat Service." Like their Allied counterparts these games showed the armed forces in victorious combat with the enemy (e.g. "Heinkel 111 bombers attacking London Bridge). The approach was quite similar between German and U.S. kids' games—only the targets and planes were different.

Wartime children's books and puzzles of Allied and some enemy nations seemed to follow the American pattern. "Boys Own Paper," a six-pence British boys' magazine that had been around for generations, published wonderful wartime editions which encouraged patriotism. Stories of the Battle of Britain and the Dunkirk evacuation permeated its pages. Cover art work was every bit as good as the American books of the period. Pictorial alphabet books are found in some terrific British series, including

British alphabet picture books are a century old. Those featuring famous artists, such as Harry Payne, are now quite expensive.
COURTESY MERV BLOCH

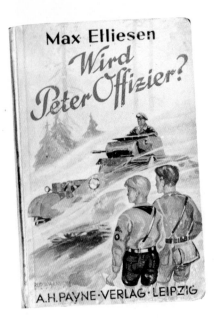

popular. One, *Wird Peter Offizier?,* described the rise of an intrepid HJ member to acceptance in the much-admired Panzer Tank Corps.

As in Allied countries, cigarette cards depicting military heroics, uniforms and heroes were avidly collected by German youth. Cigarette card collecting had a long history in Germany as in England. The cards were mounted in large very attractive, often embossed, cover books that could be purchased at low prices at the tobacco shop or obtained free for a certain number of cigarette boxes.

Some of the best included "German Armed Forces" (Die Reichsweer)—280 cards, watercolor, and the German Army on Maneuver—250 cards, watercolor. Many of the German toy and toy soldier makers based their figures and toys directly on scenes depicted in these cards.

Cigarette card books sell in the sixty to two hundred dollar range. Those featuring aircraft and Zeppelins are the most costly.

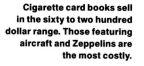

ENEMY WARTIME TOYS

This page

The German toy industry was the best in the world and the annual Nürnberg Toy Fair still is the mecca of toy buyers. Tinplate toys were far more authentic than those made in any other country; this was particularly true of the military items. Many were meticulously based on photographs of the real thing. Today they are considered the cream of the crop, selling in the thousands of dollars, an exceptionally high price range for toys made in the thirties and forties. While colorful, authentic and somewhat rare, intact sheets of wartime paper soldiers are, for some reason, not highly sought after.

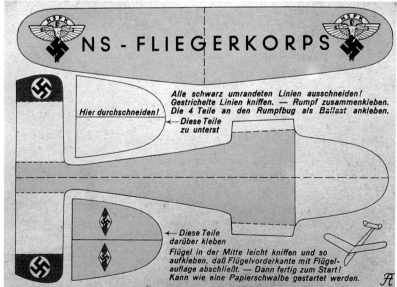

NS - FLIEGERKORPS

Hier durchschneiden!

Alle schwarz umrandeten Linien ausschneiden!
Gestrichelte Linien kniffen. — Rumpf zusammenkleben.
Die 4 Teile an den Rumpfbug als Ballast ankleben.

← Diese Teile
zu unterst

← Diese Teile
darüber kleben

Flügel in der Mitte leicht kniffen und so
aufkleben, daß Flügelvorderkante mit Flügel-
auflage abschließt. — Dann fertig zum Start!
Kann wie eine Papierschwalbe gestartet werden.

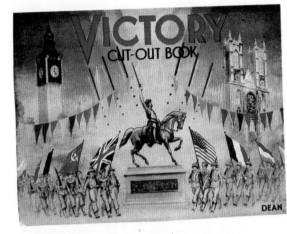

LE MARÉCHAL CHEF DE L'ÉTAT FRANÇAIS A LYON
PASSANT DEVANT LES TROUPES PLACE BELLECOURT

ALLIED NATIONS' TOYS AND GAMES

VICTORY CUT-OUT BOOK

DEAN

MODEL BATTLESHIP
12 INCHES LONG — READY TO SET-UP

TOY SOLDIERS
19 SOLDIERS — READY TO SET UP

ANNE & PAUL DRESS UP DOLLS

This and facing page **Cut-out sheets of paper war-time soldiers are also available from Spain, Finland and Belgium. Punch-out sets from Allied nations, as well as coloring books turn up occasionally, but perhaps because of paper-use restrictions appear to have been produced in far lesser numbers. Nor do any appear in the numerous volumes on toys of the 1930s–1950s that have been published in recent years.**

GIFTGAS

SEJREN

JEEP'EN

RIVER PLATE

The Greatest Naval Game ever known

THE GREAT NEW MECHANICAL NOVELTY & GAME

'ACK-ACK'

SPORT THRILLS FUN

SHOOT AT PLANES IN FLIGHT IT'S self-propelled

DOWN A NAZI DIVE-BOMBER

NO CUTTING · NO PASTING   READY TO PUT TOGETHER

· ANTI-AIRCRAFT IN ACTION ·

COMMANDO Machine Gun

REALISTIC! This full color cut-out makes up into a model over 25 in. long

A STURDY TOY...EASY TO MAKE

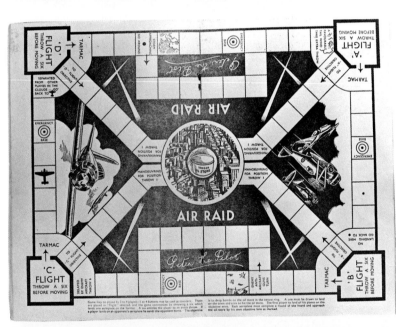

SPITFIRE AND BOMBER SQUADRON

CUT OUT · MODEL BUILDER · 6 SHEETS · NO GLUEING NECESSARY

NAVY BOBS

SINK THE ENEMY BY SHOT OR TORPEDO

A New GAME OF SKILL FOR TWO OR MORE PLAYERS PLAYED IN 2 DIFFERENT WAYS

BOMB THE AXIS!

THE COPP CLARK CO. LIMITED TORONTO   CANADA

GERMAN WORLD WAR II BOARD GAMES

This and facing page
**German boxed board games of
WWII are quite popular with
collectors of German-made
militaria and toys. They are still
reasonably available, usually at
auction and sell in the fifty to
three hundred dollar range.
Many games were based on
actual wartime events, e.g.
"Bomben über England."
So-called "target" games,
which were extremely popular
in the U.S., do not appear to
have been generally manu-
factured in Germany.**

Sprung auf, marsch marsch!

Propeller frei!

das fesselnde Luftkampfspiel

Das Eiserne Kreuz

Verlag von D. u. M. Hausser, Ludwigsburg

Wir fahren gegen Engeland

Ein neues Kriegsspiel von unserer U-Boot-Waffe

Hitlerjugend
Geländespiel

VERLAG von D. u. M. HAUSSER, LUDWIGSBURG

Klar zum Gefecht!
Das packende Flottenspiel

Der Siegeszug
unserer jungen Wehrmacht

251

VALUE GUIDE

T HE VALUE RANGES in this section are not intended to be definitive guides to the price one will or should pay for WWII military toy collectibles. They are intended to keep in perspective the prices of various items and categories and thereby to assist one who decides to build a collection. I have based prices on (1) fifteen years of searching for WWII toys at several hundred shows and flea markets; (2) perusal of thousands of pieces; (3) analysis of hundreds of price lists of miscellaneous toy dealers; (4) and participation at auctions. Prices for puzzles, books, games, and boxed punch-out sets tend to be more consistent than for other categories such as wooden toys where prices are all over the lot.

With respect to condition, unlike metal toy soldiers and other metal toys, few toys of WWII vintage show up unused or in mint condition. Toys were played with during the war and the materials are more fragile. The purist is going to be disappointed if he looks for nary a crease, crack, tear, dent or wrinkle in a paper, cardboard or wood toy. A collector's best bet for mint or excellent condition is in the paper doll and punch-out booklet categories. It is best to let your own display standards be your guide.

With respect to prices, particularly in the areas of miscellaneous paper and scrapbook items, understand that asking prices vary greatly. Recognize that there is a great deal of this type of ephemera and subcategories are a distinct approach. Two informal rules I use may be helpful in deciding whether to purchase an item. The first rule is, if it seems to be priced way too high, it probably is. The second rule, is Harry Rinker's. He says, "If you think it's 'neat' and you can afford it, get it!"

Description	Price Range
BOOKS	
FICTION	
Grosset & Dunlap, Air Combat Series for Boys (WWII reissue)	$10–15
Whitman, Big/Better Little Books	15–25
Whitman, Fighters for Freedom series	12–20
Whitman, large paper booklets	15
Miscellaneous, with jacket (Dave Dawson, Lucky Terrell, Red Randall, Yankee Flyer)	12–20
Miscellaneous, without jacket	6–12
NONFICTION	
1939–1942 small defense type, hard-bound	8–15
Whitman, Guide Books series, hard-cover	8–15
Whitman, Guide Books series, paperback	6–12
Picture books, large, 9½″×11½″ (Garden City Publishing, Grosset & Dunlap, MacMillan, Random House)	15–25
Comic-style books, paperback (U.S. Heroes series, War Heroes series, etc.)	20
COLORING BOOKS	
Medium size, untouched	10–20
Medium size, colored in	10
Large size, untouched, military subjects (Merrill, Saalfield)	25–35
Large size, colored in	15–25
Medium size, untouched, animals/children on cover	10
Medium size, colored in	5
Large size, untouched, animals/children	15–25
Large size, colored in	10
Paint/Crayon boxes, unused	15
Paint/Crayon boxes, used	10
GAMES	
BOARD, BOXED	
Large size, 14″×22″, major companies such as Corey, Lewis, Milton Bradley, Parker Brothers, Selchow & Righter	60–125
Medium size, 9″×12 to 10″×14″, smaller companies such as Advance, All-Fair, Gotham Sales, Lido, Lowe, Whitman, etc.	25–60
TARGET	
1939–1942 large metal games (Baldwin, Wolverine, Wyandotte)	100–250
Boxed, large ("Bombs Away," "Bomber Ball," etc.)	75–125
Boxed, small to medium ("Bomb-the-Navy," "Sink the Ship," etc.)	30–50

Bombing games utilizing dart boards ("Bombs
    Away," "Direct Hit," "Secret Bomb Site," etc.) $75–150
Dart boards, boxed   50–100
Stand-up, large, wood and cardboard ("Sky-
    Shoot," "Wings," "Sink the Invader," etc.)   100

OTHER
Bagatelle games, wood and cardboard, large, 30″×14″   50
Card games   10–20
Hand-held BB and marble games   15–30

MISCELLANEOUS HOME FRONT AND OTHER BOXED SETS
Air raid warden, various   75
Air recognition, various   50–75
Blackout   50
Doctor and nurse kit, Army   25–50
Map, geography   25–50
Paint set, framing or statuette   50
Uniform, children's   50–100
Victory Garden   75
WAAC set   50

MISCELLANEOUS WWII TOYS AND COLLECTIBLES
Banks, composition   50
Banks, papier-mâché   25–50
Banks, cardboard and wood   10–25
Periscopes, cardboard and wood   25
Pencil boxes   15–25
Scrapbooks   15–30
Statues, carnival   50–75

PUNCH-OUT
Booklet, medium size (Advance, Concord, Dell, Fawcett,
    Lowe, Pressman, Victory Toy, Whitman, etc.) $30–60
Rigby books, intact   50–75
Rigby, boxed set   75
Wyandotte, boxed sets, unpunched   60–80
Wyandotte "Air Squadron" boxed set   70–80
Individual vehicles, planes, or ships from punch-out
    sets, assembled   3–10
Individual soldiers or sailors from punch-out sets   .25–.50
Al-Nu cardboard soldiers   3–5

ENVELOPE
Small package, 9″×6″ (ECA, Lowe,
    National Handikraft, Reed)   25–40
Large package (Crestcraft, ECA, etc.)   40–75
"Cut, Paste & Stick" booklets   25–50

BUILT-RITE (Warren Paper)
Army hangar set   150
Fort sets, medium   100
Fort sets, large boxed, complete with soldiers   200
Individual vehicles   25–40
Soldiers, individual   .50–1.00

BILD-A-SET (Pachter)
Medium   40–50
Large   60–85

YOUNG PATRIOT (Colorgraphic)
Medium size, unpunched   40
Large size, unpunched   60–85
"Sculpturettes"   40

PAPER DOLLS
Lowe, regular size   60–100
Merrill, regular size   60–100
Saalfield, regular size   60–100
Whitman ("Our WAC Joan," etc.)   30–50
Smaller size ("United We Stand," etc.)   25–50
Magazine pages, uncut   5–10

PUZZLES
Hand-held puzzles, small   20
Map puzzles, large boxed   50
Young children's, large pieces   30–60
Older children/adult's, boxed
Multiple puzzles, boxed, 250–1,000 pieces
    Jaymar, Modern Fighters for Victory series   10–25
    J.S. Hart, America in Action series   10–25
    Perfect Picture Puzzles   10–25
    Saalfield   10–25
    TUCO   15–30
    Whitman   10–25

WOODEN TOYS
Pistols, Composition   10–15
Pistols, Wood   10–15
Pistols with Holster and Belt   25
Rifles, "Daisy Defender"   125
Rifles, "Yankee"   25
Rifles, miscellaneous   15–25
Tommy guns ("Krak-A-Jap," "Chattermatic,"
    "Yankee," "Victory")   50
Tommy guns, ratchet, miscellaneous   20–30
Tripod Machine Gun, "Rapid-Fire Auto-
    matic Gun"   40
Tripod Machine Gun, "Yank Raider"   100

ARMY VEHICLES AND PLANES (medium to large size)

Krak-A-Jap Cannon	$60
Krak-A-Jap Jeep	40
Krak-A-Jap Invasion Barge	35
Buddy L tanks and vehicles (large)	150–200
Noma Tank	30
Victory Tank	35
Aircraft (regular size)	25
Scandia and Mann-Riley ridable vehicles	150–200
Ships (small)	10–15
Trucks (small)	10–15

NAVY TOYS

Aircraft carriers and submarines, small	
Tillicum small boxed sets	50–60
Tillicum large boxed sets	75–125
Tillicum small individual pieces	5–10
Tillicum large individual pieces	15
Keystone boxed ships, large	75–100
Victory composition ships/tanks	50
Baldwin "Victory Carrier"	75

SOLDIERS

Beton plastic soldiers	5
Manoil composition soldiers	30–40
U.S. composition soldiers	10

MODEL KITS

Aircraft, small boxed, flying	varies
Aircraft, large boxed, flying	varies
Aircraft, large boxed, solid (Austin Craft, Rogers, Strombecker, etc.)	30
Vehicles, boxed, solid (Comet, E-Z Crafts, Strombecker, Testor)	15–30

FOREIGN MADE WWII TOYS AND COLLECTIBLES

Books and Booklets	10–40
Cigarette card books, German	75–250
Games, British and Canadian	35–75
Games, German	50–100
Games, German (Hausser)	100–400
Paper Soldiers, sheets, French, Italian, Danish	25–50
Paper Soldiers, sheets, German	50
Punch-out, Canadian, British and Australian	25–75

Toy Soldiers, composition, readily obtainable, German (Elastolin, Lineol)	15–75
Toy Soldiers, composition, Italian	15

PREMIUMS AND GIVEAWAYS

The price ranges listed below for radio premiums are *very* general estimates. Since WWII paper radio premiums are found so rarely at general shows and flea markets, persons interested in them are urged to consult Tom Tumbusch's outstanding *Tomart's Price Guide to Radio Premium and Cereal Box Collectibles.*

BOX TOP PREMIUMS

Kellogg's Pep "Fun at the Breakfast Table"	2–5
"Model War Planes"	10
"Wings of Victory"	2–5
"Wings over America"	2–5
"Kix Airbase"	100
Wheaties "Tru-Flite Fighter Models"	15

COMMERCIAL GIVEAWAYS

Blotters	1–10
Booklets	2–10
Gum/Cigarette Cards	varies
Stamp/Sticker booklets, complete	10
War maps	5

RADIO PREMIUMS

Captain Marvel	15–400
Captain Midnight	30–85
Hop Harrigan	10–80
Jack Armstrong	10–200
Lone Ranger	20–400
Radio Orphan Annie	50–175
Spy Smasher	20–50

PROPAGANDA TOYS

So-called propaganda toys featuring enemy caricatures are a highly specialized collectible and prices are often quite high for large games and toys found intact. Collectors are urged to subscribe to the excellent *Ted Hake's Americana Auction Catalogues* for information and price guides.

BIBLIOGRAPHY

Blum, John Morton. *V Was For Victory*. Harcourt, Brace, Jovanovich, 1976.

Casdorph, Paul D. *Let Good Times Roll*. Paragon House, 1989.

Cohen, Stan. *V for Victory—America's Home Front During WWII*. Pictorial Histories Publishing Company, Inc., 1991.

Dennis, Lee. *Warman's Antique American Games*. Warman Publishing Co., Inc., 1986.

Gifford, Denis. *Comics at War: A Look at the Children's Comics of WWII*. Hawk Books, Ltd., 1988.

———. *The International Book of Comics*. Hamlyn Publishing Group, Ltd., 1984.

Goulart, Ron. *Over 50 Years of American Comic Books*. Publications International, Ltd., 1991.

Goodstone, Tony. *The Pulps: Fifty Years of American Pop Culture*. Bonanza Books, 1970.

Green. *Britain at War*. Archive Publishing, 1989.

Hake, Theodore L. *Hake's Guide to Advertising Collectibles: 100 Years of Advertising from 100 Famous Companies*. Wallace-Homestead Book Company, 1992.

Harmon, Jim. *Jim Harmon's Nostalgia Catalogue*. J.P. Tarcher, Inc., 1973.

———. *Radio Mystery and Adventure and its Appearances in Film, Television and other Media*. McFarland & Company, 1992.

Jaramillo, Alex. *Crackerjack Prizes*. Abbeville Press, 1989.

Jones, Ken D. and Arthur F. McClure. *Hollywood At War: The American Motion Picture from World War II*. A.S. Barnes & Company, 1973.

Ketchum, Richard M. *The Borrowed Years—1938–1941: America on the Way to War*. Random House, 1989.

Kennett, Lee B. *For The Duration: The United States Goes to War*. Charles Scribner's Sons, 1985.

Koppes, Clayton R. and Gregory D. Black. *Hollywood Goes To War: How Politics, Profits, and Propaganda Shaped World War II Movies*. Free Press-MacMillan, 1987.

Lesser, Robert. *A Celebration of Comic Art and Memorabilia*. Hawthorn Books, Inc., 1975.

Lingeman, Richard R. *Don't You Know There's A War On: The American Home Front, 1941–1945*. Putnam, 1970.

McKernan, Michael. *All In: Australia During The Second World War*. Thomas Nelson, 1983.

Morella, Joe, Edward Z. Epstein, and John Griggs. *The Films of World War II*. Citadel Press, 1975.

O'Brien, Richard. *Collecting Toys: A Collector's Identification & Value Guide, Vol. 6*. Books Americana, 1993.

———. *The Story of American Toys from the Puritans to the Present*. Abbeville Publishing, 1990.

Perrett, Geoffrey. *Days of Sadness, Years of Triumph: The American People, 1939–1945*. Penguin Books, 1973.

Reynolds, Clark. *America at War: The Home Front*. Gallery Books, 1990.

Rogers, Donald I. *Since You Went Away*. Arlington House, 1973.

Satterfield, Archie. *Home Front: An Oral History of the War Years in America, 1941–45*. Playboy Press, 1981.

Terkel, Studs. *The Good War*. Pantheon Books, 1984.

The Home Front USA. Time-Life Books, 1977.

This Fabulous Century—The Forties. Time-Life Books, 1969.

Tumbusch, Tom. *Illustrated Radio Premium Catalog and Price Guide*. Tomart Publications, 1979–1991.

———. *Tomart's Price Guide to Radio Premium and Cereal Box Collectibles including Comic Character, Pulp Hero, TV, and other Premiums*. Tomart Publications, 1991.

We Pulled Together and Won. Reminiscences Books, 1993.

Weiss, Ken and Edwin Goodgold. *To Be Continued*. Bonanza Books, 1972.

Williams, Anne D. *Jigsaw Puzzles*. Wallace-Homestead Book Company, 1990.

APPENDIX

BOARD GAMES

	Manufacturer
Battle Checkers — Beat the Axis	Penman
Pursuit	Whitman Publishing
Blockade	Corey Game Co.
Ranger Commandos	Parker Brothers, Inc.
Sea Raiders	Parker Brothers, Inc.
Hornet Airplane Game	Samuel Lowe Inc.
Land & Sea War Game	Samuel Lowe Inc.
Sunk — The Navy Game	Parker Brothers, Inc.
Army Air Corps	Parker Brothers, Inc.
Ferry Command	Milton Bradley Co.
Sea Battle	Lido Toy Company
Frontline Jeep Patrol	Lido Toy Company
Ration Board	Jayline Mfg. Co.
Battaan	Milton Bradley Co.
The Battleship Game	Whitman Publishing
Bizerte Gertie	Milton Bradley Co.
Empires	Selchow & Righter Co.
Air Combat Trainer	Lewis Instructor
Pursuit	Game Makers, Inc.
Battlefield Game	Illinois Game & Toy Co.
Battle of the Tanks	Milton Bradley Co.
Fighting Marines	Milton Bradley Co.
Dave Dawson Victory Game	American Toy Works
Dave Dawson Pacific Battle Game	American Toy Works
Strategy — The Game of Armies	Corey Game Co.
Military Strategy — the Modern Game of War	GHQ, Inc.
Bomber Raid	All-Fair (E.E. Fairchild)
Air-raid Warden	Parker Brothers, Inc.
Let 'em Have It	Parker Brothers, Inc.
Our Fighting Rangers	Advance Games, Inc.
Blackout (2 Versions)	Milton Bradley Co.
Democracy Game	Toy Creations, Inc.
Victory Bomber	Whitman Publishing
Dive Bombers	Whitman Publishing
Bombers Attack	All-Fair
Flagship	C.H. Taylor
Conflict — Land-Sea-Air	Parker Brothers, Inc.
Dog-fight — an Aerial Combat Game	Parker Brothers, Inc.
Thumbs-up — the Great Victory Game	Parker Brothers, Inc.
GHQ — the Exciting Battle Game	All-Fair
H.V. Kaltenborn Game of Diplomacy	Trend Game Co.
Salute-Forces Recognition Game (2 Versions)	Selchow & Righter
Air Attack	Corey Game Co.
Victo-Victory Bingo	Spare-time Corp.
Attack	Van Wagenen & Co.
Pursuit	Van Wagenen & Co.
Defense	Van Wagenen & Co.
Spotting — the Warplane ID Game	Parker Brothers, Inc.
Tell-a-plane	B & M Mfg. Co.
Get in the Scrap	Milton Bradley Co.
Army Checkers	All-Fair
Great American Flag Game	Parker Brothers, Inc.
Radaronics	American Radar Corp.
Flag-stix	
Flags of Nations	
Cargo for Victory	All-Fair
Spy	All-Fair
V for Victory	Toy Creations, Inc.
Magnetic Mine Weeper	Walco
Spotter School	Funhouse, Inc.
Bombs Away	Armac Games
Battle	All-Fair
Battle Stations	Whitman Publishing

CARD GAMES

	Manufacturer
Squadron Scramble (2 Versions)	Whitman Publishing
Tactics	National Military Tactics Co.
Squadron Insignia	All-Fair
Spotter Cards	U.S. Playing Card Co.
Sabotage	Games of Fame Co.
Victory Rummy	Victory Game Co.
Sigs	Whitman Publishing
Zoom	Whitman Publishing

HAND-HELD GAMES

Trap the Jap in Tokyo	Modern Novelties, Inc.
Put the Yank in Berlin	Modern Novelties, Inc.
Sink the Enemy Navy	Elvin Products
Zowe	
Keep 'em Calling for Victory	
Trap the Sap	
The Bomber	
Give It Wings	
Atomic Bomb	A.C. Gilbert Co.

TARGET-TYPE GAMES

Air Defense Target	Wolverine Supply Mfg. Co.
Trap-a-tank Obstacle Course	Wolverine Supply Mfg. Co.
Junior Bombsight	Otis-Lawson Company
Direct Hit	Northwestern Products
Bombs-Away — Eagle Bombsight	Toy Creations, Inc.
Target Game Darts	
U.S. Air Force Target	Whitman Publishing
Bomber Ball	
National Defense	Louis Marx Co.
You're in the Army Now	Gotham Pressed Steel Toy Co.
Soldiers of Fortune	Louis Marx Co.
Soldiers w/Cannon Target	J. Pressman & Co. Inc.
Par-a-chute	Baldwin Mfg. Co.
Sink the Invader	Baldwin Mfg. Co.
Tidily-winks Barrage	Corey Game Co.
Push 'em-up Victory Bomber	Northwestern Products Co.
Victory Bomber Target Game	Whitman Publishing
Torpedo Attack	Allstate Engineering Service
Bomb the Navy	J. Pressman & Co. Inc.
Bazooka — Army Pinball Game	Louis Marx Co.
Rapid-Fire Pursuit	Gotham Pressed Steel Co.
Anti-tank Target Set	Louis Marx Co.
Air-Sea-Power Bombing	Louis Marx Co.
Wings — Stand-up	Parker Brothers, Inc.
Secret Bomb-site	Model Airplane Co.
5 in 1 Roller Target	N.Y. Toy & Game Mfg. Co.
Bomb-site	The Toyad Corporation
Dive-bomber Safety Darts	N.Y. Toy & Game Mfg. Co.
USAF Safety Darts	N.Y. Toy & Game Mfg. Co.
Bombardier Bomb	Kidi-kuts
Hang The Tyrants Bowling Game	
Bombardier Bombsight	Continental Co.
Set the Son Dartboard	W & L Game Co.
Bomb-a-Jap — Dart Game	Winkenweder & Ladd, Inc.
At Ease — 35 Serviceman Games	National Association Service
Attack	Wiz Novelty Co.
Aerial Bomber	Baldwin Mfg. Co.
Coast Guard in Action	Baldwin Mfg. Co.
Coast Defense	Baldwin Mfg. Co.
Sky-Shoot-Parachute	Baldwin Mfg. Co.
Air-Raid	Rosebud Art Company
Stick the Dictators	Jay Co.

Military Paper Dolls, WWII*

Air, Land and Sea #313 S 1943 92445)
American Nurse #3945 W 1941
Army and Navy Wedding Party #2446 S 1943
Army Nurse and Doctor #3425 M 1942
Babs, the Ambulance Driver L (1048)
Bild-a-set, 10 Beautiful Junior Girls in Uniforms #80 P 1943
Bride and Groom Military Wedding Party #3411 M 1941
Dick the Sailor #1074 L 1941
Edith of the A.W.V.S. L (1048)
Eleanor of the O.C.D. L (1048)
Florence the Nurse L (1048)
Girls in the War #1028 L 1943
Girls in Uniform #1048 L 1942
Girl Pilots of the Ferry Command #4852 M 1943
Harry the Soldier #1074 L 1941
Joan and Judy's Paper Doll Box #898 S 1943
Junior Volunteers #593 S Box Set (2450)
Liberty Belles #3477 M 1943
Mary of the Wacs #1012 W 1943 (3980 — Our Wac Joan)
Military Wedding #314 S 1943 (2446)
Navy Girls and Marines #4855 M 1943
Navy Scouts #3428 M 1942
Our Nurse Nancy #3980 W 1943 *box or envelope*
Our Nurse Nancy #1012 W 1943 (3980)
Our Sailor Bob #3980 W 1943 *box or envelope*
Our Soldier Jim #3980 W 1943 *box or envelope*
Our Soldiers (no number) Dell 1941
Our Wac Joan #3980 W 1943 *box or envelope*
Our Wave Joan #1012 W 1943 (3980 — Our Wave Patsy)
Our Wave Patsy #3980 W 1942 *box or envelope*
Paper Doll Wedding #3851 M 1943
Paper Dolls in Uniforms of the U.S.A. #492 S 1943
    Box Set (2445)
Pressed Board Dolls #1023 L 1942 (1048)
Red, White and Blue #321 S 1943 (2450)
Ruth of the Stage Door Canteen L (1048)
Soldiers and Sailors House Party #3481 M 1943
Stage Door Canteen #2468 S 1943
Stage Door Canteen #347 S 1943 (2468)
Sybil of the Field Hospital L (1048)

Tom the Aviator #1074 L 1941
Uncle Sam's Little Helpers #2450 S 1943
United We Stand #113 S 1943
Victory Girls #58 L Box Set (1048)
Victory Paper Dolls #2445 S 1943
Victory Volunteers #3424 M 1942
Wacs and Waves #985 W 1943
War Girls #529 L 1943 (1048)

compiled By Mary Young

Punchout and Cutout Sets

■ Rigby's

Fighting Ships
Easy to Build Model Planes
Naval Models
Book of Models
Marvel Model Book
Warplanes of the World (2 Versions)
Model of Fighting Planes
Models of Naval Craft

■ Wyandotte

U.S. Defense Boxed Set
Army Base
Air Squadron
Army Attack Squad
American Commandos
Soldiers in Action
Anti-aircraft Gun
Navy Patrol

■ Colorgraphic

Sculpturette's (2 Versions)
Young Patriot Smash the Axis
Young Patriot Invasion
Young Patriot Fighting Units
Young Patriot Army Combat
Young Patriot Army Combat Set
Young Patriot Navy Combat Set
Young Patriot Army and Navy Combat Set

■ Built-rite

Army Outpost
Fort #100a
Coastal Defense
Army Plane Hangar
Fort #16
Fort #27
Army Camp #1021
Frontline Trench
Army Battery
Fort 25a
Army Raider's Victory Unit
Army Ranger's Fighters
Army Fighters #112
Guardsman
Fort Set #252

■ Dell

Our Soldiers Cut Out Army Uniforms

■ Reed

Model Battleship
Model Flat Top
3 Flying Models

■ Bild-a-set (Pachter)

Army Fighting Force
Navy Fighting Fleet
Army Combat Units
Action for American Youth
Junior Navy Fighting Fleet
Junior Army and Navy Fighting Forces
Beautiful Girls in Uniform
Army Fighting Unit

■ Electric Corps of America ("ECA")

Land-Sea-Air Super Battle Set
Make Your Own Battle Set
American Skyhawk Squadron

Surprise Attack Fleet
Mechanized Force
Smash the Axis
Action Ace Plane kit
Super Flat Top
Battle Set, Naval Task Force

■ Samuel Lowe Co.

U.S. Stand Up Soldiers
U.S. Stand Up Sailors
Over 80 Stand Up Sailors
Over 80 Stand Up Soldiers
Victory Punchouts
Service Kit of America's Armed Forces
Harry the Soldier, Dick the Sailor, Tom the Aviator
Model Planes
Model War Planes
Model Tanks
Model Tanks Jr. Commandos (2 Versions)
Model Airplanes Jr. Commandos
U.S. Commandos

■ Whitman Publishing Co.

American Defense Battles
100 Punchout Soldiers (2 Versions)
30 Toy Soldiers-Sailors-Marines
Models of USA—Air Defense
Fighting Planes Booklet
Fighting Bombers Booklet

■ Victory Toy Company

The Captain Army-Navy Combat Set
The Colonel-Army Combat Set
Junior Commander-Army-Navy Combat Units
Complete Set-up for War Maneuvers
Junior Commander-Army-Navy Combat Set Complete
  for Land-Sea-Air Maneuvers
Sure-Fire Cannon

■ EINSON-FREEMAN CO.

Self-running Army Combat Models
Pre-flight Trainer
Sea Raiding Battleship
Secret Airplane Bombsight
Coastal Artillery Gun
Junior Bombardier

■ ALL-FAIR

Action Soldier Set
Paratroops Set

■ FAWCETT PUBLISHING

13 Toy Models
Warplanes & Tank Punchouts
9 Toy Models—warplanes and 4 Models Tanks Set

■ RAP-A-JAP (WOODBURN MFG.)

Bombing & Fighting Units
Modern Combat Units (2 Versions)

■ MISCELLANEOUS PUNCHOUT SETS

Hingees—Terry and the Pirates	Martin Picking & Son
Toy Army, I Can Make	Platt & Nourse
Soldier Cut-outs—Cavalry	
Playtime On Parade—Folder Set	
Army Cut-outs	Saalfield
Our Soldiers	Saalfield
U.S. Planes, Tank, Jeep and Gun	Saalfield
Fighting Soldiers With Jeep	Concord
United for Liberty—Allied Soldiers	Advance Games
U.S. Fighters for All Out War	Container Corp. of America
Attack Force Soldier Set	J-Mar
Camouflage Defense Force	Jay-Line Mfg. Co.
Combat Attack Set	Hasbro
Tokyo Raiders Set	American Toy Mfg. Co.

American Defense Battles Punchout Book	Merrill Publishing
Commandos Aircraft	National Handi-krafters
Army Ambulance	National Handi-krafters
Army Scout Truck	National Handi-krafters
Fold-a-Planes Sets (8)	Crestcraft Co.
Jr. Tanks Walkie-Talky String Phone	
Smiling Jack's Victory Bombers	Plane Facts, Inc.
Rat-a-tat Machine Gun	Art Skill Publishing
Swing-a-plane	J.L. Schilling
Secret Weapon Invasion Set	
Uncle Sam Fighter Set On Land, On Sea, in the Air	
Model Airplanes	Kellogs
Jack Armstrong Flying Models (14)	General Mills

COLORING AND CUT, PASTE AND STICK BOOKS

Boys and Girls Dot Coloring
Soldier and Sailor
Red White and Blue
Patriotic Designs
Our Army & Navy, Cut and Stick
Lowe, Cut, Paste and Stick
Fighters for Freedom
Warplanes, Tanks and Jeeps
Spot the Planes
Flying Forts
Rangers and Commandos
Flying Cadets
We Fly for the Navy
Girls of the Army and Navy
Submarines
U.S. Marines
The Story of Guns
Fighting Yanks
America at War

Uncle Sam at War
Flying for Victory (2 Versions)
Victory Book
Crackerjack Paint Book
Snappy
Jeepers
Soldiers and Sailors
Soldiers Coloring Book
The Bugle Call
Mascot
I Like to Play Soldier
I Like to Play Sailor
I Like to Play Aviator
Aviator Coloring Book (2 Versions)

Soldier Coloring Book
Sailor Coloring Book
Hit the Mark Playbook
Whoopie Paint Book
Hi Soldier Coloring Book
Navy & Marine Paint Book
Old Glory Painting and Drawing Book
America Coloring Book
Wet-a-brush Book
Tracing Book
Tracing Book to Paint and Color
Yankee Doodle Dandy Paint Book
Little Soldiers and Sailors Paint Book (2 Versions)
Hi-Ho Coloring Book

Bedroom & Scrapbook Collectibles

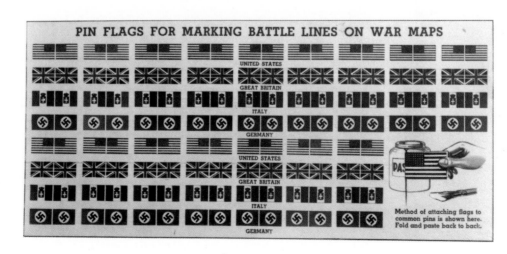

This and next page
**During WWII kids collected all sorts of neat stuff that was kept in boxes, under the bed, in scrapbooks, on bedroom walls and on bureau tops. Banks, carnival chalk figures, pennants, maps, school tablets and pencil boxes were included.
A smattering of these hundreds of patriotic items is shown here.**

261

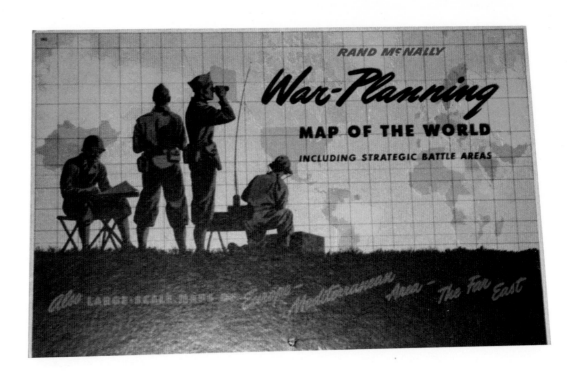

262

INDEX OF MANUFACTURERS & PUBLISHERS